InSideOut
COACHING

How Sports Can Transform Lives

JOE EHRMANN

WITH PAULA EHRMANN AND GREGORY JORDAN

Simon & Schuster

New York   London   Toronto   Sydney   New Delhi

Simon & Schuster
1230 Avenue of the Americas
New York, NY 10020

First Simon & Schuster hardcover edition August 2011

SIMON & SCHUSTER and colophon are registered trademarks
of Simon & Schuster, Inc.

For information about special discounts for bulk purchases,
please contact Simon & Schuster Special Sales at
1-866-506-1949 or business@simonandschuster.com.

TheS imon & Schuster Speakers Bureau can bring authors
to your live event. For more information or to book an event,
contact the Simon & Schuster Speakers Bureau at
1-866-248-3049 or visit our website at www.simonspeakers.com.

Designed by Nancy Singer

Manufactured in the United States of America

30 29 28 27 26 25 24 23 22 21

ISBN 978-1-4391-8298-7
ISBN 978-1-4391-8300-7 (ebook)

This book could not have been written apart from
the love, strength, and wisdom of my wife, Paula.
Paula gave me the courage
to confront, articulate, and embrace my past
and then integrate these experiences into
my life mission to build a better world.
My children, Alison, Esther, Barney, and Joey,
have been my sustaining source of joy. I love you all.

CONTENTS

PART I

INTRODUCTION

The InSideOut Process

The black sky hung heavy over Baltimore that October night. Street-lights all over our neighborhood were burned out. Clouds clung to the tops of the row houses, and as I drove, the mist rose so thickly that it felt as if the car was colliding with it.

I was driving home with my four-year-old son, Barney, asleep in the seat beside me. He rested his head on the armrest. Ice cream stained his cheek. I turned off talk radio to savor his peaceful breathing.

It was my weekly father-son night with Barney. I had a speech scheduled that evening and thought it might be fun to take him along. My wife, Paula, dressed him up in the same outfit I was wearing—blue blazer, red tie, and khaki pants. She handed me his coloring book and crayons as we walked out the door.

I sat him in the front row and told him that if he behaved, I would take him to the local ice cream shop and he could order anything he wanted.

As I spoke from the podium, I realized that I couldn't concentrate. It was a few years into my ministry. I had started to enjoy public speaking and loved engaging my audience. It gave me a sensation like the single-mindedness and adrenaline rush that I got from sports.

But tonight I felt nervous and distracted. I kept watching Barney and he kept watching me. Even though my brain was sending the right words to my mouth, my deeper mind kept focusing on my son.

I was overcome with how great he looked and how much I loved him.

After the speech and handshakes, I went over to him and hugged him.

"Dad, that was really good!" he said.

My heart was touched. It was so like Barney to be thoughtful beyond his years.

I got him his ice cream—he ordered a hot fudge sundae and a chocolate milkshake. I just couldn't say no. As the bright light of the ice cream shop illuminated the ice cream covering Barney's chin and clothes, I thought about how Paula would react to my sweet indulgence. Far too much sugar, and the stains to prove it!

Outside, the city was empty and the mist was thick; a few roaming cats and random rats spooked me.

As we got closer to home, I looked down at Barney again. Suddenly, I began to have the most mystical and magical experience of my life. It seemed as though my soul left my body and connected with his. I had an overwhelming sense of how much I loved him, how special and important he was to me. Out of all the children in the world, this magnificent boy was my son. And I was his dad.

And in the throes of this spiritual connection, it seemed as if the mist started coming in through the car vents and engulfing us. I pulled over to the side of the road and stopped. A sense of being haunted came over me, a sense that maybe there were a few shadows and ghosts lingering in the dark that needed to come out into the light.

And then for the first time in my adult life, I managed to articulate something that had always eaten at me: "My father never saw me this way."

I was acutely aware of the difference between the love I felt for Barney and what I had received from my own father. My father never felt this. Why didn't I have a father who loved me the same way I love my son?

The car arrived home that night almost driving itself—and carrying two boys. One was sound asleep on my shoulder, resting in the strength and security of my love for him. And the other was me, a four-year-old "Joey" Ehrmann wrapped in a retired lineman's body who was just starting to get in touch with the hole inside his soul.

I handed both boys to Paula. I told her about my experience and my wave of emotions—the sense of loss, grief, and abandonment that I associated with my father. Forty years of imprisoned emotion were being set free. I realized that night that a change was happening, the start of a permanent one. All the pain, hiding, and shame were ending as I saw my story laid out on the road right there in front of me. The days with my abusive father and my constant aching for his love, the debilitating sports culture in which I thrived as a teen in Buffalo, my manipulative coaches and my incessant need for their approval, and my junkie's use of sports, fame, and drugs as medication for the grief. I was beginning to see it all clearly and knew it was time to put it to rest.

Laid out before me was my life as a sports story, a narrative with each mile marker underscoring a coaching relationship. I saw the transactional coaches: the kind of coaches who use players as tools to meet their personal needs for validation, status, and identity. They held their power over us to elicit the response they wanted. I obeyed these coaches out of necessity but I never accepted their belief systems or bought into their programs. Coach first, team second, and player's growth and needs last, if at all, were their modus operandi.

I also saw the transformational coaches, who used their coaching platform to impart life-changing messages that I began to understand only decades later. Coach-power, like all forms of power, can be used either for good or for bad, for self or for others. Transformational coaches are other-centered. They use their power and platform to nurture and transform players. I followed these coaches because I sensed their authenticity; they have affected me for a lifetime. Players first, team second, coach's needs met by meeting the needs of players.

I realized my sports career had been a lifelong, often desperate, search for acceptance and approval from adults who had power and authority over me. I had been a sports hero in high school, an All-American at Syracuse University, and a star in the NFL, but the profound impact that sports has had on my life has had little to do with my performance, my awards, or the number of games my team won.

It does, however, have plenty to do with the refuge and camaraderie, even the escape that a team and a game can provide. My personal journey through sports had a lot to do with my quest for empathy and validation—acting out in front of coaches trying to get it, destroying running backs to earn it, crushing offensive linemen to win it, and reliably playing the part of the affable wild man trying to score it. I was getting validation in bits and pieces but never really filling the void that was consuming me.

For several years, I had been haphazardly trying to piece together my story in a coherent way, trying to make sense of my life. But I kept going in circles, unable to get the pieces into a straight line. That night I finally solved a huge piece of the puzzle: My sports life had been full of transactions, doing this to get that, trying to satisfy my father and coaches who wanted something out of me, exchanging my performance for their praise and acceptance.

Instead of looking back in despair, I quickly decided, with Paula's help, to look forward with hope. I wanted to become the kind of coach I had craved all those years under transactional coaches. I wanted to be transformational. A transformational coach is dedicated to self-understanding and empathy, viewing sports as a virtuous and virtue-giving discipline. Transformational coaches believe young people can grow and flourish in sports in a way that is more liberating and instructive than can be achieved through almost any other activity.

But we knew—Paula knew and kept reminding me—that moving forward would mean moving backward as well. I had to understand and accept my own story before I could understand and help transform the young people I coached. It was only as I came to understand the differences between transactional and transformational coaching that I fully appreciated the powerful influences of both in my life.

That night I started to realize that transitioning from a transactional coach to a transformational coach requires connecting the zigzagging dots of a scattered and struggle-filled life into a connected, coherent story. I could not become a transformational coach until connecting those dots and understanding my own story.

In her graduate work, Paula had come across profound research based on studies that looked at the common characteristics of parents who had raised children with healthy relationship patterns. What these studies indicated was that the parents' history, whether tumultuous or smooth, had little to do with the outcome. It was the parents' capacity to make sense of their history that determined their ability to raise children who could connect well to others. Parents who are able to make sense of their own lives can go on to help their children make sense of their lives, too.

I knew immediately that this insight translated to coaches as well. No coach could teach his players critical life skills until he learned those skills himself.

So many of my coaches were transactional: They operated on a quid pro quo basis to incentivize us to perform better; they looked for what they could get out of coaching and not what they could give; they ignored athletes' developmental needs and often manipulated and distorted the values of winning and losing. When I began coaching, I became one of them. I simply emulated what I knew.

The most compelling and durable glory of coaching, however, is to use the whistle for its transformative and not its authoritative power. Outside of parenting there might not be a better platform than coaching to transform boys and girls into healthy and thriving men and women. A coach's responsibilities include helping young people to confront and comprehend the toxic culture that is trying to seduce and shape them. Coaches have the power to teach and to affirm and to convey empathy and compassion. And, I believe, there may not be a more influential group of leaders in the world than transformational coaches.

How we make sense of our lives dictates how we live them. Similarly, how we make sense of our personal sports history and the coaches in our past influences the way we coach. Today, without this self-understanding, sporting history will repeat itself—transactional coaching will perpetuate itself. But once we understand our history, with all its feelings and emotions, we can put ourselves in our players' shoes and begin to coach for them. We can remember what it was like to be that age, and all the conflicting messages we received. As coaches, we keenly feel the social, emotional, and psychological issues that many young athletes face. We can carefully calibrate our coaching, because we are finely attuned to the effect our words and gestures have on the hearts and minds of the players we coach. We can empathically place our players' needs above our own and become what I call InSideOut coaches.

An InSideOut coach is one who has done this sort of arduous interior work to answer such critical questions as, Why do I coach? Why do I coach the way I do? What does it feel like to be coached by me? How do I define and measure success?

The interior work consists of reflecting on both our glorious and our hurtful experiences with sports and coaches. It involves tracing the unfulfilled needs we felt as athletes and determining how those unmet needs can drive us as coaches, and, finally, understanding that our obligation is to coach for our players and not for ourselves. When coaches do this interior work they come up with some startling answers to the key questions I just posed.

An InSideOut coach's answers are radically different from the responses our contemporary sports culture expects, or rather, demands. An InSideOut coach resists the transactional impulse and asserts that the right way, indeed the only way, to coach young people is to seek to transform their sense of their own worth, talents, and value. An InSideOut coach sees a younger, developing version of himself or herself in every athlete and bases lesson plans, communication, and the very structure of the program on the obligation to transform the many young athletes who need connection, empathy, and guidance.

So after years of grasping at my own chaotic life narrative, I turned my scattershot personal story into a coherent narrative with the goal of becoming a better man, father, husband, and, albeit with my fair share of failings, an InSideOut coach.

Second to parents, coaches have enormous influence over young people's lives. InSideOut coaches can achieve the goal of instructing, mentoring, and sometimes even saving kids only with a thorough and daily devotion to certain principles—nurturing community, classroom-like instruction, empathic communication, joyful competition, and the spirituality of ceremony. These principles are every bit as important as the Xs and Os, the technical expertise, and even the hunger to win. I daresay that InSideOut coaches not only help young people grow but also leave a legacy more enduring for how they transform lives than for their wins.

During my own interior workouts something powerful dawned on me: Contemporary sports are our secular religion. Sports engage more individuals, more families, and more communities in a shared experience than any single cultural activity, organization, or religion in America. Twenty to 30 million kids play recreational sports, while another 10 million teens play interscholastic sports. This means that between 30 and 80 million parents are invested and involved in their children's sports. There are at least 5 million coaches with the potential to become one of the most influential adults in a young person's life. Forever.

Our beautiful challenge as coaches is to use this awesome and sometimes frightening influence to become agents of transformation in athletes' lives. We are in a position to help them comprehend and negotiate the challenges of growing up in our culture. Because of the incompatibility of the daunting needs of our youth with the twisted culture of sports, there are many young people playing sports who feel diminished and discouraged by the very activities that should strengthen, encourage, and redeem them.

My intention in this book is to take back the spiritual and transformative side of the games our children play and restore sports to their original intent.

I believe that sports can offer the most universal and accessible venue in which to rejuvenate and embody the great virtues. And I believe that InSideOut coaches are charged with the task of virtuous instruction—not merely with offering their technical expertise—as primary agents of this social renewal.

Restoring sports as the method for nourishing and celebrating virtues and redefining coaches as virtuous instructors are the foundations of my coaching manifesto. Seeing the profession of coaching from the inside out shows us the transformative power that it holds to teach and uplift and to help athletes celebrate the joy of learning and growing.

CHAPTER 1

Stepping Inside

My recurring childhood memory is of my father holding up his bear paw of a hand and in his deep voice commanding me to snap my right wrist forty-five degrees clockwise at the end of each jab.

Upstairs, my mother nervously paced the kitchen floor. I could hear the creaking despite the rising tone of my father's voice as he instructed me. The cellar was hot from the furnace. He was swearing; I was sweating.

Having lived my life in sports, I realize it is only appropriate that my earliest childhood memory revolves around sports and coaching. This memory could have been about sports as a metaphor for fathers and sons and love, about the instruction, affirmation, and self-confidence that can come from sports, about the value of persistence and bonding and connection that good parenting and coaching can foster. It could have been a great memory.

But it wasn't. I was five years old and I couldn't snap my wrist at the end of my jabs. Or at least I couldn't do it to my father's satisfaction. The memory haunts me to this day.

My father grew frustrated. He dropped his right arm and held his hands by his sides while he stared at me. He shook his head in a way that felt like a body blow to a little boy. And then he spoke—lower, with disgust.

"How hard is it to snap your damn wrist?"

He raised his hand and jabbed the air inches from my face, snapping his wrist again and again.

"Like this! Like this! Like this!"

As each jab shot straight to my heart, tears started to come out of my eyes and run down my cheeks. I realized I was crying only when I felt how cold the tears were compared to the warm sweat dripping down my neck. Then my father started slapping my cheeks back and forth with both hands—not hard, to hurt me, but soft and silly, to mock me.

He stopped and stared into my teary eyes.

"Be a man!" he said.

I wanted to run up the stairs and grab hold of my mother, but I knew I couldn't. I knew "a man" shouldn't; therefore, I didn't. I couldn't risk being a "mama's boy" on top of my boxing failure.

I stood there blinking. He turned and stomped up the stairs, brushed past my mother, and put on his coat. I heard him pause again at the stairwell and could feel his last look at me so deeply that I see his face now even though I never saw it then. I heard the door bang on his way out as he headed to the bar on that Buffalo night.

One of the great myths in America is that sports build character. They can and they should. Indeed, sports may be the perfect venue in which to build character. But sports don't build character unless a coach possesses character and intentionally teaches it. Sports can team with ethics and character and spirituality; virtuous coaching can integrate the body with the heart, the mind, and the soul.

But as my first memory shows, sports can also beat up young people and break them down so profoundly that they barely recover as adults. I was one of those waylaid kids, and my recovery was a long, hard road.

My life in sports—being coached and coaching—was a search for a coherent narrative. Discovering it enabled me to become a transformational, InSideOut coach. My journey to coherence was a rough and tumble one, made worse by coaching that only increased my pain and confusion.

In the end a couple of transformational coaches helped turn my life around. My story shows both the awe that coaches elicit from their players and how long-lasting and deep-seated the effect of great coaching can be. Although being subjected to transactional coaching can be damaging, an athlete who experiences the awe of being nourished by a transformative coach can be transformed.

A favorite concept of mine comes from Henri Nouwen's book *The Wounded Healer.* The premise of the book is that as we travel life's journey from childhood to adulthood we acquire wounds along the way. A wound can be any unresolved social, emotional, relational issue that still impacts our lives. These wounds can be inflicted by negative cultural messages or experiences with parents, peers, or adults with power and authority over us. Unresolved, these wounds can leave us with a sense of deficiency or inferiority. We can let unhealed wounds drive us and risk hurting our players through endless self-serving transactions, or we can heal ourselves and then help heal our players. Nouwen says we have two choices: Either we deny, repress, or dissociate from the wounding and therefore wound others with our unhealed injuries, or we bring healing to our wounds and offer our healed wounds to others to heal and transform their lives. I am a wounded healer and this is the story of my wounds, their healing, and the transformation in coaching that ensued because I chose to process and grieve over my pain instead of hiding it and acting it out.

BUFFALO BOY

Buffalo is a great sports town. I grew up in a neighborhood called Riverside, along the Niagara River connecting Lake Erie and Lake Ontario. We lived four blocks from Riverside Park, where all sorts of sports were played all hours of the day and night. The bouncing and hitting of balls echoed around the park along with all the kids' shouts and laughter. In this Riverside garden, it was as if God created sports and childhood to go together.

My father, whom I called Dah, worked on drilling and dredge boats in the Great Lakes and disappeared for months at a time. My mother made up for his absence with an overwhelming presence—always cooking something on the stove that made the kitchen the warmest room in our tiny house.

Religion happened on Sundays and at bedtime. People flocked to churches in their best clothes on Sundays and kids said their prayers in their pajamas before turning out the light.

But the other religion in Buffalo was sports, particularly the Buffalo Bills. I remember hitchhiking to their training camp and going to the Bills games on weekends with my grandfather and, at age nine or ten, being more fascinated by watching him and his friends watch the game than by the game itself.

He and his friends didn't chat but rather conferred: They analyzed each play in serious tones and with grave faces, or sometimes, if things seemed to be going right out on the field, with a twinkle in their eyes.

And I sensed with that basic but uncanny childhood intuition that these men were communing. The game in front of them and the crowd around them broke down many of the masculine barriers they and their culture had built up. I had my first, primitive sense of sports as something spiritual.

But more often than not I saw the dark side of sports—that twisted way in which men use sports to establish, define, or demonstrate their masculinity and assert themselves.

One Saturday every July, yellow buses lined up along Riverside Park and took the whole neighborhood across the Canadian border to Crystal Beach, an amusement park near Lake Ontario where we held Riverside–Black Rock Day. As a young boy I loved these trips because we rode the roller coaster and played games all day long. The men headed off to the bars when we arrived in the late morning, mothers shepherded us from ride to ride and game to game, and at the end of the day the whole neighborhood gathered in a little stadium for the annual family tug-of-war battle.

My family had a long tradition of winning at Crystal Beach. My little brother Billy won the Pretty Baby Contest two years in a row. I won many athletic contests in my age bracket. My little sister Susie won the pie-eating contest. And my father's clan would usually win the tug-of-war.

The summer I turned ten, I discovered that this event was not the idyllic retreat I had imagined it to be. That was the summer that I realized for the first time where the men went in the morning and what they did. They returned from the bars wobbly and cursing with abandon. I smelled the alcohol on their breath and the alcohol-flavored sweat coming out of their pores. I was beginning to understand why our mothers seemed perturbed as the men trickled onto the stadium field and took their places.

I stood with my mother and brother at a comfortable distance from my father's team and watched as they won contest after contest. Shirtless, they seemed like drunken Charles Atlases, but with their biceps thick from hard labor, not from weight rooms and nutrition drinks.

Dah's team made it to the finals that July and crowds of people encircled the two remaining families as they took their places at the ropes. The other family won the first of three matches after a ten-minute struggle. One man vomited and others laughed as the women scowled.

Suddenly, just before the second of the best-of-three contest, the front two tuggers dropped the rope and stood face to face shouting at each other. I moved closer to my mother; we all seemed to huddle closer together, and the men in front of us started to grumble.

Then the brawl broke out. As the women evacuated the children and the casserole plates, the two families began clobbering each other and fighting as if their manhood depended on it. Security guards arrived, and the bloodied men slowly staggered away from one another.

No one spoke on the bus on the way home; some men held ice to their heads or towels to their cuts. My father sat in front with the other men; my brother and I sat behind my mother. She didn't stop looking out the window.

The day had all the attributes of a comedy about men behaving badly, women being frustrated, and an afternoon at the ballpark gone awry. But we were kids and there was nothing funny about it.

Throughout my childhood, Dah believed his sole obligation was to make me into a man. Using physical punishment and emotional manipulation, he emphasized strength, stoicism, and silence. There was no room for emotion, warmth, or failure. An undefined but overwhelming notion of masculinity filled most of my encounters and relationships. Inevitably, most of the boys of Riverside were chasing some impossible image of manhood like dogs chasing their tails. My self-image could never match the masculine image Dah held out for me. It was unattainable, unhealthy, and inherently false. But I chased it and chased it hard.

On days like the tug-of-war debacle, the little voice inside my head found its own version of distorted logic. Negative self-talk, I call it—my head talking to me about how I didn't size up, match up, or man-up to meet this culturally warped definition of masculinity. My father's love was conditional, and I felt tremendous pressure to perform to receive it. Even as a young boy I knew my father's love was based on his estimation of my performance on the masculine field of life.

Lacking the emotional skills to discern the damage to my sense of self, I sought approval from Dah through sports and my achievements on the field. I continued to think that if I played well, he would give me acceptance and a gesture of approval. It was an unabashed transaction, a conditional relationship that my father used to try to turn me into the man he wanted me to be. And I complied.

But there is not a more flawed measure of a child's value than sports. The playing fields are uneven; genetics skew the results in favor of the proper body type for each sport; dedication and determination can do only so much. And yet some parents and coaches use performance as the measure of a child's worth.

In my case, I was born to play football. I had plenty of desire and determination and was blessed genetically, being big and fast. And though I kept winning at the games we played, I was convinced I was not man enough to win at life.

THE GAME CHANGERS

Two sports-related game changers and one much more serious event forever altered my life. Looking back at these incidents through the prism of adulthood, I can now see clearly that although my father laid some questionable groundwork for me, a number of coaches and other grown-ups repeatedly blasted holes in my already distressed foundation.

TWO GAME CHANGERS

Game changer number one: the winter of 1961. For the first of many times I hurt another human being intentionally. I was eleven years old. It was during a youth league basketball game, and I was in-bounding the ball from under the basket. But the opposing player was all over me and I could not get the ball in. The coach called two consecutive time-outs to avoid a five-second call that would have cost us possession of the ball.

The jumping-bean kid guarding the in-bounds pass was too close to me and the ref wasn't giving me room. Coach pulled me aside after the second time-out, gripped my arm, and would not let go as the referee's whistle summoned us back to the court.

He put his face very close to mine so no one could hear and looked me straight in the eyes without blinking.

"Bring the ball back over your head with both hands and smash it into his face," he said.

He put his right hand on my left shoulder and squeezed it so tightly that it hurt.

"Smash the ball as hard as you can in his face. You will teach him a lesson about who he is playing against."

I remember walking to the space below the basket and looking at the kid whose nose I was about to break. I remember knowing I was going to do it even though most of me didn't want to. The bulk of my consciousness resisted the instruction, but something inside of me won out.

I looked at my coach as the ref blew the whistle and handed me the ball. The coach kept staring at me without blinking. I gripped the ball, slammed it into my hands as my teammates broke in zigzags, lifted it above my head, and brought it down with all my force right into the kid's face. Blood shot everywhere and the kid's mother came rushing from the stands screaming at me as her son lay crying on the court.

The whole gym stared at me the same way my coach did before the beastly act. The fifty or so people there became like one big eye looking straight into my wicked heart. It made me sick to my stomach. After the game, Coach praised me in the locker room, upholding that play as something positive, and "the way the game was to be played!" Something I should feel good or manly about. Shame engulfed me even as my teammates congratulated me. Shame became my constitution. I was not angry at my coach. I did not pity the poor kid on the floor below me. I was confused and consumed with myself and my shame.

Game changer number two: Because of a single play, I walked away from baseball forever. I was twelve and nicknamed Moose after the Yankee first baseman Moose Skowron. I could dig most balls out of the dirt, and like Moose, I was big, hit with power, and could move pretty fast, too.

One summer afternoon with two outs during a tied game in the final inning of a Babe Ruth championship, a perfect throw from the third baseman coming straight at me ended the tie. I watched it. I focused on it. I missed it. It hit my glove and rolled several feet behind me. As I ran for it, a run scored, the other team won, and I walked off the field trying not to cry, because I had cost my team the championship and had let everyone down.

I walked back to the bench, fighting back tears, and our coach stared at me as he walked past with the bag of bats. One teammate hit me on the shoulder; others were crying, or angry or stunned. I don't remember that coach's name, just his face and his big belly passing by as I longed for a hug, a pat on the back, or a consoling word. I craved some coaching affirmation, anything to make me feel better. But I got nothing.

Although my mother came to most of my games, she was not at the game that day. I walked home from the park and sat on the front porch for a long time. I swore never to play baseball again and I didn't. I swore never to put myself in a position again where my failure would be so visible to others.

That fall a school nurse sent home a note informing my mother that I needed to get my eyes examined after failing an eye test. I remember being seared by what the optometrist said to me: "I am surprised you can even see a baseball coming at you." Too late.

ONE LIFE CHANGER

The event that forever changed my life happened the fall after my failed baseball experience. The crisp October night began with nothing but the innocence of childhood. I was running around with a group of friends, prepubescent boys playing a fun-filled game of tag at the edge of some big pines in a church-sponsored campground south of Buffalo. We ran into some local kids who lived near the campground, and they joined in, all of us taking turns chasing and being chased, both competing and laughing at the same time. When we finally took a break, we all sat down together, and that was when something happened, pretty much meaningless at the time, that would soon lead to pure hell for me. Someone in the group—I don't remember if it was one of my friends or one of the locals—asked a little girl who was there to drop her pants. She was only four or five years old, and so she immediately obliged, at which point one of the boys shined a flashlight on the most private area of her body. We all looked and giggled, but nobody did anything more than that. And then we all went right back to our game of tag.

The locals eventually left, but the rest of us kept playing under the moonlight. After a while, we noticed two men approaching from a distance. They were running toward us—they were clearly angry about something—and so we all took off as best we could. Unfortunately, I got a late start, I slipped, and I knew I was going to be caught. One guy tackled me and both men started to kick and punch me as I curled up into a ball. I had no idea what this was about, but with each blow—and with their hostile words—they made it more clear. They apparently thought that something more had happened once the girl had dropped her pants because they kept calling me a rapist and a pervert. I soon came to realize that one of the men must have been the father of the young girl.

The men dragged me by my wrists to a nearby shack, and it was like being taken to a slaughterhouse. It didn't matter what I said or how I tried to defend myself. I knew I was in trouble. But I never could have anticipated what was about to happen. One of the men yanked down my pants and violated both my childhood and my masculinity. He raped me. It was an impossibly disproportionate penalty—impossibly horrific and brutal—given the relatively minor incident that had triggered it. And yet this was my new reality. Bloodied and confused, I was now the victim of a violence that would never make any sense.

I remember lying on the ground for a long time after those men were gone, wondering how I could possibly go back to camp. What had just happened to me? At the age of twelve, I certainly didn't know it was called sodomy or that such a vicious thing could be done to a boy. All I can remember thinking was: What would my father say? What would he think if he knew I never even threw a punch? I knew his masculine code could not accommodate such behavior. I knew that the son of Dah could not reveal such utter weakness and defeat. For decades, I never spoke of what had happened in that shack. I could not even speak of it to myself. The rape produced a shame in me that left me wounded, isolated, and alone for decades to come.

The shame-driven sense of manhood I carried with me undoubtedly helped push me to be a tough guy, an All-American collegiate athlete, a professional football star . . . and one of the unhappiest "successful" men you could ever find. I was always trying to accomplish away my pain and humiliation by claiming new victories on the fields of sport, new sexual conquests with girls and later women, and new heights on the ladder of social status. Ultimately, when none of that proved potent enough to erase the pain, I turned to alcohol and drugs to medicate the pain.

These events were among the lowlights of my childhood, but many other incidents incrementally pushed me further and further toward confusion and incoherence. The big themes that dominated my adulthood arrived early and viciously: an absent and angry father, abusive and violent adults, and transactional coaches uninterested in changing their players' lives. Sports quickly became the arena in which they all converged. Shame became the fuel that drove me to make sports a place to act out my childhood chaos for a growing audience to witness and applaud. It also provided a place for me to hide.

Looking back, I realize that much of my anger arose from my unprocessed grief. As I aged, grief morphed into rage. With no voice to share my hemorrhaging and no adult to discern it, I hurtled toward an incoherent adulthood.

HONEST ABE

Acting out became my act. And a decent actor I was. My preferred persona was the insolent tough guy, which allowed me to cover up the dead spot in my soul and hide the shame in my life story.

Young people's ability to sense and compensate for their own shortcomings is startling. I knew that the things that had happened to me were going to set me back for years to come. I was convinced my life was going to end very badly one day. After getting into a fight or mouthing off to a teacher, I somehow knew that shame and a corresponding anger drove me to each outrageous act. And I cared less and less about controlling my negative emotions. I was a pressure cooker. I simply did not know how to stop. I didn't know how to talk about my experiences or who to talk to. I needed some sort of shock therapy by age twelve. It arrived one winter day in the form of a substitute gym teacher.

Eddie Abramoski, affectionately known as Abe, was a burly trainer for the Buffalo Bills. He had played football at Purdue and had been an athletic trainer at West Point and for the Detroit Lions. He was barrel-chested with a prizefighter's face and a gait like a bull's. I could imagine him taking hold of a player's dislocated shoulder and snapping it back into place with one twist; I could imagine a big lineman leaning on Abe with all his weight as Abe helped him off the field.

When Abe showed up one day as our substitute gym teacher at PS 60, I sensed a special opportunity to act out. I could show this big man that I was a big man, too. I could show this former college football star, this Bills trainer, that I was a man among boys.

The gym was a full-length basketball court with little out-of-bounds space in front of the concrete walls. It was the same gym where I had smashed the ball into that other boy's face.

On Abe's first day substituting, we played kickball. I played like a banshee. I probably played the best game of kickball in the history of American physical education. Booming kicks, spot on target. Pounding people. I ran like a lion.

I noticed Abe watching me. He stood in the middle of the court against the wall with his whistle in his mouth the whole time.

When he whistled the end of class, I knew he was still watching me as we ran to the locker room.

During the first weeks he was there, I never spoke to him but kept going into each gym class as if it were the Super Bowl. I craved to impress this guy. I would go to sleep at night rehashing my heroics from that day and rehearsing what I would do tomorrow.

And then one day I took it too far for Abe. We were playing basketball, six on six, to get more kids into the game. I was driving for a layup and trampled a kid; in keeping with my pattern, everyone stopped and stared. But Abe didn't even look at me. He stopped watching me for the rest of the class. We continued playing, I kept dominating, but I grew enraged that he was paying no attention to me whatsoever. Zero.

After gym class, we all ran off to change, and as I came out of the locker room and walked down the hall I felt someone following me. It was Abe.

I was ready for another Buffalo-style assault and this time I wasn't even scared. I felt like a wave in the ocean was coming at me and I just waited for it to take me under.

But Abe surprised me. Finally, he looked me in the eye, and I could tell by the oddly kind look on his face that this wasn't going to be a blaster.

"I'm not sure why you ran over that kid. But I've been around sports for a long time," he said. "I have never seen a kid your age with your athletic ability. And everyone follows you. You don't even realize how much of a leader you can be. I hope someday you realize it. Get your act together, young fella, and use your gifts for the good."

He smiled kindly, stepped back a bit, and nodded at me. Then he walked away.

I stood there looking at the lockers on the wall across the hall. Abe saw something in me that I didn't see myself. And for the first time in my history with coaches, I felt like someone had my best interest in mind. I felt like someone cared about more than how I played or how tough I was. The word I use today for what Abe did is "affirmation," but then it was just "care." A coach had used his platform to try to make a difference in my life. He deftly disciplined me and showed that he cared about me at the same time.

Many times during my tumultuous years at Riverside High, I got sudden, unplanned visits from Buffalo Bills players. I was usually called out of the classroom or approached on the field. "Coach" Abramoski was sending them over to mentor me, more as a person than as a player. They were surprise visits, flattering ones, intimidating ones, but ultimately inspiring. They helped to corral a wild stallion.

Honest Abe started something. It was a brief encounter that provided me with a long-lasting resiliency. He may have done more to transform my life and self-concept than any coach I ever had. He did not realize it, but he was the first transformational coach I ever came across. He affirmed me, allowed me to attach to him; he put my well-being before his needs, and he provided a sense of my human, not just my athletic, potential. That meeting didn't set me straight, but it gave me the abiding sense that sports could be good for me and I could be good for sports. So I played on.

FRIDAY NIGHTS LIGHTS

Abe gave me permission to dream big dreams.

Just like all teenagers, I longed to belong and be a part of something. To have an identity, to be known and accepted for who I was—or at least who people thought I was—was what I craved. During my freshman year at Riverside High School, I fulfilled the fantasy of most boys in Buffalo. I made the high school varsity football team.

I earned a new nickname, too, an affectionate one: Rookie. None of the older players knew my name, and during one of the first practices someone referred to me as the rookie. The name stuck and to this day I am still called Rookie by friends and family.

For the next four years, our team went undefeated. I got my first taste of the power of connection and commitment that comes with belonging to a team.

It would never get better than this—the carefree communion of high school football. It was something I would never experience again.

My coach in high school was Charlie Dingboom. What a perfect name for a coach: Ding! Boom! He was by far the most respected person in Riverside and a father figure to many. Like Honest Abe, he taught me a great lesson that would take me many years to appreciate.

It was my junior year and I was a star player. We had been undefeated for two seasons and were about to face our stiffest competitor—South Park High School.

I had been out on Friday night drinking and fighting alongside some of my teammates in another section of Buffalo. Coach Dingboom found out and threw me and three other starters off the team just before the game. When I arrived at the locker room, he was waiting for me at the door and would not let me enter.

He wanted me to learn that no one—no matter how good a player you were, no matter how important everyone thought you were to the team—was bigger than the team. I had to buy a ticket to the biggest game of my life and watch from the bleachers my teammates slug out a 6–0 victory.

What I remember most was the immediate sense of loss—lost identity and lost community. Coach Dingboom's lesson kept me in check for the rest of my playing days. I would party too much, fight, but I would never cross the line that would keep me from suiting up. I needed a team, any team, more than adulation and fame. I loved the latter, but I needed the team more. I didn't ever want to not belong again. I vowed never to allow myself to be so abandoned. Training rules became my Ten Commandments.

ORANGEMAN

When I got to Syracuse University in 1968, I learned about a whole new level of transactional coaching from a World War II paratrooper named Ben Schwartzwalder. Ben was my coach during one of the most tumultuous eras in American cultural history. An old commando and the social chaos of the 1960s were not a good mix—not for him, the team, the campus, or me.

Coach Schwartzwalder had been the head football coach at SU for

more than twenty years when I arrived. I remember a game of my sophomore year when Ben took the game program into the pregame locker
room and counted the number of opposing players with long hair and
mustaches. If they met some unspecified quota of his, he would call the
team "pinko commies," and we would soon be fighting for America,
Mom, and apple pie.

Not surprisingly, Ben was an authoritarian coach. Like many
ex-military coaches of his generation he regularly made connections
between sports, war, patriotism, and manhood. Real men went to war;
real men stoically sacrificed their bodies for the good of the team. The
team was always first; the opponent was the enemy; and his players were
"soldiers" and "warriors" who would "take no prisoners" and "never
surrender." And like all good soldiers, we obediently followed orders,
never questioning the chain of command.

Because of the power of the whistle, Ben was a father figure for me
and I played to win his approval. His attitude toward sports and players
was reminiscent of my father's. I became that five-year-old in the cellar jabbing at Dah's big hand again. I was seen as a big, tough guy—yet
I still felt and acted like a little boy seeking approval. I see now that
Schwartzwalder was a transactional coach. He knew what he wanted
out of me and he knew how to get it. He loved my anger, leveraged my
needs, and used my "mean streak" to serve his mission perfectly.

We were headed for a collision, and it came during the spring before the 1970 season when his authoritarian style reached a breaking
point. We were a preseason Top Ten pick and were hyped for a national
championship. But in spring practice, eight of our African American
players walked off the team. They demanded racial equity on the team,
better medical treatment for all athletes, and integration of the coaching staff.

Ben quickly dismissed them as troublemakers. Colleges all over
America were canceling spring classes because of the Kent State shootings and continuing protests concerning civil rights, women's rights,
and the Vietnam War. The "Syracuse Eight," as they became known,

were aware of the potential consequences of losing their scholarships and not being allowed to play the game they loved. The stakes were high, but the Syracuse Eight were correct in their claims. African American players were given fewer scholarships and had to fight depth charts that were stacked against them. They were confined to certain playing positions and were treated differently from white players.

Despite the risks, they maintained their protest and made the difficult decision to leave the team in hopes of reforming the coach, the athletic department, and the university.

Jim Brown, the great Syracuse and NFL Hall of Fame running back, tried to act as mediator between Schwartzwalder, the boycotting players, and the rest of the team.

"I was there trying to work it out," Brown told the local Syracuse paper. "I listened to them [Syracuse Eight] and they made all the sense in the world, so I went to Ben and tried to represent the fact that these youngsters were making sense and he should take into consideration what they were doing. Ben had no clue, no understanding of what they were doing. He told them they were football players; they weren't black and all that other stuff. He didn't budge."

"You're not black men or white men—you're Orangemen," Ben used to say. I can hear him loud and clear to this day.

I knew our season would suffer without the African American players. I knew the right thing would be to join them, but my own agenda took precedence over theirs. I don't remember Ben ever bringing the team together to talk about reconciliation or rebuilding our broken community. It felt like every man for himself.

I had responsibilities and needed to play so I could get into the NFL. I kept quiet and played that season. We finished 6–4. I made All-American, but my failure to support my black teammates tainted that recognition for me. I regretted my ignorance and my selfishness and also regretted that as a team, we weren't brought together, educated, and given the opportunity to understand our teammates' claims of injustice and to respond together as a community.

Later that year, a committee of students and faculty published a report titled "Allegations of Racial Discrimination in the SU Football Program." The committee concluded that "racism in the Syracuse University Athletic Department is real, chronic, largely unintentional, and sustained and complicated unwittingly by many modes of behavior common in American athletics and long-standing at Syracuse University."

I always wondered what would have happened if Ben had chosen to unite the team to resolve the conflict rather than dividing us to protect himself. I've learned coaching demands overcoming personal prejudices and developing a commitment to lifelong learning. Ben and the white players, myself included, could have learned valuable lessons about courage, commitment, and conviction from our black teammates.

Thirty years later, Syracuse University called me to say it was giving me the Arents Award, an honor given to the university's most distinguished alumni. I paused before I responded, thinking to myself: Do they remember what kind of student I was? Didn't they know those were some of the worst years of my life?

I had not been back to campus for thirty years. But the words of Dr. Martin Luther King Jr. rang in my ears, "We remember not the words of our enemies, but the silence of our friends." I said something that surprised even me. It came out of some distant, wounded past.

"If I come, can I speak?"

I had decided that I had to break my silence. I knew that one of my greatest educational experiences in college was the Syracuse Eight's act of civil disobedience. I didn't realize it at the time but their boycott had taught me as much about justice, courage, and integrity as any event, course, coach, or teacher at the university. Fighting racism had become part of the foundation of my football afterlife and in fact was one reason the university had chosen to honor me! And I intended to say so and to make amends publicly.

I invited two people to join Paula and me that night—John Cherundolo, a teammate and now a judge in Syracuse, and my lacrosse coach,

Roy Simmons Jr. That evening I was able to accept the award on behalf of the Syracuse Eight and publicly repent my lamentable conformity to a culture of silence. Unwittingly, I also put the ghost of Schwartzwalder to rest, and, with one big hug, thanked the lacrosse coach who had taught me that sports and spirituality go hand in hand.

COACH SIMMONS

Honest Abe gave me a taste of what transformational coaching could be. A lacrosse coach named Roy Simmons Jr. gave me the full-course meal.

While rehabbing my knee from an operation the winter before my senior season at Syracuse, I picked up a lacrosse stick for the first time and fell in love with the game. I decided to play lacrosse that spring. I believed it would be much better for me physically and emotionally than going to spring football practice every day. And I was enchanted by the carriage and coaching style of Coach Simmons.

I knew Schwartzwalder would try to stop me for fear my playing lacrosse would interfere with football, but in my senior spring no one had a hold on me. So I tried out for the varsity lacrosse team, and once again my size and speed turned the coaches' heads.

Lacrosse is a wonderful combination of the athleticism of basketball, the physicality of football, and the hand-eye-foot coordination of hockey. I had never seen a lacrosse game played and I was immediately befuddled by how Coach Simmons talked in a way that was completely antithetical to my experiences in other sports and with other coaches.

One clear spring day, I arrived to practice behind Manley Field House and saw a Native American standing with Coach Simmons waiting for the team to assemble for practice. The man wore tribal regalia, and as I approached I naively assumed he was the father of one of my Native American teammates from the Onondaga Reservation just outside Syracuse.

I sat down beside the guys and Coach Simmons introduced the visitor as Chief Oren Lyons, an All-America lacrosse goalie in the 1950s. Chief Lyons is Faith-Keeper of the Turtle Clan of the Onondaga Nation and a Chief of the Six Nations of the Iroquois Confederacy. As Faith-Keeper, Chief Lyons was entrusted to maintain the traditions, values, and history of the Turtle Clan and uphold the Great Law of Peace of the Iroquois. One of those traditions was lacrosse. He was the first person I ever heard make the connection between sports and spirituality. Native Americans call lacrosse "The Creator's Game." Lacrosse was played to honor the Creator and promote peaceful relationships among the various tribes. Some Native American traditions hold that when you cross the great divide into the afterlife you pick up your lacrosse stick on the other side.

My memories of that season were more atmospheric than incidental. There was no shouting, screaming, shaming, or use of sarcasm to control players. Instead, there were these sensations: finesse instead of force, camaraderie instead of combat, and an abiding memory that playing and feeling alive and free were still connected.

As the coach who had the greatest impact on me, Coach Simmons's influence in my life is an example of how a coach integrated sports with life and spirituality. He took my personal vision from the playing field and turned it up to the sky. When I later decided to do the inside work I needed to improve my outside coaching persona, I turned to Coach Simmons as my primary role model. He was that coach who sought to transform and not transact. The virtues of the game—fraternity, skill, spirit—were primary for him. Winning was by no means an afterthought—Coach won six NCAA titles—but actually a consequence of his transformational coaching.

WILD HORSES

In the spring of '73 I was the tenth pick in the first round of the NFL draft, chosen by the Baltimore Colts. "Baltimore?" I couldn't believe it. "The heart of the South!" Or so thought the naive Orangeman from

Buffalo. Joe Thomas, the Colts' general manager, said he "really liked my mean streak." I went from the most transformational sports experience of my life, playing lacrosse, right into the most transactional one. Professional football is business and therefore based on the quid pro quo. You do this, you get that. A great game gets you adulation, a bad one warrants immediate skepticism or dismissal. A good practice gains you more playing time; a bad one can get you cut.

I had the privilege to play a great game in a great football town and be a hero to thousands of kids. But in retrospect, I approached the experience with barely a quarter of my heart. I had a symbiotic relationship with the Colts fans, turning their adoration into my motivation on Sundays. But jovial Joe was telling them a lie every time I appeared on the field, at a public event, or even at a bar. I was a drug addict. It began when I was given a Valium Demerol one-two punch before knee surgery following my junior season at Syracuse. I had never felt anything like it—all the pain, and not just the physical pain, went away, at least for a while. This medication continued on an almost daily basis, and once I was drafted, drugs became the way to medicate past emotional wounds and soften the new and overwhelming pressure of professional football.

When the Colts ended training camp my rookie year, final cuts had not been made. The team put us up in a motel for the last week of preseason. I was smoking marijuana daily, using speed to get up for games and barbiturates to come back down after them. One day a knock on my motel door startled me from a midmorning nap. I staggered up to open the door. It was the maid, and I told her to go ahead and clean the room. I sat on the bed to put on my shoes and realized I had drugs spread out on the nightstand table by the bed. I didn't even care. I walked past her and left them there.

"Twenty minutes," she said.

"Take your time," I said as I walked down the hall.

I went out for lunch and when I came back the door was closed and the maid was gone. I opened the door and went in and started to laugh.

The maid had even tidied up my drugs and paraphernalia. So I lay back down for my postlunch nap, and just as I was dozing the phone rang. It was the assistant to our head coach telling me to come to the coach's office immediately.

As I arrived, the assistant invited me in. I sat and we looked at each other without speaking. I was expecting a pep talk or praise. But my heart started pounding as he informed me that the maid had called the office saying I had a room filled with drugs.

He paused and I prepared myself to be told I was being cut. Then he shocked me even more.

"Listen, Joe, you don't need to say anything," he said. "You've got a great career ahead of you, but if this is true, you need to clean up your room and clean up your life. If it's not true, then we will forget about this conversation."

And then he dismissed me. As I reentered my room I grabbed the pipe lying on the table. I got up and lit it and took a few tokes to calm my nerves.

I played at a time in the NFL when there were no drug tests, few behavior policies, and almost no interest in the well-being of talented but troubled young men. The only concern was winning. If you couldn't perform, you were released. Even the press that covered the teams seldom reported players' misbehavior.

So I became a bit more discreet with my drug use, performed well enough on the field, and gave the press and public what they wanted.

"I really want to get Namath good. I want to knock his head off. I could really build up a tempo for smacking him in his face." That was a statement I gave to the *New York Times* before playing the Jets. Today I'd be fined a lot of money for that statement. These days some football players talk big before games, but we know it is entertainment. The press eats up the bravado, the opposing players respond, and a lot of the supposed rivals laugh together once they get on the field and see the frenzied crowd thinking that what was said was meant.

I, on the other hand, was not trying to be entertaining. I meant it. I thought that way and I played that way. As part of the veterans' hazing, each rookie was forced to stand on a table in the dining room and sing his alma mater's fight song. I refused. They could tell I would rather fight than submit. So I didn't. I thought that validated my manhood.

Baltimore is one of the greatest football towns in America, and the fans loved a hard-nosed lunatic. I loved the adulation in return and tried to give the crowd the show it came to see. To get what I needed, I gave them what they wanted. It seemed like a win-win.

During the week, I provided a different sort of entertainment. I was a reliable regular in the Fells Point bar district on weekdays. Beer, pot, coke, and once in a while things far trickier and more scary-sounding filled my nights. I was wild but friendly, big but approachable, and I loved being the life of the party.

In retrospect, my playing suffered immensely—I am certain I could have played much better. I always tell my high school players that the worst thing in sports is to have a case of the regrets. I wish I had . . . I could have . . . if only I had. . . . I have a lot of regrets about my career, but I was in too much pain, too alone, and too afraid to get the help I needed. But the fans thought I was great and that was enough for me.

Coach Simmons's lessons and the spirituality of sports receded into the background of my life. I harnessed all the old anger and shame that Schwartzwalder had tapped into and I lived a blissfully hazy life of denial, moving from one Sunday performance to the next.

The greatest Sundays of my life came in 1975. In 1974, we finished 2–12. Our philosophy, or at least mine, was: "When we win, we celebrate and when we lose, we party." In '75 our new head coach was Ted Marchibroda, one of the finest people I know. Ted was not a mentor or guru in a Roy Simmons sort of way, but he deftly developed camaraderie among us by simply being himself. He was the Favorite Uncle type, so guileless and genuine that everyone wanted to play hard for him. I have tremendous love and respect for Ted as a man and a coach.

We won our first game, in Chicago against the Bears. They had a highly touted rookie running back from Jackson State named Walter

Payton, whom we held to eight carries for no yards. Someone made the comment that he must have been highly overrated!

We then lost the next four games. We had allowed ourselves to become conditioned to losing and seeing ourselves as losers. But something started to change. Ted believed in us and kept convincing us that we were capable of much more. We started to like one another. We started hanging out and partying together, and suddenly things began to turn around. We won game after game. I toned down my bar-hopping with each game we won and started to host poker games and team parties at my house.

Within the individualistic culture of professional football, I sensed myself trying to foster the development of a community, a band of brothers. Honest Abe's affirmation of my leadership ability came to fruition as I helped lead us on and off the field. We won one, then two in a row, then six, seven, eight, nine! We grew closer and closer as a team and the town sensed it. Our season ended at 10–4, and we won the next three division titles. Nineteen seventy-five was a standout season for Baltimore, for the Colts, and for me.

In fact, we had a reunion of that '75 team in 2009, hosted by Jim Irsay, the owner of the Indianapolis Colts. Jim was a teenager during that turnaround season when his father owned the team in Baltimore. He wanted to honor and celebrate the memory of that year and the players and coaches who made it happen. So he flew all the players, coaches, and wives to Indianapolis for a banquet and a ball game. It was amazing to hear my teammates, thirty-four years later, talk about how that year was one of the most exciting and amazing years in their lives. Every speech was about the relationships we had developed on and off the field. It was our relationships that transformed a losing team into an NFL powerhouse that year.

Back in 1975 I also met someone else whom I would eventually come to think of as a coach—a tall, skinny flower child named Paula Peach.

My growing popularity landed me an invitation to Commander Jim's Singles Radio, a local, extremely popular broadcast modeled after the television show *The Dating Game* with a host named Jim Lange. It was marketed as a "celebrity call-in," and I was the mystery date for the "lucky" local lady who called in and could guess who I was! Over the air, with much of Baltimore listening, host Commander Jim gave the "innocent" Paula some hints about who the mystery man might be.

"He's part of the famous Sack Pack on the Baltimore Colts and he's the best-looking one."

"Uh . . . John Dutton?"

"No . . . he's a great guy. He's really well-known . . . a great player . . ."

"Is it Freddie Cook?"

I was on the other end of the line thinking this stupid show wasn't such a good idea. Little did I know I'd been set up and listeners were getting a real chuckle at my expense. Paula didn't know anything about the Colts' defense; she was playing along with the script they had given her. She named every other player on the Colts' Sack Pack before she finally conceded.

"Oh—it must be Joe Ehrmann!"

Much of Baltimore, including many of my teammates, enjoyed the joke and looked forward to seeing how this dating game fix-up was going to turn out.

Following the show, the radio station set up our date. I left two tickets for Paula at Will Call at Memorial Stadium, the last game of the season. We played the New England Patriots that day. The game ended with us beating them in a terrific battle, winning the divisional title. After showering, I walked outside the locker room and reluctantly searched for my blind date. I was surprised when I found her; a shaggy-headed five-foot-ten nineteen-year-old in jeans and a hooded sweatshirt. I invited her into the clubhouse for the team Christmas celebration, and we have been together ever since. This would turn out to be the most surprising game changer of my life, as I ended up learning more about becoming a man from Paula than from any other person in my life.

Memorial Stadium is one of my most memorable places. It was built in 1954 to honor the war dead of World War II. It was a holy place for

Baltimoreans, a sacred space cast in concrete and exposed beams that galvanized the state of Maryland. Unlike stadiums today where people sit according to economic status, Memorial Stadium obliged all sorts of people to sit alongside one another. Every Sunday people left their seg-regated churches and neighborhoods to cheer together as they watched black men and white men, Northerners and Southerners, Republicans and Democrats try to model for a nation how to play as a team.

And for the next three years, the Colts approximated the recently ended era of Johnny Unitas in Baltimore. We were appreciated and needed. I kept partying, but with less venom and more collegiality. Honest Abe was proud to know I was named cocaptain but would have been far more proud of my leadership skills.

The fun continued until the summer of '78, my sixth year in the NFL. My brother, Billy, was preparing to go to college for his fresh-man year of football. I got him a job in training camp with the Colts. I wanted him to spend the summer with the team to learn the work ethic of a professional athlete. I wanted him to learn the skills and techniques of a defensive lineman from the best.

One day in late July, I was sitting on the table getting my ankles taped for an afternoon practice when Billy walked up to me with a mas-sive black-and-blue mark on his chest. Our trainer, Eddie Block, was so concerned that he sent Billy for a blood test. Jim Irsay, Billy's friend, spent the day with him while I practiced. That night I got a call from Johns Hopkins Hospital. "Bring your brother immediately."

As they checked him in, I was sent to the oncology floor to await his room assignment. I didn't know what the word "oncology" meant. I will never forget asking a nurse what it meant and hearing her spine-tingling response: cancer. Later that night a doctor pulled me aside and said, "Listen, Billy's got cancer and it's a type of cancer where there's virtually nothing we can do to help him."

Billy had something called aplastic anemia, a bone marrow cancer that stops the making of new blood cells. As I watched my nineteen-year-old brother confront his own mortality with tears in his eyes, I realized that everything I had invested my life in—the applause, awards, and accumulation of material things—none of this really mattered or provided help or hope for him. I tried a few locker-room style pep talks in the early days of his illness but soon forsook those empty words. Touch became our main form of communication, because of my stunted emotional vocabulary. I think we both knew where and how it was going to end.

I had a cot placed next to his bed and slept there most nights during the season except for our away games.

Every day for five months, I joined other families with sick and dying children in the waiting room of that oncology floor. I soon discovered a caring community unlike anything I had ever belonged to. The presence of courage and teamwork was as strong as in any locker room. The families celebrated each improved blood result, supported each other when bad days came, lined up to face devastating reports together with gallantry and grace. In that waiting room it was no longer just about "my" child—it was about all "our" children.

We knew Billy would die—his descent was so rapid and irreversible, so predictable, so tied to the calendar that it was like a pregnancy in reverse. Just before the last game of the season I made a decision to bring Billy to our home in Baltimore so he could die in the presence of the people who had loved and nurtured him. I got him discharged and took him one last time to a place he loved. I put him in my car and drove over to Memorial Stadium, where the Colts were practicing. My teammates came out to the car and lifted up this former defensive lineman, who was probably down to about 120 pounds. They carried him into the locker room, helped him undress, and put him in one of the whirlpools. As he sat in the pool soothing his aching body, my teammates came in one by one to say good-bye. He kept leaning his head back, closing his eyes, and licking his lips as if he wanted to taste his last moments.

I took him home that night. The whole family was there, including his dog, Benji. His friends came down from Buffalo and we celebrated an early Christmas. The next morning he died on our waterbed. I had

had five months to prepare for his death, but the reality and finality of it devastated me. We took his body and flew it back up to Buffalo for his funeral. My teammates and coaches came, too.

Standing in that cemetery in the middle of December was the turning point in my lilfe. The snow was blowing in my face. Hundreds of people came out. At the end of the ceremony I stood next to the casket, next to the open grave. I heard the priest say the final "Amen." And with that, everybody turned and just started walking away. And I remember wanting to scream. I wanted to say, "You mean this is it? You have some good times, some bad times, you live, you die, and then everybody just walks away?"

I was twenty-nine years old. I was six years into my NFL career and I was angrier and more lost than ever. A few weeks after Billy's death, a new kind of coach entered my life. He had as great an impact as any sports coach I ever played for. I received a call from a psychologist in Baltimore named Dr. Jay Levenson who specialized in death, dying, and bereavement. He had read about my brother's death and suggested we have lunch.

That day at the table he handed me Viktor Frankl's book *Man's Search for Meaning*. Jay Levinson had been Dr. Frankl's graduate assistant at United States International University in San Diego and remained a close disciple and friend.

Dr. Frankl had been imprisoned in a Nazi concentration camp with his wife, parents, and brother. His father died of pneumonia in Treblinka, his mother and brother were gassed at Auschwitz, and his wife, Tilly, died of malnutrition at the Bergen-Belsen concentration camp, two days after it was liberated by British troops. He alone survived.

In *Man's Search for Meaning* Frankl writes that everything can be taken from a man but one thing: the greatest of all human freedoms, the ability to choose how to respond to any given circumstance. Frankl said that we retain the freedom to choose our attitudes and actions in response to whatever life deals us.

I wrote that statement over and over in a notebook.

Jay and I met again to discuss the book, and he helped me realize I could choose how to respond not only to my brother's death but to all the trials and tribulations facing families with seriously ill children. And Jay handed me the perfect response to Billy's death. He envisioned a place for the families of sick and dying children where their basic needs could be met, a place that would provide a caring community in which families could help and support each other as well. I remembered the camaraderie among the parents and family members who spent those hard nights together in the oncology ward at Hopkins. So many of them came from all over the country and could not afford to stay in a hotel room. They had no place to shower, let alone close a door and escape. Jay invited me to use my athletic platform and visibility to transform my grief into a transcendent cause.

So Jay and I brought together a diverse team of compassionate and committed people to make a difference in the lives of others. Under Jay's transformative coaching, our team built Baltimore's Ronald McDonald House. The doors opened on June 28, 1982, on what would have been my brother's twenty-third birthday. Each of the thirty-five thousand families from around the world who have walked through those doors have seen a plaque that reads: "In memory of Billy Ehrmann, whose life brought together those who built this House."

I was beginning to take control of my life, to unshackle myself from the past and choose the future I wanted to live. I asked the Colts for my release to get a fresh start, and my football days in Baltimore ended. I was picked up by the Detroit Lions, and there I started to deal on a deeper level with some of my issues. I was sad leaving Baltimore and the Colts, but knew I needed to leave town in order to grow. I was a local celebrity and a good teammate. But the zenith of my life as a professional athlete was my response to Billy's death and the relationships that I developed because of it.

Billy's death had been a rock bottom experience for me, leaving me with a clear view of what was and wasn't important in life. I had teammates during that season who worried about Paula and me, prayed for us, and invited us to the team Bible study. They were shocked when we actually showed up and even more shocked when I ended up in seminary less than two years later. Larry Moody and Dave Kruger of Search Ministries were the leaders of the Colts Bible study, and two of the first men who loved and accepted me unconditionally.

I remember going to that first Bible study, sitting in the driveway getting high, trying to build up the nerve to enter the group. After I took a chair, one of my teammates stuck his nose in the air, sniffed around the room, and declared, "I smell marijuana." Larry quickly quieted him, wanting me to feel accepted where I was at that time in my life. They taught me and modeled for me the truth that *people don't care what you know until they know that you care.* There was no pretense and no hidden agenda. It was the perfect place for me to express my pain and explore my questions about God's involvement in suffering and the meaning and purpose of life. Larry and Dave shaped not only my theology but also my coaching philosophy: It's all about relationships.

OPEN THE DOOR

I enrolled in Dallas Theological Seminary during the off-seasons of my first two years with the Lions. I was on a spiritual quest and looking to find answers. Upon my retirement from football, I went to Westminster Theological Seminary in Philadelphia to pursue a degree in Urban Ministry. Paula and I joined Refuge Evangelical Baptist Church, a small, struggling storefront church where we were the only white members. Under the leadership of Reverend Wilbert Richardson, we were loved and mentored, and I learned more about practical theology there than in any of the many seminary classes I had taken.

After seminary, Paula and I moved back to Baltimore and I began my new Sunday game with Search Ministries. I preached on Sundays and spent weekdays trying to teach and coach young people in one of the most battered neighborhoods in Baltimore, a place where the television show *The Wire* would later be filmed. I preached the way I led on the field: booming, raucous, and self-involved. Paula called my preaching style "early locker room."

We developed a community-based ministry called The Door. We started by trying to help meet the basic needs of the community—food, shelter, help with evictions, after-school programs, and family counseling. Eventually we addressed more systemic issues such as racism, job training, economic development, and housing. But I knew that my greatest and most satisfying impact was as Coach Reverend Joe.

I was coaching a Pop Warner football team in the neighborhood and took kids to games all over the city. In contrast to all the preaching and social justice work that was so difficult, I felt like these kids on my team were alive and changing and feeling joy. I felt like transformation was taking place inside the minds of my players—the kind of powerful change I wasn't achieving so well in my other endeavors.

As the local crack wars intensified, I grew more worried for my players' safety. Some started missing practice because they were too scared to cross the newly created gang boundaries to get to the field in the late afternoon. One kid, nicknamed Chink by the others, jokingly said that the best way to come to practice was on a bicycle because it made him harder to catch.

Chink never missed practice, and then one day he didn't show. A stray bullet had hit him in the chest as he rode to the field, and he died on the way to the hospital. I will never forget the faces on the boys standing before me that day at practice as the news of his death hit us all.

A few days later, we met at The Door as a team and drove across town together for Chink's funeral. On that trip, as bus driver and coach and consoler, I had my clearest realization that transformational coaching was the most direct and powerful way to connect and convey empathy and guidance to young people.

SEASON OF LIFE

I first met Biff Poggi while playing with the Colts. He was a great high school lineman in Baltimore who looked like a thirty-year-old even at sixteen. He used to sneak into the Colts' weight room, and I remember thinking we must have claimed him off waivers. He went on to play at Pitt and Duke. The next time I saw him was twenty years later when he and his dad brought a carload of food to help fill our pantry at The Door. He had coached several years at the college level and was now an assistant coach at a local private boys' school.

We reconnected immediately and started to meet for breakfasts on a regular basis. The conversations inevitably turned into mutual reflections on how more inspirational coaching would have helped us avoid many pitfalls and much self-sabotaging behavior. We were an odd couple united by our sports regrets.

Biff, too, had suffered through his share of adolescent hardships and likewise had compounded them by acting out. Now he was working as hard as I was to understand what had happened to him and to line it all up into a coherent narrative. We saw the destructive coaching around us as well as our own errors. We determined that we wanted to create a football program that applied what life had taught us about the game, about coaching, about being teens, and about ourselves.

At these weekly breakfast meetings, we had heated discussions about seemingly irreconcilable issues. Is football violent or merely aggressive? Can you really love your players and win? What do you replace the so-called killer instinct with and will a player and team be as effective if they learn true competition instead of a winning-is-the-only-thing approach? Can a cohesive team built on brotherhood and a new form of masculinity and empathy win championships?

We grew confident that our answers to these questions would defy the orthodox expectations about kids, coaching, and winning. And we decided to undertake the experiment to prove our hypothesis.

Gilman is a sprawling campus in one of the wealthiest neighborhoods in Baltimore. It is a great school academically and its kids get into the best colleges around the country. But in Baltimore it is also known as a rich kids' school. Indeed, it is an expensive place to attend and there are lots of fancy cars in the student parking lot. But it is also a diverse school racially, religiously, and economically.

Gilman's headmaster at the time was Reddy Finny, whose own icon-oclastic approach to boys, diversity, and sports is legendary. A trans-formational coach in Biff's life, Reddy endorsed our experiment and was instrumental in getting Gilman to hire Biff to put our theories to the test.

The Gilman program took off. Then one day I got a call from an old friend, Jeffrey Marx. Jeffrey had been a ballboy for the Colts when I played. He was writing an article about former Colts and came to a coaching clinic I was teaching at the University of Maryland. Jeffrey was initially interested in writing a book about my life and how he and I had reconnected. Several weeks into the Gilman football season, he came to realize that the focus of the book should be the coaching philosophy.

Jeffrey's terrific book about a year of Gilman football, *Season of Life*, became a *New York Times* bestseller. It feels funny to read about yourself as if each page you turn is a day in your life or a part of your soul. The book helped to put my life's narrative on sequential pages. Holding the book somehow gave me the sense that I was beginning to know myself.

Every coach has a story that fits between two book covers. To be empathic, to be instructive, and to have an impact as coaches, we have to find our own narratives first—understand them, contain and bind them. If you want to be a better coach, you have to become a better you. The coach's journey took me almost thirty years and the clock is still running. Just about every part of my life story revolved around sports—all the big events, highs and lows, even the moments of life and death. And with the prominence of sports in our culture, I would guess that many coaches might say the same thing.

I have told the story of my sports life in this chapter as a way to introduce the big themes that drove me to reframe coaching and try to help reform sports. This reclamation of an inherently sacred profession—coaching—is based on a bold conviction that sports can help transform our young people. Sports are a rite of passage in a country that has few transformative rites. While our social ills are plentiful, I believe that coaches have the power, platform, and position to be the linchpins in individual and social transformation—player by player, team by team, teachable moment by teachable moment.

Sports are all about stories—recounting the great play, arguing about strategies employed, and marveling at the courage of athletes. I lived my story hard—to the brink and back far too many times—and coaching became the perfect ending to my own story. Coaching was my destiny. It took me a long time to realize this, but, once I did, I discovered that my sports story finally made perfect sense.

The keys to redemptive sports are the thousands of potentially transformational coaches, the numerous men and women who understand the importance of coaching from the inside out and the power that comes from understanding their own past in order to coach wholly in the present. Coaches have to get their own story down as coherently as possible before turning to the sacred task of transforming young people. The best way to start, I realize now, is to pick some heroes—some InSideOut coaches from any field who help us understand our own stories, go beyond them, and show us how to coach for others.

CHAPTER 2

My Heroes Have Always Been Coaches

One of the highlights of my week is a breakfast club. My companions are gentlemen in their seventies and eighties and I am the honorary youth in the group.

Wisdom and age tend to go hand and hand, and I acquire a lot of wisdom from these men. World War II tales; old Baltimore stories; family triumphs and tragedies; farming, banking, and fishing stories; there is rarely a pause in the hearty conversation.

As an ex-Colt, I am often asked to tell football stories. And they love those. But one morning I asked to hear their sports stories. There were five of us at that breakfast and I heard about plenty of sports injuries that worsen with age, about a few heroic shots, and about one classic goat moment where a guy ran the wrong way after an interception during a high school game.

But each member of the breakfast club shared one similar memory: a snapshot of an exchange with a coach that he remembered vividly, word for word, as if it had happened on the way to the diner that morning. As each gentleman spoke, I realized that the snapshot was really a mental video they had been playing over and over for decades.

One guy remembered, from more than forty years ago, the anxiety and anguish of waiting for final cuts to be posted on the gym wall. He recounted how he slowly slid along the opposite wall in the hall waiting for a solitary moment to see if he had been cut. He had, and he cried and turned from some approaching students to hide his tears. He told how, after a sleepless night, he summoned the courage to speak to the coach to try to understand why he did not make the team.

The coach said, "You're just not good enough!"

My breakfast mate has carried this memory with him all these years. Another fellow recounted having to go to the foul line for a potential game-winning free throw while in high school. As he told the story you could see his pulse quicken and his face redden.

As the referee handed him the ball, his coach called a time-out and motioned to him to come over to the bench. Coach locked eyes with him and said, "I know you will make this shot," and sent him back to the line.

He made the shot and won the game but says he felt more pressure at that moment than even as a fighter pilot during World War II.

Both these men, in their eighties, were forever shaped by these momentary interactions with coaches.

As an ordained minister, I have preached in churches for decades. That morning at the diner, I wondered how often the members of my congregation will remember a sermon of mine thirty or forty years from now.

But I have coached hundreds of players by now and I am certain of this: 100 percent of them will remember my name, the words I spoke to them, and the emotions generated by our conversations and interactions. Forever! This is part of the awesome power and responsibility of coaching: You give your players memories, for better or for worse, that stay with them until the day they die.

So I started to ask men and women I met this question: When you were younger, what person made the biggest difference in your life?

The answer was invariably someone who mentored, taught, advised, affirmed, or inspired. That person was often a coach.

When I meet with coaches I am pleased to share this very unscientific poll with them. It flatters them; then it usually gives them pause. As they contemplate the magnitude of their position and the lifelong consequences of their words and actions, I sense a shock of recognition.

Then I ask some probing questions: Given that you are so prominent and powerful in the memories of so many young people, who are your coaching role models? Who do you aspire to be as a coach? After whom do you pattern your method of mentoring, teaching, advising, leading, and inspiring? On what do you base your coaching philosophy?

Until a few years ago, I might have given the same pat answers they usually do. I might have said that good coaches are judged more on wins and losses. You know the ones—the sages and tough guys and gals whom the media crown geniuses because they win a lot of championships. I can't label them transactional coaches because I don't know most of them. Most of us would agree that they are famous for their winning record and not because of their transformational ability to mold and shape the character of their players. We know their names because they win.

But I wonder if we have any idea what these coaches' real purposes, missions, or values are. What kind of men and women are they off the field and out of the limelight? What is the moral and ethical composition of their program? What are they teaching about living an honorable life? Or do they focus only on the win-loss record, mastery over the Xs and Os, and promotion of their own images and reputations?

When I started coaching I hadn't thought through the need to clarify why I was coaching or how I was coaching. I just coached the way I had been coached—or the way I had seen others coach—for better or,

more typically, for worse. I occasionally connected but usually trans-
acted with my players.

When we were children many of us had moments when our parents
said something to us and we thought to ourselves, "When I become a
parent I'll never say that to my kids." Then we become parents and our
children hear those exact words come out of our mouths!

I think it is the same with coaches. Some of us remember being
shouted at or shamed. We recall moments of stomach-turning pressure,
praise withheld, or simply brutal criticism from coaches.

Yet when we coach, we often find ourselves replicating the same
harmful drills and repeating the same hurtful words and ways of interacting. They just come out of our mouths or get written into a practice
schedule as unconsciously or unmindfully as breathing and walking.

Early on as a coach I threw in a little Dingboom here, some Schwartzwalder there, dashes of Abe's affirmation and Coach Simmons's inspiration, balanced by Vince Lombardi's aggression—all in the name of
realizing my father's objective of turning my players into men!

My coaching was a hodgepodge of unsorted, memory-driven impulses thrown at my players. I gave little forethought to their effect or
effectiveness. I did not look inside, account for my behavior, and adjust
it before it reached the outside and turned into lifelong, and sometimes
hurtful, memories for my athletes. Being unaware of myself, I stayed
unaware of my effect on players or their feelings and reactions. That
lack of awareness can turn potentially positive learning experiences
into nightmares that haunt athletes for a lifetime. Just ask my breakfast-
club buddies.

I began the InSideOut coaching process by recalling and trying to
understand the experiences, feelings, attitudes, and behaviors of coaches
and adults who impacted my life. Chapter 1 is my autobiographical history that unfolded from doing this inside work. Some experiences were
easy to recall, others more difficult, and some extremely painful. I knew
that to change the way I was coaching, I had to make sense of the way
I had been coached. Understanding myself and how others influenced

me ultimately produced insight and empathy in me, for myself and for my players.

I also learned that to become transformational coaches, we often need to seek models outside traditional coaching archetypes and think beyond personal experiences. Coaches exist in all walks of life. Some of the best models are not even found in sports history. They are found in literature and world history. When I ask my audiences about coaching models, they often throw back that question at me. "Joe, which coach influenced you the most?" I immediately name Coach Simmons. He was a sculptor of a coach—he chiseled and carved us into thoughtful young men, just as Native Americans carved wooden lacrosse sticks out of tree branches.

The next question audiences ask is, "Who are your coaching role models?" It took me time over the years to identify them. I finally settled on Dorothy from the Wizard of Oz and Moses—two coaches far removed from the world of sports who nevertheless perfectly fit my aspirations. Am I joking? Not at all. Think about it. One, a young coach full of affirmation and empathy, exhorting and encouraging her players to reach their greatest potential. The other, a biblical liberator building players and a team based on moral and ethical principles.

Coach Simmons gave me firsthand experience—he touched me emotionally in a way that made me want to imitate him. As a coach, I wanted to help restore the spirituality, honor, and sacredness of sports. I played for a gentleman who showed me how to do it. Then, in my quest to broaden the dimensions of transformational coaching, I needed coaching models as big as Dorothy and Moses to satisfy my intellectual and social ambitions for coaching.

After a few years of coaching, I realized I had the power to take young people, crippled by their supposed personal deficits and deficiencies, and help them discover the power within themselves to overcome and to achieve. Dorothy gave me a coaching model for a travel team. The Yellow Brick Road of every season is an opportunity to affirm, and encourage, rather than demean and defame.

I also realized sports could liberate young people from their shackles of fears, doubts, anxieties, and social pressures. So I studied the techniques of one of the greatest liberators of all time, Moses.

All my models—Coach Simmons, Dorothy, and Moses—are limited, flawed, and therefore all the more accessible to my imagination. All three demonstrate the courage that it takes as a coach to transform lives, communities, and culture. They show that coaching cannot be reduced to strategy and technique. Great coaching demands introspection, integrity, and integration of the coach's life history. All three help me to step outside the standard "coaching box" and coach according to the needs of my players.

COACH SIMMONS: THE DREAM CATCHER

The Syracuse lacrosse team was struggling that day. They had had a long bus trip, the April rain and chill made the field sloppy and the ball slippery, and a flu bug had hit the team, to boot.

The Orangemen were down 7–3 at halftime and their opponents were sensing a huge upset victory.

Coach Simmons walked into the locker room and surveyed his team. They were dripping with rain, wiping mud off their uniforms, listless.

They grew silent, waiting for his halftime speech. He opened his mouth, paused, and studied them again.

Then he went over to the blackboard and wrote the following in big, thick figures: 118–24.

He turned, looked each player in the eye, and suddenly smiled.

His players looked shocked for a moment, and then started to smile slightly, too. They didn't know what to make of it—was this a play or formation that Coach had just come up with?

Coach spoke: "Psalm 118, verse 24. 'This is the day that the Lord has made, so rejoice and be glad in it.' "

He noticed the players' shoulders easing, their bouncing legs grow still, and he heard a few exhalations and chuckles.

"That's it, men. Win, lose, or draw; enjoy. Let's get back out there and play like you love the game and each other."

He shocked them, and the players shocked the crowd and the opponent by dominating the second half. Coach Simmons quietly taught a lesson those young men will, no doubt, remember for the rest of their lives: Sports are meant to be enjoyed regardless of the score. Sports are a gift, an honor to play. Sports foster a satisfying sense of community. And when you enjoy what you're doing and enjoy who you're doing it with, team performance automatically improves.

After that game, Coach discovered the numbers 118–24 written on the chalkboard before every game for decades. He never knew who started the tradition—or which players continued it year after year. But he clearly remembers the lasting impression that verse made on his players on that muddy April day.

Coach Simmons will turn seventy-six soon. His wife, Nancy, died a tragic and untimely death in his arms three years ago. Nancy was the love of his life, his "seraphine angel." After fifty years of marriage the loss is a deep struggle. But art and sports still renew him daily and help him, he says, "to mend the hole in my heart." He travels with the lacrosse team regularly, follows all the SU sports, and humbly remains confident that his way of coaching is part of the legacy that lives on in me and other players he has coached.

Playing lacrosse for Coach Simmons required a consuming devotion to rejoice and be glad. His approach to the game, his manner with players, and his view of the role of sports in life made lacrosse both the sport it was intended to be by its Native American founders and an experience far more rewarding and spiritual than we typically expect from sports today.

Coach laughs recalling another anecdote about that psalm. "Years later," he says, "the coach of a team we beat regularly came up to me at a coaches' convention. He said, 'Roy, I just want to ask you one question. Every other year, you come and beat us on our field and after a few years I started to go into the visiting locker room to see if I could discover any secret from something you left behind. And there is always this play on the board: 118–24. What is that play, Roy?' "

Coach Simmons put his arm around the coach and laughed. He shared his secret play willingly, and the coach shook his head and laughed, too.

Another anecdote: At practice, Coach was always shouting the word "Dig!" At first I thought it meant get lower for the ball. As a football lineman, I always thought in terms of leverage as I battled offensive linemen. I always tried to dig as low as I could when the ball was snapped. But I soon realized "dig" had many meanings for Coach. It indeed could mean dig for the ball—lacrosse parlance for getting your stick under it. It could mean dig deep—his practices were tough and required regular gut checks. But to Coach it always meant: Dignity, Integrity, and Grace. D-I-G. Coach Simmons became my primary coaching model because this three-word paradigm defined his program.

By thinking through our story and my relationship with him, I realized he connected with me in a way no other coach ever did. His acute awareness of his players' needs grew out of his own self-awareness, which made it easy for young men to connect with him. That connection is what I seek to provide as a coach, so my InSideOut work required a thorough study of the master.

Dignity

In 1988, Coach Simmons thought he had a special group. Fall workouts showed him a team that seemed more cohesive than most, fun-loving but serious and charismatic, if such a word could be used to describe a team.

It had talent from top to bottom, a nice mix of veterans and freshmen, and a good grasp of the fundamentals of the game.

The team met one last time before Christmas break and Coach sensed a championship spring coming.

But then everything changed. The terrorist bombing of the Pan Am 103 plane over Lockerbie, Scotland, killed thirty-five Syracuse students, including one lacrosse player, coming home for Christmas from studying abroad. The campus and community were devastated with grief.

"People often ask me to name my most memorable moment as a coach," Coach told me. "They expect some scoreboard-related memory or a coaching honor. It takes them aback when I say it was our team trip to Lockerbie."

The trip arose out of Coach Simmons's conviction that sports should heal.

"I sat in the crowd at the Carrier Dome with thousands of people at the memorial service and kept asking myself, 'What can I do to help address all this grief? I'm a coach, what should I or could I do?'

"I decided to take my boys to Lockerbie, to make lacrosse, this great game, the ambassador to these poor people who also suffered so much on the ground, with airplane parts crashing into homes and bodies hanging everywhere," Coach Simmons told me.

The team played the season in honor of the victims and community, but all the while Coach and his boys were raising funds for their trip once the season was over.

They arrived at the Lockerbie Academy and a solitary bagpiper met the team. They were all weeping. They played an exhibition game that day and gave lacrosse clinics to the local kids over the next several days. They brought equipment as gifts. And they laid a wooden lacrosse stick covered with roses at the memorial built for the dead. Coach has gone back several times with players and has maintained an equipment pipeline to sustain their presence. Scotland now has a national lacrosse team and the sport has spilled over into Wales.

Dignity pervades Coach Simmons's approach to the game. Just as the Native Americans used lacrosse to honor their Great Spirit, Coach used the sport to honor the Lockerbie dead and their mourners. His players were quickly educated in the brevity of life, its sacredness, and the power sports have to enrich relationships, and in this case, to honor and uphold human dignity.

Coach Simmons is an archetypal coach for me because he recognizes and uses this sacred power of sports. From global tragedies like Lockerbie to the individual struggle of a player in search of life's meaning, dignity was always the name of the game for Coach Simmons.

Integrity

Coach Simmons played lacrosse with Jim Brown at SU. Jim was not only one of the greatest running backs in the history of the NFL, he is also considered by many to be the greatest lacrosse player in history, too.

"I figure I got knocked over by Jim Brown more than any athlete ever," Coach said, reminiscing about his practice mate.

But it was Jim's relationship with Coach Simmons's father that left the biggest impression on him, instructing Coach in the imperative of integrity and social responsibility.

Jim Brown still points to Roy Simmons Sr. as one of the most instrumental men in his life. Roy Sr. coached football, lacrosse, and boxing at Syracuse. One day, Roy Sr. received a call from a judge from Manhasset, Long Island. It seemed Jim couldn't get a football scholarship at Syracuse because he was black, so the judge asked Roy Sr. if he could give Jim a lacrosse scholarship. Roy Sr. gave Jim the scholarship funds he had left and convinced the track coach to supplement them.

The rest is history, of course. But the deeper part of the history is the effect it had on Roy Jr. His father essentially adopted Jim. He took Jim's side when it deserved to be taken within the athletic department; he defended Jim when the faculty and staff would unduly criticize him, and he often convinced Jim not to leave despite the racist attacks he was experiencing.

As a teammate and the coach's son, Roy Jr. soaked up this integrity. When he came of coaching age, Coach Simmons, like his dad before him, used lacrosse as a platform for developing character in young men and for teaching social justice.

Coach Simmons incorporated the Onondaga Native Americans into his program, both literally and philosophically. He engaged the nearby reservation throughout his coaching career, recruiting kids from the reservation and arranging scrimmages there. He brought players to the "res" to watch the wooden lacrosse sticks being carved and invited Native American families to Syracuse games. He encouraged his players to understand the injustices that had been done to Native Americans and to reach out to those on the reservation.

He became so close with the Onondagas that a year after his wife's death, he invited his friend, former teammate, and current Onondaga chief, Oren Lyons, to consecrate the Nancy Simmons Wisdom Center at Coach Simmons's Episcopal church outside Syracuse. Chief Lyons asked Coach to meet him at the center alone on the day of its inauguration. Oren had much more in mind, though. He arrived in his beads, bangles, and feathers and brought sacred tobacco, which is traditionally burned before lacrosse games. He lit the tobacco, said Native American prayers and chants, and stood with Coach as the two watched the sacred smoke float into the sky.

"It is rising up to your wife," the chief said to Coach as he looked up toward the heavens. This was the highest honor Oren Lyons could bestow on Coach Simmons and his wife. The old chief no doubt was also honoring the lifelong integrity of the old coach, too.

Grace

I came to lacrosse during my redshirted senior year at Syracuse. I admired the game—the stick skills, the speed, the hitting and dodging that made contact a part of the game, but not its essence. I tried out, impressed the coach, and, at six-four, 260 pounds, was given a handcrafted stick, custom-made for my body type. My teammates called it an oar! Coach commissioned it at the reservation and it felt alive when he handed it to me.

But I could not shed my football mentality, let alone my incessant anger. I began clobbering people with the stick. I remember our spring trip to Baltimore to play various colleges in the area. We were playing Washington College in one of the first games I saw, let alone played in, and I was guarding a speedy attack man.

During one play, I unintentionally slashed him across the head trying to strip the ball out of his stick. I saw the referee throw the flag and knew the play would not end until we got possession of the ball. I figured since I already had one penalty, they wouldn't call another. So I took two more swipes at his head, landing my "oar" cleanly on his helmet's air hole.

The ref threw his hat and a handkerchief from his pocket and he called three penalties on me in one play. To top it off, I got an unsportsman-like call, and he threw me out of the game.

In football I had never heard of three holding penalties on one play—you hold, get the flag, and keep holding. As I marched through the penalty box, Coach came up to me and patiently pulled me aside.

"That is not how this game is played," he said. "Dignity. Integrity. Grace. DIG. This game is about artistic beauty and grace."

That lesson meant much less to me then than it does now, but it did slow me down and kept me focused on developing skill and finesse.

But what struck me most during the course of that season was Coach Simmons's slow revelation of his life as a sculptor and painter and how art nourished the gracefulness of his coaching. He started at Syracuse as a physical education major like his father but always felt the pull of the arts. A mentor convinced him to give it a go, and he flourished in that department. He went home after our games and disappeared into his studio in back of his house and painted or chiseled for the afternoon.

Here I was—having long accepted, yet suffered from the image of masculinity that sports sells—encountering a coach I truly admired who was undermining all the masculine clichés.

When I first peeked into Coach Simmons's art studio, I got my initial sense that sports could be as much about grace as the arts. That encounter started a spiritual reformation in me that took a long time to complete.

We give sports an elite status, but culturally we diminish them by commoditizing sports and hyping that funny thing called victory. Entertainment, winning, war metaphors, and other malarkey taint sports' dignity, integrity and grace.

Grace is a slow-paced thing, elegant and insistent on its own timing. Coach Simmons graced my life for a season, but his lessons grew with time. I think of him often now as I coach and teach coaching. I realize I studied with a sports version of Michelangelo—his methods artistically driven by logic and integrity. But it was his graceful delivery of these lessons—never preachy or forced—that made them so long-lasting. He suggested, he spoke softly, he lived by example. He knew he was a role model and he gracefully modeled the values that he wanted us to live by.

This archetypal lacrosse coach Roy Simmons Jr. has instructed me daily for more than forty years. The longevity and grace of his lessons are sweet antiseptics to all the damage done by the transactional coaches who had power and authority over me.

DOROTHY: THE SUBTLE LIONHEART

Coach Simmons was my most influential coach and he certainly helped me imagine the sort of coach I could become. But after I started coaching, I also wanted to reach into the realm of myth and heroes for coaching models. I am a big reader, and many characters in the stories that inspire our imaginations also merit imitation in our daily lives. That sort of striving after heroes is one thing sports and literature have in common.

When I was a child, every Thanksgiving my family would feast at my aunt Ag's house. Although she had no children of her own, Aunt Ag was so maternal in her every move that she seemed born to care for us. After turkey dinner and parfait sundaes soaked in her homemade chocolate syrup, we would all settle down to watch *The Wizard of Oz*.

Initially terrified of the monkey-birds, I started to fantasize about riding on them. As a young teenager, I also started to admire Dorothy's courage and grit. I identified with Dorothy, who, like me, felt ignored. I loved the sense of team and camaraderie that Dorothy and her companions developed. But Oz, the Wizard, was a different story—his ultimate authority, his intimidating voice, his disappearing act, and his final abandonment of his charges. He reminded me too much of my father.

Then, one humid summer night, many years later, in our row house in East Baltimore, Paula brought the memory of Aunt Ag sweetly back. We were sitting in our den listening to the Orioles game on the radio. Paula was typing—I actually miss the sound of that typewriter—a paper for her Master's degree in psychology. And she turned to me and said, "It was a dream about someone having a dream."

She had been studying Sigmund Freud's *The Interpretation of Dreams* and had to write a paper on psychoanalytic theory and the Oz story. She was referring to the idea that the story was developed based on the author's dream. She explained Oz to me in such a way that all those Thanksgivings at Aunt Ag's finally made sense. The Oz fable is a dream (remember: Dorothy gets hit on the head and knocked out). All the characters she encounters are projected parts of herself that she has not integrated. Oz and the Wicked Witch are her rejecting parents; the Good Witch is an idealized mother; and the Scarecrow, Tin Man, and Lion are the various parts of Dorothy that she sees as deficient.

Growing up in a patriarchal world in which masculinity appeared to be everything, I never considered Dorothy as a coaching archetype until I started to learn from Paula and see how poorly girls were being coached and taught. My daughter Esther was involved in many sports at that time and I couldn't help but see how her coaches were failing to build her self-esteem, encourage her confidence, and help her treat sports as an escape from the pressures of encroaching womanhood.

I also recognized the Wizard of Oz in myself. Like too many coaches, the wizard defined his role with power and authority. He feared people getting too close and discovering who he really was. He built a power structure where he alone was at the top. Every day the wizard hid in a tower with a bullhorn and barked out orders. I started out my coaching career as the wizard.

But Dorothy doesn't build a power structure with herself on top— she weaves a team into a web of authentic relationships, compassionate interaction, and common goals. Coach Dorothy assumes the fundamental responsibilities of every transformative coach. First, she builds authentic relationships with her players that allow her to understand their deepest fears, needs, and longings. She then creates a caring community based on self-esteem and mutual support. Finally, Coach Dorothy tries to help each player reach his fullest potential.

Team building is most often thought of in terms of breaking down players, cutting the least talented, creating a hierarchy, and then acting with the authoritarianism of the wizard. Coach Dorothy does it differently: She deftly weaves together a team of insecure, needy, and desperate players. Their unique gifts, abilities, and histories complement one another and flow into one another. Her honesty, courage, empathy, and genuine concern for her players become the team's very ethos. Dorothy is a cinematic creation, but she satisfied my imagination as a coach who aspired to transform and enchant young athletes.

I began to sweat even more that night when it became painfully clear that I was coaching like the wizard. I was trying to get kids to do great things at The Door and on my teams, and I used whatever tricks were necessary to get them to believe in me.

I began to realize a fundamental truth about sports, coaches, and athletes: Players will do what they're told by a Wizard of Oz–type coach but they will only truly follow someone whom they believe in and who believes in them. Coaching is all about relationships. It doesn't happen on chalkboards, with titles, or in newspaper articles. Transformational coaching occurs only when people believe in you and choose to follow because they know that you believe in them, too.

That's the magic of Dorothy's transformational coaching. Thirsty young people attach to Dorothy-style coaches because they sense her acceptance, availability, and advocacy. They see clearly that she places their needs above her own.

The Scarecrow thinks he is not smart enough and wants a brain. The Tin Man believes himself to be heartless and wants a heart. The Lion thinks of himself as a coward and desires courage. In many ways they resemble every team in America, each player questioning himself. Who am I? Who will love me? What can I do with my life? Am I smart or dumb? Am I athletic or nerdy? Am I a winner or loser? Like every young person, Coach Dorothy's players had acquired a destructive sense of personal deficits and inadequacies from the prevailing culture, their peers, and even their parents.

Dorothy empowered her players by questioning them. She questioned their self-doubt, pointed out evidence to the contrary, and used a mix of empathy, firmness, and affirmation to convince them of their worth. Something remarkable started to happen—they became a team. Individual self-confidence begat collective confidence, and the whole group developed the capacity to initiate remarkable transformation.

Once I understood this and made the Dorothy archetype a part of my coaching approach, I started to see real transformation happen. I stopped being the transactional wizard and started emulating the transformational Dorothy.

With my Door team, I began each practice with Dorothy in my head. Who were the Lions, the Tin Men, the Scarecrows, and how could I help them believe in themselves? Such an act of imagination made coaching magical for me.

I had one player who particularly reminded me of myself at his age. I saw tremendous potential in him as an athlete and leader, as Honest Abe saw in me, but I could tell that he saw only failure, rejection, and loneliness in his life. I decided to pull a Dorothy on him.

After practice one day, I asked him what he thought I thought of him.

"Huh?" he said, surprised and slightly irritated.

"What do you think I think about you as a person?"

"I dunno."

"Think about it? Do you think I like you?"

"Yeah, sure."

"Why?"

"I don't know, Coach."

"Would you like to know?"

"Yeah, I guess."

"I think you are this incredible human being. You are kind, smart, and I can tell you will be a great husband and father someday. You have the ability to lead and make a difference with your life. Your teammates all respect and like you, and my goal this season is for you to understand and believe all of this, too."

He looked down and I thought I saw one of the corners of his mouth shift a bit. I think it might have been a lot for him to take in. He wasn't used to hearing such direct and positive feedback.

After a while he started to walk differently, his posture changed, he smiled more, and he led. And he started to fulfill all the potential he had.

Of the many Scarecrows I have coached, one player will always stand out in my mind. The vast majority of students at Gilman receive the benefit of attending Gilman from elementary school on. This student applied to enter Gilman's ninth grade and took the entrance exam. He had come from Baltimore's struggling school system, and his test scores didn't match his innate intelligence and Gilman initially rejected his admission. His mom requested an opportunity to reapply, and after much tutoring and studying, he was accepted on the condition that he repeat the eighth grade. He struggled in school, thinking he just did not have the intelligence the other students possessed. We knew from his IQ test that he had the brain power to succeed and then some. But during those first weeks of classes, as he was exposed to peers who were simply better prepared than he was, his self-doubt doubled.

I shared with him an interesting study published by Stanford sociologist Carol Dweck in her book *Self Theories*.* She postulated that what people believe about themselves determines how they live. She stated that some people believe their intelligence is genetically determined while some believe intelligence is acquired through effort. Your beliefs ultimately shape the outcome of your life.

African American freshmen in college have a higher dropout rate than their white and Asian classmates. Dr. Dweck ran a study in which she showed a thirty-minute videotape stating that intelligence comes from neural connections in the brain and that these connections in the brain can be changed through effort. One group saw this thirty-minute videotape while a second group saw a video unrelated to intelligence or the idea that through effort you can change yourself. Those who saw the intelligence-work tape had an extremely low dropout rate, and the other group had the usual high dropout rate.

I pointed out to this student all the misinformation young children of color living in underserved communities like his receive. He needed critical thinking skills to understand the role race, economics, and ZIP code played in his identity and education and to understand his success or failure would be based on hard work, not genetics, finances, or ZIP codes. It took two years of daily affirmation and Dorothy-like coaching to get him to open his mind and see that he could learn as well as anyone once he mastered the basics that he had missed at his previ-

---

* Dweck, Carol, S. *Self-theories: Their Role in Motivation, Personality, and Development* (London: Psychology Press, 2000).

ous schools. He then began to thrive. He went on to become a B-plus student at Gilman, graduated from one of America's most competitive universities, and is working on Wall Street as an investment banker. Not bad for a once self-identified Scarecrow.

I had many Tin Men, too—young men who had disconnected their hearts from their heads. They had been taught as young boys that men don't feel, men don't touch, and men don't cry. They saw emotions, feelings, and tears as signs of weakness and masculine failure. They lost touch with the very thing that makes them human—their hearts. So whenever boys share emotions, feelings, and tears on the field, I always encourage and affirm them.

I remember one particularly difficult loss. At the end of a game, the boys circled around my coaching partner Biff. One player was outside the circle struggling to hide the tears of disappointment. Biff saw him and said, "Come into the center of the circle. When one of us cries, we all cry together as a team."

And as the player ashamedly walked into the circle, Biff said to the team, "Those are the tears of a man. A man who cares deeply."

As the player settled into the middle of the circle, Biff then said, "I want everyone to give him a hug." That to me is an everlasting example of weaving together the hearts and emotions of a team into one big heart. Biff weaves like Dorothy.

My favorite Lion: One morning I received an anxious call from a Gilman mother whom I did not know. She spoke with a thick accent. She explained to me that her freshman son had been so physically and emotionally bullied by other boys that he didn't want to go to school. She said he was sick to his stomach every morning. She had gone to the administration several times, but the bullying had continued. Not knowing where else to turn, she called me for advice. I told her I would be glad to meet her son and see if we could find a solution.

When I met Tommy I noticed he was reed thin, short, and nervous. His mother was Chinese. His birth father was Jewish and his stepfather was Italian. His slight frame, mixed heritage, and distinct physical appearance led to his being called a variety of abusive names. Biff and I met with him and heard the fear and shame he felt at being bullied and not having the courage to fight back. We decided to have our star quarterback befriend him.

So the next day our quarterback invited Tommy to sit with him and other members of our football team. We had a rule that if you were a member of our team you did not allow any other student to eat alone in the cafeteria. So our players knew the drill. They befriended Tommy and invited him to a regular seat at their table. Tommy—a wiz at math—ended up tutoring some players, and eventually, they invited him to become the team student-manager. Tommy was woven into the fabric of the team.

The final week of the final game of his senior season, Tommy approached Biff and me and asked if he could dress for the game! Talk about courage! He not only dressed for that game but also practiced all week. We even taught him how to run a down-and-out route so we could throw him a pass.

Everyone was so jacked to see Tommy in uniform on game day that it lifted the energy and enthusiasm of the whole team. I will never forget watching him run out onto the field and enter the huddle, to the sheer delight of his teammates, and run the pattern. Tommy had become a Lion for life!

Dorothy is the perfect match for Coach Simmons in my pantheon of InSideOut coaches. Coach's dignity and Dorothy's directness, his integrity and her cajoling, his grace and her generosity make them coaching complements. I experienced Coach Simmons; I imagine Dorothy. The practical and the imaginary both enrich my coaching.

MOSES: THE ANGRY AGENT OF CHANGE

Through all my InSideOut exploration, I realized that anger had driven much of my athletic success. Coaches leveraged it—they fired me up and charged me up by angering me. I thought anger was my fuel, but it was really my time bomb. It was driving me into drinking, drugs, and despair.

My theological studies led me to another model for the transformational coach I wanted to become. Coach Simmons provided me with the practical foundation for transformational coaching and Dorothy awoke my coaching imagination. Moses, however, was the archetype whose historical stature spoke to the sort of change I think sports should achieve.

I identified with Moses' anger and his isolation, his exile and his leadership. Moses wanted to live on the outside—he wanted to act, fight, lead, and transform poor and oppressed people. But his frequent chats with God taught him that he had to go inside first to be a transformative coach. Like Moses, I wanted to skip that grueling work, too. It was too introspective, too hurtful, and absolutely too hard! But I knew it was the right thing to do and I knew I had to do it.

So I studied Moses as a transformational coach for the techniques he developed to fulfill his role as the liberator God had called him to be. "I have seen the misery of my people crying out because of their oppression and I am concerned about their suffering. So I am sending you!" God told Moses.

That verse accosted me one morning as I was preparing for a staff meeting at The Door. Me? Yes, you! My own childhood had a lot to do with the way that verse from Exodus rang in my head. I identified with the thousands of young African Americans who were suffering from cultural and familial oppression. Young black male students have the worst grades, the lowest test scores, and the highest dropout rates of all students in the country. When these young black men don't succeed in school, they are much more likely to graduate from the nation's criminal juvenile justice system into the penitentiary system.

I realized two clear reasons why Moses became a model for my attempt at InSideOut coaching. First, he accepts the "call" to coach. The concept of "call" is rooted in the idea that each person has specific gifts, talents, and life experiences that direct him or her toward specific purposes and routes in life. Like teaching, the coaching journey begins with a calling. Transformational coaches often have "burning bush" experiences, calls that we seldom expect but that always demand an answer. Someone can confront you like Honest Abe and challenge you to achieve new heights. Or the call can come from observing and hearing the cries and miseries of young people being eaten up by oppressive cultural images and messages. The call can come from an inner dissatisfaction or discomfort with the status quo of coaching. Or it can come from an urge to atone for damage done by coaches in the past. In my case, all these "burning bushes" met in one big flame.

Second, Moses showed me that the call to transformational coaching demands a journey of self-discovery. I related to Moses' flaws. I started to appreciate how his call to coach forced him to address these flaws once and for all. In times of solitude and contemplation, he came face to face with the long-ignored memories, thoughts, and feelings that kept him from fully connecting to others and realizing his leadership talents. Like Moses, I had to face all those nightmares, self-doubts, insecurities, and life experiences that seemed easier to repress than process. The call to coach required that I understand myself in order to understand my players' lives, feelings, emotions, and behavior.

I also found in my study of Moses a precise technique for liberating my athletes from the oppressive culture that undermines their ability to flourish. I started by helping players critique the culture in which they live and the confusing messages they receive from movies, music, magazines, media, and Madison Avenue. Moses helped his team of followers develop the critical thinking skills necessary to understand the role race, politics, and economics played in the negative and nasty messages his followers received. Their sense of self-worth and the opportunities they envisioned in life were severely undermined by the messages they took to heart.

I could do the same thing for my athletes.

Next, I encouraged my players to personally and publicly embrace and articulate their pain. Moses had to get his followers in touch with all the assaults on their self-esteem and share the pain caused by accepting these falsehoods. Moses could not change his players until they articulated the pain and hurt inflicted on them by misinformation. As a coach, I wanted to hear clearly from players what hurt them and how it hurt them. Be it their peers or their parents, a teacher or a brother, racism or sexism, I wanted to hear clearly what the trouble was so that together we could use sports to help overcome the problem, not exacerbate it.

In addition to critiquing the culture and articulating the pain, I try to help players reframe a new vision of themselves and their teammates. Moses liberated his team by helping them imagine reinventing themselves. Moses knew that people move toward and become that which they believe about themselves. His players had ingested racist, anti-Semitic, sexist, and dehumanizing messages. His players were not acting in accordance with their potential, value, and worth, but with the cultural biases they believed. His team lived in a culture that taught them they were worthless, hopeless, deeply flawed, and unworthy. They internalized what others said about them and performed well below their capabilities and capacity. Moses as liberator knew that all meaningful, lasting growth and change begins on the inside and then works its way out. I set out to do the same for my athletes by rebuilding their beliefs and self-esteem.

Coach Simmons helped me realize just how much a coach can accomplish with his platform. Dorothy's empathy, encouragement, and inclusiveness helped me see how enchanting and magical transformational coaching can be. And Moses' leadership skills and liberation technique taught me that coaches can be agents of cultural change as much as transformers of individual lives.

With these three archetypes I had my models, and I strove to incorporate their lessons into my vision of an InSideOut coach. Now, having identified my coaching heroes and how I could emulate them, I needed to clearly identify my bad coaching habits and their sources. By labeling these habits I hoped that I could banish them.

CHAPTER 3

A Complex Transaction

Just before *Season of Life* was published, Jeffrey Marx wrote a story for *Parade* magazine. The story focused on how we coach to help boys become men for others at Gilman. The story, titled "The Most Important Coach in America," ended up on *Parade*'s front cover with a picture of me and some of my athletes. I was uncomfortable with this elevated title and embarrassed at being singled out. I had encountered so many great coaches striving to build a better world through sports; I felt I wasn't the most important coach in Baltimore, or even on our staff. But Jeffrey captured our vision of a team as a cocurricular community based on empathy, geared toward ethical instruction and social and emotional development, and filled with the joy of belonging and competing together. The article also captured the attention of a lot of people.

The overwhelming reaction to the article—thousands of emails, phone calls, and letters—soon startled Paula and me in a different way. We kept asking each other why this was such a big deal. All I had been advocating was using sports and coaching to guide, nurture, and train boys into manhood and girls into womanhood. Why that simple message caused such an outpouring of letters and emails from people seeking some sort of connection with me was initially baffling to us.

Parade had brought to the surface a crisis: destructive coaching had become too common in American sports. It was as if thousands of people finally found an outlet to verbalize the grief, pain, and confusion that so many bad coaches had caused or exacerbated decades before.

Paula and I started to tally and analyze the correspondence, and we noticed two predominant types: adults describing their negative experiences as youths and parents watching their children suffer under transactional coaches. The coaching culprits fit into relatively distinct categories. Based on these disturbing stories, Paula and I developed labels for the transactional coaches we kept hearing about. We called them dictators, bullies, narcissists, saints, and misfits.

I looked at this spectrum of coaching categories through the lens of my experiences as a player, coach, sports enthusiast, and parent. My own experiences validated the experiences of the individuals who were writing to me. I was also struck by the fact that as a young coach, I, too, had acted at various times like a dictator, bully, narcissist, saint, or misfit.

My objective in this chapter is to present an early and perhaps idealized model for athletic competition and then to compare these transactional coaching types to show how they have hurt our children and tainted our games.

THE MENTORING GREEKS

Some of the most important coaches in history were Coach Socrates, Coach Plato, and Coach Aristotle. They created one of the world's great coaching staffs based on their radical philosophy of mentoring their players.

Coach Socrates was the James A. Naismith or Pop Warner of his time. His legacy is seen in the lives and writings of his assistants and former players.

Rather than using a top-down authoritarian coaching style, Socrates believed in interacting with and engaging his players. The most powerful teams are those in which every individual is allowed a voice, in which athletes can speak and share their unique perspectives, insights, gifts, and talents.

For Socrates, a team was a virtuous community critical to the civic, moral, and spiritual development of the city-state. Friendship was the foundation of a team and self-knowledge was a prerequisite to becoming a true friend.

His best-known statement was the challenge "Know thyself." As a coach, he understood the imperative of knowing one's inner moral landscape. He challenged coaches to struggle and interact with each other around key questions: "What is the goal and role of sports?" "How can sports serve a society?" "Who determines what is good, important, and valuable about sports?"

Plato, a former graduate assistant of Socrates, knew the gymnasium could be the center of Greek society by marrying intellectual, ethical, and physical education. Platonic coaches understood that sports should develop character and civic awareness, teamwork and togetherness. Athletics provided the platform for instructors to teach the virtues and values that build a just society.

Athletes were trained to strive for excellence, not merely victory. The goal of civic athletics was to create citizen-athletes based on the Greek concept of *arête*, meaning "excellence" or "virtue." *Arête* means aspiring to excellence in every area, be it athletics, academics, or the arts.

To Plato, a great player was not just a "gamer," but a person of high character who was not only determined to achieve a goal but also knew precisely why that goal was noble and important to the community.

Coach Aristotle, building on Socrates' and Plato's playbook, also believed that sports should entail the pursuit of excellence. And excellence demanded that the athlete develop balance—intellectually, morally, and physically. Coach A said the three components of a virtuous player are friendship, justice, and contemplation.

Contemplation—think about that! Coach A taught his players that personal reflection lays the foundation for relational, athletic, ethical, and civic excellence. His coaching challenge was to get each team member to examine his or her life and the impact the team members have on their teammates, community, and country.

Sounds a lot like one of the greatest transformational coaches of our time—former UCLA basketball coach John Wooden! One of my favorite Wooden quotations is, "How you run the race is more important than winning the race!"

Speaking of legendary Greek coaches, Homer, a Hall of Fame sportswriter, provides us a description of perhaps the most famous coach of his time, Mentor. Around 1200 B.C., as Odysseus, king of Ithaca, was getting ready to leave home for the Trojan War, he asked his wise and trusted friend Mentor to serve as protector and steward of his household. During the decade of the war and the additional decade that it took Odysseus to return home, Mentor became a teacher, advisor, role model, and coach to Odysseus' son, Telemachus.

Mentor nurtured his mentee so well that his name became synonymous with the word "coach." English word-pickers centuries ago should have used the word "mentor" instead of "coach" to describe the person who heads a team. Imagine if coaches today thought of themselves as mentors or aspired to the ideals of mentoring: I am the head mentor or I'm the mentor of the defensive line. Think how much that might have changed the coach-player relationship—a title conveying an undeniable obligation to care for players' welfare, instruct them in virtue, and guide them toward an adulthood of citizenship and contemplation.

But somehow through the centuries—and at light speed in recent decades—organized sports have almost entirely lost this vision of sports as a tool for mentoring, teaching virtue, and fostering citizenship. The moral code of the Greek citizen-athlete was devoured by the Romans' depraved and commercialized approach to sports as an end in itself.

In the movie *Gladiator* "Coach" Proximo tells his rookies, "I shall be closer to you for the next few days, which will be the last of your miserable lives, than your mother who first brought you screaming into this world! I did not pay good money for your company. I paid it so that I might profit from your death. And just as your mother was there at your beginning, I shall be there at your end. Thrust this sword into another man's flesh and they will applaud and love you for that. You may even begin to love them for that."

When we think of sports in America today, does it make us think of the Greek Mentor model or the Roman gladiator model? When we think of coaching in America today, do we see Aristotle and Mentor? Or do we think of Proximo and his gladiators?

Sports today obviously involve much more than the pursuit of athletic and moral excellence. The mere financial value of victory—from the pros down even to the youth level—creates enormous incentives and pressures to win, reducing ethical creed to sentimental rhetoric. Add to that the prevalence of ego and transactional coaches' self-involvement, and we are left with a shell of a once virtuous athletic culture.

The most regrettable consequence of this change is that sports have lost much of the value and virtue needed to foster the healthy development of our youth. Let's face it: Our "future" is in trouble, more than we care to realize.

We hear the data regularly—but it never ceases to make me wince. Every twenty-six seconds one of our children drops out of high school. Thirty-two percent of all ninth graders do not graduate from high school in four years. The rate is 50 percent for minorities, and that number jumps to 66 percent if the minority student lives in poverty! When a child enters adolescence his or her mortality rate doubles; 26 percent report a sexually transmitted disease; 21 percent are diagnosed with mental health problems; 17 percent are obese; 28 percent engage in binge drinking; almost 25 percent are victims of violence; and 20 percent of teenage dating relationships involve physical or sexual violence.

And don't think it's just poor and minority children who are struggling and suffering—it's all our children. In her book *Price of Privilege*, Dr. Madeline Levine writes that America's newest "at-risk" group is children from affluent, well-educated families. Her research shows that money, prestige, private school education, and material goods often offer little or no protection and can even contribute to mental illness and unhappiness. Addictions, anxiety disorders, depression, eating disorders, and self-destructive behavior are epidemic among "well-off" children and families.

In a groundbreaking study, *Hardwired to Connect*, thirty-three doctors, research scholars, neuroscientists, and youth service professionals issued a report most startling for the simplicity of its suggested solution. These experts stated that much of what is causing the crisis of our youth is a lack of meaningful relationships and connections with moral and spiritual meaning. It sounds like some time spent in an ancient Greek gymnasium with a transformational coach could make an impact.

This report makes the case that young people have three basic needs. One, they need someone to believe in them and to affirm and validate their inherent value and potential. Two, they need a belief system. According to the study, our youth are seeking some kind of spirituality to help them find meaning and purpose in life. Third, they need a place to belong—a community built on well-defined principles with expectations and boundaries that provide structure and safeguards in the treacherous journey to adulthood. They need to belong to a team! They need a teacher-coach, a mentor.

I am making a big claim for athletics here, and indeed a very demanding one by contemporary standards. But just think of the needs and pressures facing young people today. Is it really so revolutionary to think that we could restore the virtuous foundation of sports and retrain coaches to act as mentors in their players' passage into adulthood?

I played for coaches for twenty-seven years: from my childhood, to high school, to college and thirteen years of professional football. I have coached for more than twenty-five years. I have four children, all of them athletes, three of whom have played Division I sports. Growing up, they played a variety of sports including T-ball, soccer, baseball, lacrosse, basketball, swimming, volleyball, and football. I have watched them interact with transactional coaches—dictators, bullies, narcissists, saints, and misfits—at all levels. I have seen the good, the bad, and the ugly faces of the coaching vocation. I am certain of one thing: Coaches can either break young people's psyches or build their souls.

THE DICTATOR: MY WAY OR THE HIGHWAY

Channel surfing one night I came across one of my favorite performances—Robert Duvall in *The Great Santini*. I first saw the film when it came out in 1980. In fact, I saw it when it had a different name, *The Ace*. At that time, my football career was ebbing, my brother had recently died, and the film summoned all the regrets and anger I held toward my father.

As it ended, I turned to Paula and told her the original title of the film.

"Why did they change it?" she wondered.

And I did, too. As a title *The Ace* captured so well a father-coach's effort to use his son to relive his glory, real or imagined. Duvall had pulled off one of the great depictions of a man who was just plain transactional, both as a father and as a coach.

It was heartbreaking to watch Duvall's son realize that his father was attempting to use their relationship for his own self-aggrandizement. It is even more heartbreaking to watch it in person, when a coach does the same thing to his athletes. I have been in and around the NFL for more than thirty-five years now, addressing teams and coaches as part of the NFL's ninety-minute mandatory player-conduct seminar. I am convinced that the number one common denominator among professional football players and athletes in general is father-son dysfunction. And I think it is just as true in the boardroom as it is in the locker room.

The marriage of the military and sports is apparent in most coachspeak. Martial language and metaphors saturate our sports vocabulary in every age group.

I remember one day climbing those paratrooper ropes at Syracuse for Coach Schwartzwalder. We had to climb them just to be allowed on the practice field. He had them installed at the front of the field and I suspect they reinforced his connection between commando and coach.

One day I stopped at the top and held on to the crossbar for several minutes. Everyone had finished climbing and was walking to the practice field, but I just kept hanging there breathing what felt like cleaner air.

I looked out at the fields across the way where intramural athletes were laughing and horsing around playing Frisbee. I saw the lacrosse players shooting on the goal and playing catch just for the fun of being together outdoors. I saw the women's cross-country team running in unison through a path that led to a park.

And then I looked down and saw Schwartzwalder. His demeanor contrasted sharply with the games going on all around us. He looked up at me for a moment, snarled, and resumed his trudge to the field. My arms started to burn, so I wrapped my legs around the rope to better support myself. I wanted to swing the rope, launch myself, and land just in time to snag a Frisbee or run in stride with the cross-country team, but the reality of getting back to practice took both me and my mood back down.

The movie *Patton* came out that year and I went to see it with some teammates. The film clarified for me the philosophical basis of dictator-coaches. It all seemed so close to home: George C. Scott's unbending posture; his slapping of a fearful soldier; his prebattle speeches to fire up his command.

That famous opening scene begins with Patton standing on a stage with a huge American flag in the background. His pregame speech to the troops includes his explanation of why America will never lose a war: "America does not tolerate a loser."

World War II helped forge this genre of coaching based on military leadership models: turning boys into men by breaking them down in order to rebuild them into fighting machines. Team training camps were based on military boot camps: toughness, discipline, stoicism, and a rigid chain of command were the key tenets. Good players, like good soldiers, always went beyond their perceived physical limits, sucked it up to prove their manhood, and were deemed expendable in the pursuit of victory. The coach as dictator determined the team's mission, policies, and values, based on a win-at-all-costs mentality.

As portrayed in Jim Dent's book *The Junction Boys* and the televised ESPN movie of the same name, Paul "Bear" Bryant is a classic example of the marriage of dictatorial military leadership and coaching. In 1954, Texas A&M University hired Bryant as head football coach. Bryant thought his team was physically and emotionally weak. He took the players off-campus to Junction, Texas, and held ten days of commando-style boot camp designed to "separate the men from the boys." At the time of the camp the Texas hill country was experiencing a hundred-degree heat wave—and Bryant refused to allow water breaks!

Athletics slowly assumed its financial and commercial power under this generation of coaches. The result was the marriage of a military style of coaching with football, an increasingly popular and lucrative American pastime.

Ponder this quotation from Vince Lombardi, the legendary coach of the Green Bay Packers:

> The leader can never close the gap between himself and the group. If he does, he is no longer what he must be. He must walk a tightrope between the consent he must win and the control he must exert.

I have a hunch Schwartzwalder lived by this one. Does an affirmation or an encouraging hand on a shoulder close the gap? Does holding a player's hand when he has suffered an injury or lost a loved one? Look at the intensity of the words—"tightrope," "control he must exert," "no longer what he must be." These words describe a robot more than a human being. How do players have a relationship with this distant, dictatorial person? How does distant, dictatorial coaching affect the healthy development of players?

THE BULLY AND HIS BULLHORN

Like the Wizard of Oz before his unveiling, the bully coach often seems like a huge head surrounded by fire. Coach Bully roars at players, parents, and associates to keep them at a distance. The bully-coach's repertoire includes shouting, cursing, personal denigration, and humiliation. So intimidating is the bully-coach that few young people dare to summon the courage to approach him, let alone challenge his technique or pronouncements.

When Dorothy's dog Toto pulls the curtain back, the Wizard of Oz is exposed for the mere mortal he is. Bullies act tough in order to hide feelings of insecurity and self-loathing. Coach Bully has an incomprehensible need to dominate his players.

My daughter Esther played for a bully-coach, and the damage took a long time to repair. There are few parenting experiences more heartbreaking than realizing that a coach has hurt your child. In Esther's case, we fell for the seduction that transactional coaches can summon. The Division I women's head basketball coach who was recruiting her sat at our kitchen table. She was as warm as the chicken soup we were serving her for dinner. She spoke of the importance of academics and a nurturing environment for young female athletes.

She was a convincing person! "This is a good school and I am the right person to look after your daughter and her basketball career in college. I come from a close family in the Midwest and I understand the importance of relationships and good values."

Esther was our first Division I athlete—she was elated to feel wanted and we were happy that she was happy.

So we packed her up and took her to college to play basketball for this seemingly impressive coach. But early in her freshman season Esther's feet started to hurt. The coach ignored her pain and demanded that she keep practicing.

"Keep running!" the coach would yell. "What's your problem?"

The trainer told her she had shin splints, and they would eventually get better. But one day during warm-ups, Esther hurt so much that she took off her sneakers, threw them to the floor, and said she just couldn't run anymore.

We brought her home to see an orthopedist in Baltimore. "Multiple stress fractures and two collapsed arches," he told her. "I'm shocked that you've been walking, let alone running and jumping." The extensive damage from the continuous pounding of her broken bones required total reconstructive surgery on both of Esther's feet. It took almost two years of surgery and rehab to rebuild her arches and heal her fractures.

Esther wanted to stay on the team, support her school, and honor the obligations of her scholarship despite her injury. But this coach, determined one way or another to get her pound of flesh, started to hammer our daughter emotionally to get her to quit because the coach wanted to free up her scholarship money. She intimidated Esther repeatedly with direct attacks like, "Are you happy being a practice player? Because that's all you'll ever be!"

Her coach became so abusive verbally and emotionally that, by her junior season, Esther walked away from the sport altogether.

The coach was eventually fired, but not before I had one last meeting with her and the athletic director.

Our visit this time looked quite different from the warm and cozy sales job at our kitchen table. The face that I saw that day was the face of someone who had no regard for the welfare of a young female athlete, let alone my daughter. The face I saw had a hardened expression, with cold eyes and no empathy. The person I saw was a quintessential bully. And like most bullies when they are confronted by someone they can't dominate or intimidate, she couldn't even look me in the eyes.

To this day Paula and I blame ourselves for our blindness to the damage this bully-coach did to our daughter. This coach turned sports into a hell for Esther and, no doubt, for many other young women. And to my great regret, I know the cold face of this coach lives on in Esther's memory as vividly as Dorothy's Wicked Witch of the West.

There are thousands of young adults like Esther who have been damaged emotionally and often physically by a bully-coach. The bully-coach has been accepted by schools that look the other way if these coaches generate wins and revenue.

I understand this type of transactional coach because I was bullied, and as a coach the deeds I most regret came when I bullied my players. When a player or parent triggered the part of me that had been bullied in the past, the bully in me would rise up and rage as a bully-coach. As part of my InSideOut work I am ever mindful of this impulse and I am happy to say it rarely happens now. When I feel it coming on, I try to comprehend the emotion and regain my rational self. I refuse to let unhealed wounds dictate my behavior or coaching style. I know all too well the long-term damage it can do to my athletes.

One of my players was prone to what I believed was laziness. He seemed to raise sloth to an art form and his impressive talents made this all the more frustrating for me.

One time during a football game, I called a blitz near the goal line. I expected an easy sack for him from his cornerback position. I stood there and watched the play unfold and saw him stop in the middle of the play. The other team completed the pass, scored a touchdown, and I ran halfway onto the field and blasted him.

"If you ever do that again, you will never play on my defense again!"

That's not me—it's not how I talk to players or how I think of our team. I am not a bully-coach. But I said it and I felt it and at that moment I was indeed a bully-coach. I thought I had made a great call and wanted it executed. He didn't give me what I wanted so I threatened a devastating punishment. Yelling at him only reinforced his already struggling self-image.

There is always something else going on underneath the bullying. I perceived myself as fat and lazy, labels my father reinforced all too willingly. I saw myself, the self I didn't like, in this player and projected my disdain for my own perceived laziness onto him.

Bully-coaches in youth and interscholastic sports have plenty of institutionally accepted role models whose fame condones such behavior. Bobby Knight, the controversial former basketball coach, is known for his infamous chair-throwing incident when the Indiana Hoosiers met Purdue's Boilermakers on February 23, 1985. But it wasn't until September 10, 2000, that Indiana president Miles Brand announced he had fired Knight for a continuing pattern of "defiant and hostile" behavior.

We had seen Knight get in kids' faces, grab them by the arms, and spray his spit onto their cheeks as he ranted at them. We had seen him show disrespect to referees. He used his body, his eyes, facial gestures, and words to intimidate in the hope of affecting performance or decisions. I have heard that Knight has a compassionate side and that many former players admire him. But his public bullying not only damaged his players, it also set a public example that amateur coaches inevitably mimicked.

Watching these public displays from coaches, whether famous ones like Knight or unknown ones at the youth level, makes me feel like I am watching a train wreck.

What's the effect on the kids? Few eighteen-year-olds, let alone younger kids, are wise enough to disregard the words of a bully-coach. I still have moments when tiny flashbacks sneak into my brain, like being told to smash a basketball into a kid's face. The memories do not devastate me anymore, but they remain as deep regrets.

How about the effect on coaches? Coaches emulate and imitate other coaches, much as ballplayers imitate the latest dunk or adopt the latest shoe style. Bully-coaches on ESPN's *SportsCenter* set an example that youth league coaches tend to follow the next day.

The private consequences of this type of behavior, however, are the real story here. In my breakfast club, eighty-year-old men still talk about their bully-coaches. Eighty-year-old men still feeling the bruises from their bullies! I believe that many bully-coaches would conduct themselves differently if they comprehended the long-term effect of their behavior. But that would require a degree of contemplation and self-assessment, a commitment to InSideOut work, that many coaches are not courageous enough to undertake. So the cycle of sports bullying goes on. It hastens the decline of civility in sports and fuels the nightmares of thousands of kids and the laments of eighty-year-old breakfast club members.

THE NARCISSIST: THE TEAM IS YOUR MIRROR

The narcissist coach craves the center stage. He gloats on the sideline as the clock ticks down, full of pride in himself, not in his players.

Narcissism is defined in the Merriam-Webster dictionary as "excessive preoccupation with self and lack of empathy for others." Is there a worse description for someone who spends hours every day in a lead role with children? The narcissist is a stranger to InSideOut work, for this thing we call "the self" consumes him, blinds him, makes self-critique nearly impossible.

An email I received as a result of the *Parade* article came from a parent whose son played for Coach Narcissist. He played competitive baseball through the ranks: T-ball, Little League, Babe Ruth, and various travel teams. He had also played on his school's team for the past five years, from seventh to eleventh grades. He attended all the practices, lifted weights, and took hitting lessons on his own. With his senior season coming up and with a new coach, he worked especially hard and even quit his after-school job.

As the final "cuts" were being made, the coach called him into his office and said, "I am going to build a powerhouse here, raise the level of performance, and I'm sorry to say I won't need you this year."

Stunned, the boy replied, "But I am a senior and we don't cut seniors!"

The coach said, "I don't care what grades players are in—when you play for me, you've gotta be a star."

The boy's mom painfully described the total rejection her son felt—his sense of embarrassment, shame, and separation.

Many of the emails we received in response to the *Parade* article were from individuals who had experiences with this kind of coach.

Many of the stories were like love stories gone awry, individuals and parents who had been drawn in by a coach's charisma and then blind-sided by that same coach's capacity to turn cold and detached.

"He just stops talking to me," says a college lacrosse player about his coach. "When I have a bad game, he won't even look at me. Sometimes it goes on for days. It's kind of embarrassing. He makes sure everyone knows he's disappointed in me and he does it by acting like I don't exist anymore."

One female college athlete recently told me how her narcissistic coach operates. "She gets a couple of girls on the team believing they are really close to her. They start telling her all of the personal stuff that's going on with the other girls on the team. Then she uses the personal information against the girls on the field, calling them out about boy-friends and private interchanges that occur between each other, 'Mary, if you weren't so involved with your boyfriend, you'd probably be work-ing a lot harder on the field!' " Pitting players against each other, this coach gets them to compete for her attention. This miraculously intact female athlete instinctively knows that her coach is feigning concern and using her athletes as pawns. Her narcissist-coach manipulates by pulling her athletes' emotional strings adeptly to get what she wants.

THE SAINT GOES MARCHING IN

I was out to save the world and transform it in the process. Three years out of professional football, I still had the adrenaline, still loved the limelight, and still felt invincible.

The Door became my path to canonization. I was addressing so-cial issues by day, coaching in the afternoon, and preaching at night. I thought I was living for the young people around me, but I was really just trying to save myself.

My true aspirations became most apparent the night that my wife confronted me. I had been working on lead-paint-poisoning issues that were devastating young lives in our neighborhood, where all the row homes were more than one hundred years old. I had my children tested in the process of compiling data. All of them had lead levels that surpassed the toxic threshold.

When Paula found out, she said, "You have a Messiah complex! You are worried about saving the world and you are losing your family! I don't want to be married to a Mother Teresa with muscles!" (A local television sportscaster had dubbed me that some years earlier.)

I had never heard the phrase "Messiah complex" before but I knew immediately what she meant and the source of the pathology. I was devoting myself so completely to a cause that I was sacrificing my own family. I was chasing the things that made me feel like a saint, as if I were saving the world. But I was still transacting and not transforming; I was getting high on sainthood.

Coaching can draw in the type of person who wants to save the world and actually *excessively* empathizes with players. Players need boundaries, rules, and regulations—saints are often more concerned with being liked by players than with doing what's best for them. The impulse to help is pure—players need to be helped, but part of that help is teaching them how to resolve problems on their own, instead of rescuing them so the coach can feel needed.

During The Door years, my Messiah complex was driving me to seek acclaim for each life seemingly changed and each kid saved. It wasn't saintly work; it was using other people to meet my own needs. Although I didn't recognize it at the time, I believed it was my sole responsibility to fix what was wrong with the world.

The urge to be loved and appreciated and to be a do-gooder is the curse of the saint. Coaches are there for players—players are never there to meet the needs of coaches, not even supposedly saintly coaches.

I remember during those days a young football player walked off the field in tears. He fumbled the ball toward the end of a close game and we lost. "We really needed to win this one for the coach!" I heard him mumble. "He believes in us so much and we just let him down!"

I didn't realize it then but I do now. It's not unusual for players to want to please their coaches. But it is certainly harmful for coaches to generate this need in their athletes. I would never want a young athlete to feel that way. As I did my InSideOut work, this boy's comment became my best critique. I was still coaching from the outside without going inside to understand the thoughts and emotions that were driving my behavior.

THE MISFIT: LOOKING FOR A HOME

Coaching can satisfy the human urge to belong to something that provides identity and meaning. That's why sports can attract a coaching type that I call the misfit. The misfit-coach needs his players' acceptance and obedience. He needs to feel a part of the team even more than his players do. This type of coach gravitates toward youth league sports because status and title are easily obtained there. You are instantly dubbed "Coach," and you are handed a group of young developing minds heeding every word you say. Parents generally fall in line, not wishing to jeopardize Junior's playing time.

Most people, especially after they become parents, express bafflement at the fact that parenthood requires no license or training. Raising kids is the most complicated job in the world, but untrained coaches get easy access to young developing brains. Because most youth and recreation leagues are largely dependent on volunteers, there is usually little screening of the coach and training is rarely provided. Between their deficiencies in emotional intelligence and their lack of knowledge of players' developmental needs, misfit coaches can snuff out a player's enjoyment and development before preseason ends.

Our oldest son, Barney, has been an amiable guy from the get-go—always well-liked by his coaches and seen as a coachable athlete. We were shocked when one day our very coachable son turned defiant.

One thing about Barney as a kid was that if something didn't add up for him he would call you on it or keep asking you questions until it made sense to him. When he was four, Paula's mother jokingly called him a "Philadelphia lawyer," because of the persistence with which he would question the logic of things, keeping her on her toes.

When Barney was twelve, his lacrosse coach was a businessman from downtown Baltimore who claimed a storied lacrosse history. He was always the best-dressed guy on the field—donning the latest sports apparel week by week. And his vanity license plate displayed how hard he tried to fit in with the lacrosse socialites.

Lacrosse is huge in Baltimore, and this coach worked pretty hard putting together his ideal team of little lacrosse players. He had big plans and grandiose speeches to match them. But there was a major disconnect.

Barney picked up on it immediately. "He doesn't make sense," Barney would say in frustration.

We struggled to understand what he meant, so we started to watch the coach more closely. It became clear that he wasn't connecting with the kids. In teaching such fundamentals as passing, cradling the ball, and aligning on the field, he would seem to go into his own world, unable to read the signals of boredom the kids were giving him. His responses to their questions were off-kilter. It was initially hard to pinpoint, but there was something about him that seemed to upset the boys.

So Barney, as was his fashion, began to question the coach, not out of disrespect but more out of confusion. Threatened by his questioning, the coach made Barney a target. At that point, it became clear to our young son that this coach was all image and no substance. Barney's questioning was peeling the veneer.

There was one boy on the team who was Barney's friend. Game after game the coach would blatantly refuse to play him. In the middle of one game the coach randomly started shouting at this kid whom he never played. Barney just stopped in his tracks. He'd had enough of this coach. He walked off the field and packed up his equipment. We followed him to the car and he told us he would never play for that coach again. We supported his decision.

We realized that the unsettling traits of misfit coaches can sometimes be detectable only by children. Knowing our children and listening to what they say about a coach are fundamental to protecting them and helping them make sense of nonsense-making coaches.

A misfit-coach thinks the ball fields and courts are places for him to fit in, find an identity, climb up the social ladder, or simply feel needed. He can be well-intentioned and charming or completely awkward and clueless. Either way, his goals and behavior can be destructive to a young athlete.

TRIGGERS

What I have just described is not a rigid classification system of transactional coaching. Some coaches show more than one of these characteristics. As coaches our vulnerability to these characteristics depends on our personal histories. Many coaches mean well, but because they have not come to terms with their life histories, their concern is with their own problems and needs and not those of their players. Without accountability, the cycle is perpetuated, especially when the media glorify coaches who should not be role models.

My coaching behavior slid in and out of these categories during my early coaching years. When I was coaching my team at The Door, it consisted of players who lived in a violent community. Shootings, beatings, and sirens were part of their daily life.

One September game, as I paced the sideline, I heard a parent screaming at one of my players.

He kept shouting: "Kill him! Take his head off! Don't take any shit from that boy!"

I kept finding myself trying to scream over this man with words of affirmation and encouragement to my team. But all the while my blood was boiling.

Then in the third quarter the boy got run over on a sweep and sat there on the ground. He was hurt and breathless.

His father yelled: "Get your ass up—you're no punk-ass bitch."

I lost it. I went over to this man, pointed my finger in his face, and told him to get off my sidelines and keep his mouth shut while I was coaching my team. And he grabbed my wrist and told me never to put my finger in his face.

Then I really lost it! That sensation of a hand gripping my wrist triggered a deep, vicious, and unconscious memory of my rape. I lost control. I attacked the guy. A group of people separated us and the referees stopped the game.

After the game, I gathered my players and apologized to them. I had been teaching them that violence resolves nothing in life, yet here I was acting violently! I wanted to be part of the solution to help these boys, but my poor emotional management and disconnections were getting in the way.

As I reflected on my reaction to this "fan," I dismissed my behavior as my wanting to protect my players. But I started to recognize a pattern. I remember in college playing against West Virginia. I sacked their quarterback and as I slowly got off him, he grabbed my wrist and tried to push me away. I remember grabbing him by the Adam's apple and squeezing as hard as I could, telling him if he ever touched me again I would break his neck.

To this day I can still see the horror in his eyes. He knew and I knew this was no idle threat. That memory haunted me—the loss of control, the rage, and the reality that I was fully out of control in that moment.

In both these stories, being grabbed by my wrist triggered memories of when I was raped as a boy. One of the men who attacked me kept hold of my wrists. That experience triggered violent reactions later in my life. When triggered we often lose control of ourselves: our heads, hearts, bodies, and behavior. A trigger can be a thought, feeling, or situation that taps into an old injury or insult, igniting overwhelming feelings of anger, shame, or anxiety. Triggering can lead to distorted reactions and uncontrolled outbursts of anger, rage, and abusiveness and an assortment of reactive behaviors. Not to mention tons of regret.

Traumas large and small live in the body as well as the mind and the body often remembers better what the mind tries hard to forget. The traumas may be overwhelming, like mine, or what seemed like trifling coaching criticisms that grew bigger with time.

Without undertaking the InSideOut process, I would have kept passing on my behavior to my players and the next generation of coaches. Coaches often stand on the sidelines feeling exposed, naked, for all to see and judge. The fans behind us are evaluating us based on the performance of the team on the scoreboard. Not only are fans grading our value and worth, but subconsciously we, too, are comparing the team's performance to negative feelings about ourselves, to that continual whispering in our ears, "Will I ever be good enough?"

All coaches are vulnerable to triggers when placed in situations that awaken traumatic memories. At those times coaches revert to defensive behavior. An unhealed wound can trigger us to wound others. Or better said, hurt people hurt people. The solution is to identify the wound, be mindful of it, and control our tendencies so that we don't act out even when that trigger is pulled. In gaining control of our emotions, we change from boiling thermometers to regulated thermostats. If we want to be in control of our programs, we need first to be in control of ourselves.

An InSideOut process produces a coherent narrative that helps us recognize and understand the triggers we each face. This coherent narrative helps us master the reflexive power of these triggers. There are coaches whose daily behavior fits the labels in this chapter. The types define their personalities. But there are far more coaches who merely have dictatorial, bullying, narcissistic, saintly, or misfit moments. Because of the power that coaches hold, those mere moments can become lifelong, life-shaping memories for young athletes.

CHAPTER 4

The Play's the Thing

Play hard. When I was playing for the Colts, Bethlehem Steel employed thousands of people at Sparrows Point in the Baltimore harbor. The company produced the steel for the Golden Gate Bridge. Its dirty smokestacks shot fire and smoke into the sky all day and all night. Steelworkers helped manufacture Baltimore's blue-collar reputation.

Wearing Colts blue, I also zealously embraced the town's tradition. I played hard all day—and most nights. You could count on Joe Ehrmann to show up every Sunday and play hard. "Blue-collar" was a phrase I heard attached to my name as often as "hard-nosed." And from talk radio to the local pub, it was a label I enjoyed.

The irony of it all: The last time I played hard was decades earlier when I was on a toboggan with five friends in Buffalo. Snowy Buffalo seemed even snowier in those days. I remember deluges of snow. Though the city rarely canceled school, there were days when Mother Nature defeated even the relentless Buffalo snowplows.

The toboggan chutes were on a hilltop at one edge of the park. At the first sign of snow, my tobogganing team awoke simultaneously. One guy brought the toboggan his parents had splurged on, another brought candles so we could wax the bottom of it, and another guy and I always made hot Ovaltine and brought along bags of Oreos.

And then we played hard—all day long up and down the hill until our hamstrings burned and our calves cramped. On the toboggan, we wrapped our bodies around each other like Olympic bobsledders. Toward the end of the day, we even pulled each other up the hill on the toboggan, so we could take turns resting.

We rejoiced. As night fell, we scrambled home for supper. Even now on those mornings when I wake up rested, I feel something like the contentment that I felt the day after sleeping off my hard play in the snow.

How often today do young people get to play creatively, freely, and joyously? From what I've seen, rarely! How often do they feel that great sensation of play during organized sports? Even more rarely. Play, as much as any other activity, fuels the social, emotional, and physical development of young people. It is through play that children learn about themselves, others, and life. But then suddenly it's gone, vanished. And with the loss of play often comes an increase in a child's stress, anxiety, and isolation.

We still use the oxymoronic phrase "play sports" but "playing" in organized sports has become almost impossible for our children. Kids today get a rude awakening when they transition from the toboggan to the ball field. They go from the unbridled joy of creative play to the performance-based world of driven parents and overly competitive coaches.

I often say that the most competitive sport in America is parenting—sitting in the stands competing with each other for a better seat in the bleachers of life based on one's child's performance. These parents have forgotten the pure, unadulterated pleasure of their own play as children—if they ever felt it!

Young people get caught in the riptide of sports that adults create for them. Adult culture abruptly summons tobogganers nationwide with a booming Wizard of Oz–like voice to step off their toboggans and get with the real program of life. Stop playing and start conforming and competing.

On the toboggan, everything is okay. Kids are free to be in the moment when they engage in creative play. It's a time when we're actually human "be-ings" free from the self-consciousness that arises as we morph into human "do-ings" measured by our feats, tasks, and accomplishments. Kids join a team and then learn that they are not okay unless they are always a starter, an all-star, or the top pick. The demise of play is a loss of the innocence that the world and adults strip from our children.

In an article published by the American Academy of Pediatrics, Kenneth Ginsburg, M.D., highlights the importance of free play in the healthy development of children. "Despite the numerous benefits derived from play for both children and parents, time for free play has been markedly reduced for some children. This trend has even affected kindergarten children, who have had free play reduced in their schedules to make room for more academics."*

Somehow, in all the craziness of life, we have lost the meaning and significance of play. Bruno Bettelheim, the psychologist and author, wrote of this parenting problem back in 1987. He argued that developing minds need space and open time to think and contemplate the many problems and facets of life. Modern culture and parenting trends are keeping children so busy, says Bettelheim, that it becomes difficult for our young people to learn problem-solving skills and to fully realize their true creative potential:

The biographies of creative people of the past are full of accounts of long hours they spent sitting by a river as teenagers, think-

---

* Ginsburg, K. R. "The Importance of Play in Promoting Healthy Child Development and Maintaining Strong Parent-Child Bonds," *Pediatrics* 119, no. 1 (2007): 182–91.

ing their own thoughts, roaming through the woods with their faithful dogs, or dreaming their own dreams. But who today has the leisure and the opportunities for this? If a youngster tries it, as likely as not his parents will fret that he is not using his time constructively, that he is daydreaming when he should be tackling the serious business of life. However, developing an inner life, including fantasies and daydreams, is one of the most constructive things a growing child can do. The days of most middle-class children are filled with scheduled activities—Boy or Girl Scout meetings, music and dance lessons, organized sports—which leave them hardly any time simply to be themselves. In fact, they are continually distracted from the task of self-discovery, forced to develop their talents and personalities as those who are in charge of the various activities think best.*

So why do we adults act as thieves—stealing play from our children? Perhaps because many of us coaches and parents never integrated our own sports careers into a coherent narrative. We could be compensating for something we perceive as missing, atoning for something, chasing something still. We may see our children as extensions of our own needs for validation, acceptance, and approval. Their performance has the power to aggrandize or minimize us. The social status of the parents of the star players increases; parents can beam; parents can be proud of their genetic product—a part of themselves out there performing well. What's worse, I see many parents subconsciously make their displays of love conditional by showing more approval and affirmation if their child performs better on the field and less approval after a bad game.

In the best light, I think many of us see organized sports as a way for our children to develop character, strength of purpose, courage, and the

---

* Bettelheim, B. "The Importance of Play," *Atlantic Monthly* (March 1987): 35–46.

like. But one of the big myths in our culture is that sports builds character. As if doing a handstand, running a marathon, hitting a curveball, or simply suiting up are sufficient to strengthen a young person's moral fiber! Unless a coach teaches and models character and encourages its development in his athletes, it is more likely that organized sports and contemporary culture will spoil play and undermine the development of the very character and virtue they claim to build.

With plenty of encouragement from a sports-crazed adult culture, I bought wholeheartedly into three sports myths: acceptance, status, and performance-based identity. I viewed my athletic prowess, and the plaudits it produced, as a way to receive acceptance—a false acceptance because it was based on my performance and not on my character. I craved the status of being one of the best players on the field. I attached my identity to sports success; "Joe Ehrmann, football star" somehow satisfied me so much more than just being "Joe Ehrmann." I know my father felt the same way. These myths can manifest themselves later in adolescence in the form of sexual conquest, status consciousness, and a craving for the sense of power that winning generates. All these attributes got wrapped up in my sense of what it meant to be a man as I reached adolescence. You get girls, you make big bucks, and you win. The ball field, the bedroom, and the billfold are how you earn your masculinity. Pretty simple plan for a young guy who was big and could run. And pretty numbing—just the way I needed it at the time.

Sports culture, and its wayward high priests, blessed my poor behavior. And few coaches challenged conventional sports culture by trying to fight the messages and teach "countercultural" concepts like values, virtues, and successful relationships.

Even a calculator couldn't calculate the number of times my father, coaches, and other adults clearly mandated that I "Be a man!" All across America, toughness and so-called "rugged individualism" are considered primary masculine virtues. A boy is encouraged to start acting like a man by age five. I learned it boxing with my father in the basement, and an awful lot of adults like me are still walking around today wondering what happened to their childhoods. This mandate to separate our hearts from our heads teaches us that basic human emotions like love, sadness, fear, and self-doubt are not masculine. And if we act contrary to the code, we're chastised with words like "sissy," "mama's boy," and other names far more vulgar and hurtful.

It wasn't until I met Coach Simmons that I realized that a coach has a unique platform from which to beat back these myths and build self-esteem, character, and virtue in young athletes. And guess what? With Coach, I felt as if I was back on the toboggan. I was playing again! Lacrosse was lots more fun than football, even though I could barely catch and throw. Yet I experienced a new permission to play, compete, and belong, as a person, and not just an athlete. Coach Simmons helped reconnect my heart with my head—a magical combination on the field.

Any coach with self-understanding can make the same choice that Coach Simmons made, to transform instead of transact. Transactional coaches lead through negotiation, inducement, manipulation, and threats to achieve a desired productivity, efficiency, and effectiveness. When players perform well, they are rewarded. When they don't perform well, some kind of punishment is inflicted, be it yelling or the withholding of praise, playing time, or participation. Contingencies, carrots and sticks, rewards and punishments are the Xs and Os of transactional coaches. The relationship between coach and player is a quid pro quo, with the coach holding the power to give and to take.

In contrast, a transformational coach realizes the power of the coaching platform to inspire, motivate, and produce positive change in his or her followers. He or she is acutely mindful of the moral, social, emotional, and psychological needs of young people. Transformational coaches offer individual support and encouragement to each player and have a clear vision for the desired impact on their players' lives. And not surprisingly, a transformational coach, even in organized athletics, allows and encourages young people to simply play.

BOYS AND GIRLS:
CAN WE ALLOW THEM TO BE JUST THAT?

Alcohol. Drugs. Violence. Sex. More than ever, these enticements are enmeshed with and marketed by sports.

Think about the media-saturated world in which young people are growing up today. Our children are exposed to a tainted form of human sexuality. It is estimated that 94 percent of American children ages eight to seventeen consume some form of sports media; one in three do so daily, and seven in ten do so at least twice a week, with boys far outpacing girls. Football is America's favorite family sport to watch together with almost five and a half million kids under age seventeen tuning in each week.

Common Sense Media recently reviewed nearly sixty NFL games— more than 180 hours of coverage—and watched nearly six thousand commercials played during time-outs. They found the majority of commercials used sex, violence, and alcohol to promote products. Forty percent of the games included advertisements for erectile-dysfunction drugs.

President Obama, in his book *The Audacity of Hope*, said, "I wasn't too happy with ads for erectile dysfunction popping up every fifteen minutes whenever I watched a football game with my daughters in the room." I would add to that comment my objection to the degrading form of female sexuality presented with a frequency and volume unimaginable not long ago.

At a bare minimum, every coach should model and teach respect toward the opposite sex and the value of self-respect and respectful relationships. I believe coaches can be part of our society's solution to the crises in masculinity and femininity for three reasons. First, as I have said repeatedly, coaches have an unparalleled platform, power, and position with which to model, teach, and redefine masculinity and femininity. Second, athletics is an appropriate venue in which to critique the false messages of our culture and help reframe confusing issues for young people, helping athletes in their struggle to make sense of all the confusing messages targeted at them. And third, as Paula has taught me through her work as a psychotherapist, brains can be rewired at any age. The brain is neuroplastic, which means that new experiences and relationships can change the shape and function of the brain for better or for worse. An InSideOut coach has the power to provide the experiences that can bring back the innocence of play and guide players in having respectful relationships with the opposite sex.

BOYS TO MEN

I was recently sitting in a booth at a local deli. Four high school boys were seated in the booth in front of me. They wore varsity jackets, laughed and teased each other affectionately, and for a few minutes I was heartened to see them laughing, sipping sodas, and eating huge plates of food together.

They were swapping stories about their practice—I could tell some played soccer and the others football. They seemed healthy and happy; they seemed to enjoy their friendship, and for a moment, I thought that this is what sports can do. I was reminiscing as I eavesdropped. I was jealous of their camaraderie, because for me high school sports were a highlight of my career, and I haven't been able to re-create that sense of brotherhood and community in my adult years.

But then, one of them pointed to a fancy car that pulled up and parked outside. And they stopped their sports chat and started speculating about what the driver who got out of the car did for a living. Or, more accurately, what the size of his paycheck must be. The car chat ran its course and then one of them asked if the others wanted to see pictures of his girlfriend. They all moved closer together as he held them over the table. It didn't take me long to realize that they were looking at provocative photos that his girlfriend had texted him. My first experience of "sexting" at the local diner!

They were seemingly happy and well-adjusted kids, but in one sitting they exhibited what I consider symptoms of masculine identity confusion. They were associating masculinity with the idea that real men play sports, drive fancy cars, and date hot girls.

I tell myself that it wasn't that different when I was young. But today technology and the media have sexualized youth culture to a greater degree than ever. When I was a boy, the lingerie section of the Sears catalog was as close as you could get to seeing something provocative. I would have walked a mile to see a *Playboy* magazine. Today pornography is a few mouse clicks away for young men and women, degrading their understanding of each other in the process. To the shock and chagrin of the audience members in my seminars, I quote these statistics from Liz Claiborne, Inc.'s Love Is Not Abuse program:

> Fifty percent of teenagers in a serious relationship have compromised personal beliefs to please a partner. Forty-five percent of teen girls know someone who has been pressured or forced into having intercourse or oral sex. Thirty-three percent of teens experience some kind of abuse in their romantic relationships, including verbal and emotional abuse. Twenty-seven percent of teenagers have been in a dating relationship in which a partner has engaged in name-calling and disrespect. Twenty percent of teenagers report having been hit, slapped, or pushed by a partner. Twenty percent of teenage girls are physically or sexually hurt by a dating partner.*

Add in the growing epidemic of dating abuse via technology, sexting, and social media and the statistics are even more frightening. Young people find creative (and sometimes destructive) ways to release the tension and energy in their developing minds and bodies. With a scarcity of free play, over- or underindulgent parents, and other culturally

---

* Liz Claiborne, Inc., Love Is Respect.org.

based mixed messages, distorted relational styles can develop, as seen in the statistics above. Audiences at my seminars often look confused when I roll out one of my big theses, that the greatest crisis in America today is the crisis in masculinity. Take just about any social problem and you can tie it back to masculinity. I don't care if it is things as seemingly unrelated as boys with guns, girls with babies, dating abuse, or boardroom greed. Okay, maybe you are saying, "We are in the middle of an economic disaster. There is a health-care gap. There are scores of political problems around the globe. And here is this guy saying a crisis in masculinity is substantially responsible for many of our societal troubles today?"

The young jocks at the diner that afternoon were typical. They seemed a little nervous and insecure, talking in a way they probably thought they should. So many kids are faking it, trying to present an image of someone they think they're supposed to be. What I've learned over the years from my many conversations with people is that many of us still feel this same way. Deep inside, we think we're frauds. We feel inadequate and incomplete, as if we're missing some essential element.

Around the same time that I ran into those athletes in the diner, the media industry was consumed with Tiger Woods's fall from grace. During that initial period of incessant coverage and commentary on Tiger's behavior, I didn't see anyone point to the issue that was at the core of the saga: the fact that Tiger's entourage, many of his friends, and obviously he himself, bought into the myths of masculinity.

People really didn't see his downfall in the context of socialized masculinity. In fact, some connected promiscuity with virility and saw his women as the privilege that comes with power and fame. "What a stud!" some men say to one another and chuckle. "What bad taste in women," others said. Surprisingly few critiqued his behavior and called it what it was—a dishonor to his wife and children and a disservice to our young, impressionable athletes.

The whole scandal was a teachable moment for coaches, given Tiger's fame and the social issues involved. Tiger's text messages indicated that he was a pornography fan; they also reinforced how widespread, brutal, and misogynistic porn has become. The more men are exposed to pornography at an early age, the more desensitized and bored they become with fidelity-based sex. Pornography has become normalized in our society, so that all too often it seeps into sports culture, too. The average age of a first-time viewer of pornography is twelve. These early experiences can impair and distort the capacity to engage in and enjoy fidelity-based sex for a lifetime. Not exactly something to wink at and dismiss.

Sometime after the Woods ordeal, my youngest son, Joey, told me about an episode of *South Park* on TV. I had never seen the show before. We had been talking about the rash of celebrity scandals and he thought the TV satire added an interesting perspective. In this cartoon several famous politicians, sports heroes, and various celebrities are portrayed attending a mandatory support group meeting for "sex addiction." Butters, a goofy little fifth grader (and a regular of the show), is identified as a "future addict" and sent to the group by his teacher. The group leader teaches the lesson of the day which is, "Don't Get Caught!" When Butters raises his hand and asks, "But what about personal responsibility? Shouldn't we be learning to take responsibility for our behavior?" the crowd is shocked by his naïveté. "Throw him out!" they yell.

The creators of *South Park* seem to capture the lunacy in many of the messages we are sending our young people. I thought to myself, *This cartoon seems a lot more honest on this topic than the six o'clock news.*

The reasons coaches don't seize the opportunity to step up during these times can be complex but generally fall into one of three categories. We may be in denial and think it's not our role or position to step in and address the issue. Or we may be involved in similar behavior or activities or know others who are. Our guilt or confusion about what is right and wrong can justify or rationalize our silence. Other reasons include feeling incompetent and not knowing what to say or how to handle something that is touchy or complicated. However, resources are fairly abundant for those who really want to find information and support.

When I speak to coaches, young men, and my players, I draw a box on the chalkboard and entitle it the "Be a Man Box." I ask my audience to call out the words that stereotypically define what it means to be a man in our culture. The words I commonly get are: tough, strong, stoic, pimp, athletic, muscles, dominate, power, conquer, and bling. When I ask what are the social rites of passage boys engage in to prove their masculinity, I most often hear: alcohol, drugs, sports, and sex. I lived inside that box myself for a long time and enjoyed the praise and adulation of other men promoting the "Be a Man Box." I also realized the world can be a lonely place for boys who live outside the box. When I ask players what are the names boys are called who don't manifest these inherently false concepts of manhood, they immediately respond: weak, bitch, faggot, girl, gay, and other adjectives. I try to help them see that all these derogatory names can be put in two categories: women and homosexuals. When you view a group of people as inferior or defective, you treat them as such. Think of the pain being inflicted on women and young gay men because of derogatory labels. Imagine, I ask, what it feels like to be defined by one or more of these names. Then I ask players what will a boy who is called any of these names do to get back into the Be a Man Box? Every boy replies—whatever it takes. It is too painful to be out of the box.

Every boy is fed three fundamental cultural lies about his value and worth as a man. They learn the first lie by the time they are eight years old. They learn it on playgrounds, on ball fields, and during recess all across this country. Boys are taught that their value and worth has something to do with their athletic ability. Our culture associates masculinity with size, strength, or a skill set that allows boys to compete, win, and be accepted. The boy who can hit the hanging curve or catch the down and out is elevated. His skill allows others to see him as having more promise and potential than others. He is simply more "manly." Men who have grown up attempting to define their masculinity by their athletic ability are set up for tremendous failure and frustration in life. A boy's athletic ability alone, often genetically driven, seldom correlates with the development of the character traits, skills, and strengths that it will take to negotiate his life successfully.

Every boy receives the second lie about his manhood by the time he is in junior high. In our culture adolescent boys learn that being a man has something to do with sexual conquest. What does it mean to be a man? It means seducing girls to gratify physical needs and to validate one's masculinity. That certainly doesn't make anyone a man; instead, it makes one a user of other human beings.

The third lie our culture imposes on boys is that masculinity is defined by economic success, as if the measure of a man can come from a job title, position, and possessions, rather than from the content of his character.

Based on the cultural lies about sports, sex, and money, who do you think is the masculine role model for great numbers of boys? (And remember, a role model is someone you model your behavior after.) It's the professional athlete. Why? Not because we teach young kids to evaluate their character and how they use their fame on behalf of their families, communities, and others, but because professional athletes have ability and skill. They compete against other men and win. They have opportunities for sexual conquest and economic success.

So the cultural call to "man up"—the myths of athletic ability, sexual conquest, and economic success—confuse the purpose of sports. These myths overwhelm and drown notions of team, honorable competition, joy, and creative play. Coaches need to provide a clear and compelling definition of what it really means to be a man who exhibits empathy, trustworthiness, friendship, ethics, respect, and joy.

GIRLS TO WOMEN

I was in an airport news store a couple years ago and a young girl— twelve at most—asked me if I could hand her a magazine that she couldn't reach. She smiled, said please, and pointed up to the top shelf.

As I reached for it, I was startled by its cover. A well-endowed

woman in a skimpy bikini overwhelmed the headline that said something about getting the body you want in thirty days. Another, smaller
headline said: "What your man really wants in bed." I paused as I
touched the magazine, looked down at the girl, and turned to her.

"I think your parents better get that for you," I said.

Her mother promptly arrived, told the girl they were going to miss
their flight, and grabbed the magazine for her as she pointed at it.

As I returned to the magazine rack, I stepped back and surveyed the
scene. It was a nightmare for the healthy and holistic development of
girls into women. On the center shelf was *Sports Illustrated*. It was February and a one-hundred-pound airbrushed top model was beckoning
me on the cover. Not a female athlete, but a model. For a moment, even
at my age, I felt seduced. Then I thought of all the pleasure I had got-
ten from *Sports Illustrated*'s writers over the years—Frank Deford, Steve
Wulf, and Rick Reilly, to name a few. And I wondered why on earth
the publisher with the greatest platform in sports journalism, no matter
how much money that issue earned, would endorse this sort of degra-
dation of women and sex. The message to female athletes, of course, is
that no matter how well you play or perform, it boils down to what you
look like.

The *Sports Illustrated* swimsuit issue reinforces the objectification of
women and encourages boys to view women through demeaning stereotypes of beauty. Men are socialized to place appearance at the center
of women's value and worth and to place the possession of such women
at the center of their own value and worth.

As the father of two daughters, I detest how we shackle young girls
with all the wrong concepts and definitions of womanhood. In *The
Beauty Myth*,* Naomi Wolf describes the pull of culture demanding
that girls look perfect. The myth is that in return, they can expect to

---

* Wolf, N. *The Beauty Myth: How Images of Beauty Are Used Against Women*
(New York: HarperCollins, 2002).

be loved and accepted. Most girls are conditioned to believe they must sacrifice parts of their true selves in order to be accepted by others. They struggle with the dilemma of either being authentic and honest or being loved and accepted. When a girl disavows her authentic self, her self-esteem is compromised. The freedom to be and the freedom to play are replaced with self-consciousness and fear of rejection. For a girl to be loved and accepted at the expense of being true to herself means handing over her locus of control to others and to the cultural norms.

Girls begin to lose parts of themselves as three cultural lies define standards that make relentless and unreasonable demands of them. These are the lies I refer to as the "Prince Charming Myth," "Beauty and Body Type," and the "Abandonment of Authentic Self."

Little girls learn the Prince Charming Myth when they are very young. This not-so-covert message begins when little girls are told stories like "Cinderella," "Snow White," and "Sleeping Beauty," stories about beautiful princesses who are rescued by handsome princes and live happily ever after—all because they were beautiful and good! This Prince Charming Myth sets up young girls to believe that if they are beautiful enough and good enough, they will indeed be "worthy" of a handsome prince charming who will come and make life complete. When that doesn't happen, girls and women often feel that they are flawed. With age, single men become committed bachelors while single women are labeled old maids or spinsters.

The second cultural lie that disrupts the development of healthy self-images in females is the unrealistic standard of beauty for women portrayed in the media. By the time girls are eight or nine years old, they see their value and worth as human beings as dependent on what they look like. The number of nine-year-olds already dieting or thinking about dieting is epidemic. *The Journal of the American Academy of Child and Adolescent Psychiatry* reports that 40 percent of nine-year-old girls diet regularly. The Harvard Eating Disorder Center in Boston reports that 42 percent of first-, second-, and third-grade girls want to be thinner. These young girls view their bodies not from the inside out, on the basis of how their bodies perform for them, but from the outside in, on the basis of how other people appraise their physical appearance. Advertising sends the message that females are judged more by their body parts than by any other quality or characteristic. The more discontentment that advertisers can breed by displaying unrealistic, airbrushed, and computer-enhanced images of women, the more likely women are to buy into the need for and promises of their products.

The third lie that pervades our culture about femininity promotes the abandonment of the true self and the use of feminine wiles as the path to acceptance, status, and identity. It doesn't take long before girls understand the pressures to look sexy and appear skilled at attracting and pleasing men. Girls learn their lessons just like boys. They know that "pretty" for girls is like "athletic" for boys. It gives them a step up on the ladder of acceptance. By adolescence, girls have learned to hide parts of themselves they believe are inadequate or lacking and instead reveal a false, painted face that they believe others find more acceptable.

My wife tells a revealing story from her girlhood. She was four years old, the sixth child in a middle-class Irish Catholic family, and accustomed to being last in line in terms of material things. One day her mother took her shopping for shoes.

"Ladies, what can I do for you?" the middle-aged male clerk said.

"I need new shoes," Paula said, no doubt sweetly.

She clearly remembers the clerk getting down on one knee so that he could be closer to her. Face to face, in fact. It was unnerving.

"Young lady, with those beautiful blue eyes you can get anything you want!" the clerk replied.

My wife remembers having a "wow!" moment at age four. She remembers clearly thinking, "Anything I want?" She was unaccustomed to such attention, but even then was able to make the link between her eyes and the potential satisfaction of her needs. I still tease her and say she has been using those eyes ever since, but the bottom line is this: Just as we bombard our boys with messages about conquest, power, and winning, we overwhelm our girls with variations on the same themes.

By the time a girl gets to high school, the pressure to abandon her authentic self for a persona that promises acceptance, status, and popularity is almost unbearable. When girls are forced to hide their true selves, their self-esteem and ability to have authentic relationships are compromised. It takes an extraordinary amount of inner strength and self-confidence to withstand the pressures to conform to the cultural standards. There is an urgent need for coaches to teach girls how to develop the critical thinking skills and the media literacy that they need to understand the harmful media messages that focus on the sexualization of girls and women.

In my InSideOut coaching seminar, I ask coaches to draw a box on a piece of paper and entitle it "Be a Woman." I ask them to respond as they think their female players would to the question, "What words stereotypically define being a woman?" I prod them to think about words and images the media uses to define a "real" woman's physical attributes, relationships with men, sexuality, and the careers and activities in which women engage. We then fill the box with the words and concepts that summarize contemporary definitions, images, and roles of women, words like skinny, pretty, submissive, soft, sexy, desirable, and nurturer. Coaches are astounded when they see these answers on a piece of paper. When I do this exercise with female athletes, they lament the inherent conflict in being strong and successful in sports versus traditional ideas of femininity. It always breaks my heart to hear the emotional pain caused by the cultural imprisonment of girls and women.

As the expectations for females remain unrealistic and out of reach, girls are left feeling insecure and inadequate. This often breeds self-destructive behavior as girls struggle to express their unhappiness with the pressure of living up to the contradictions of femininity. The unattainability of the standard becomes the breeding ground for an epidemic of self-harming behavior such as drinking, drugging, purging, starving, cutting, smoking, and promiscuity. The pervasive sense of lacking or missing some critical piece leads to shame and eventually to attempts to hide and cover what girls believe they cannot change.

Organized athletics for them should be a liberating time on the field or the court, a time free of messages whose intent is to sell something false, unattainable, or destructive. Coaches can use their powerful platform to help lead this liberation of our girls, to teach them new words, such as respect, play, authenticity, trust, devotion, camaraderie, and enjoyment.

I believe sports should be a sanctuary, a place apart from the cultural messages and mind tricks that many social interactions involve. Sports are not movies, concerts, or magazines. In sports, young people aren't being entertained; they are entertaining themselves. They aren't watching; they are participating. They aren't being seduced by an image or a fashion or a gesture; they are engaging themselves with play and focus and camaraderie. They are *playing*. And yet, we have lost all sense of play. The notion of creative play is critical to cognitive, intellectual, spiritual, and physical development, yet organized sports and their all-too-adult messages confuse and even prohibit play.

The opportunity for coaches to encourage creative play is the unique strength of athletics. Sports played under an InSideOut, transformational coach can offer children the moments in which their minds, bodies, and souls can align and they can be beautifully authentic and carefree.

CHAPTER 5

The WHY:
The Way and the How

After thirteen years of professional football, my body finally gave out. My spirit was willing, but my flesh was a mess. I was completing seminary in Philadelphia. One of my last seminary classes studied how philosophers through the centuries have dealt with the ideal of social contract theory. The core of this theory is the concept that people elect to give up certain individual freedoms in order to make life and society work better for the whole. Social contracts compel people to think and rethink their relationships with and responsibilities to one another.

That phrase struck me and stuck with me. Once I had established The Door, in Baltimore, I decided to flesh out the notion of a Sports Social Contract. This contract would focus on the rights of children and the responsibilities of adults to provide and protect those rights. My vision centered on sports as an incubator for the healthy development of young people, a plan that eventually would help repair and rebuild a broken community.

Sports, with an appropriate purpose and solid coaching, I knew, could become a tool for community development. I also knew that sports could enhance the physical fitness of participants *and* teach citizenship, commitment, and character, as well as teamwork. In fact, sports, I believed, could create collaboration among parents, schools, and educators and create communal pride.

But what agreement should be reached between sports, coaches, schools, and adults to ensure the healthy development of young people? As I pondered this question, I realized there was a vast gap between my vision of a mutually beneficial social contract and the current contract among sports, coaches, and young athletes. It is incredibly lopsided; young people have no vote, no voice, and no power. They are thrown into the world of athletics without full disclosure or informed consent. Athletic directors, league officials, and coaches define the contract. Parents passively sign it and the children have to live with it.

Childhood is a unique time of life to be honored with certain inalienable rights critical to children's development. All children are entitled to far more than they are receiving. All children merit a positive identity based on their inherent value—not based on their skin color, creed, performance, or ZIP code. They merit being cared for simply because they exist and not because they perform. They are entitled to a safe environment and protection from violence—whether that violence is in the home, in school, on the streets, or on the athletic field.

Children who play sports, like all children, are also entitled to be free from adult sexual demands, exploitation, and exposure. Sadly, the contract is repeatedly broken and few provisions and protections are provided. We need to write a contract mandating that young players' security, well-being, self-esteem, and joy be primary and absolute in our coaching and programming. In my version of the Sports Social Contract, administrators, coaches, and parents provide unconditionally for the needs of children. Communities prosper because future generations undergo the moral, ethical, social, emotional, and physical growth that sports can provide.

Any person in a position of power or authority over young people has a moral and implicit contractual responsibility to protect and nurture those young people and strive to see them flourish. Coaching affords a key opportunity to restore and honor this social contract. To undertake this awesome responsibility, each coach can begin the InSideOut journey by asking and answering these four key questions:

Why do I coach?

Why do I coach the way I do?

What does it feel like to be coached by me?

How do I define success?

WHY DO I COACH?

Why do you coach? Think of all the time, energy, and sacrifice it takes to coach. Why do you do it? What is the purpose of your coaching? Every coach should have a definitive statement that answers this question. Coaching shouldn't start with Xs and Os but with Ys. This "WHY" should be a clear and concise statement defining the impact we are trying to make in our players' lives. WHY directs the expenditures of our time, energy, and effort and provides a final destination. Answering the question Why do I coach? can help a coach identify selfish agendas and develop a purpose that transcends personal, vocational, financial, or ego-driven needs.

WHY prompts us to answer the questions of when and how to use the power of coaching to affect players for their lifetime. As coaches we spend an inordinate amount of time on the technical and tactical aspects of performance and often lose sight of a grander purpose of coaching. When our purpose is clearly defined, it provides a unique source of passion and perseverance and a focused path to follow. But, as the Cheshire Cat told Alice, "When you don't know where you are going—any road will do." Too many coaches have no clear, concise purpose other than winning and choose a path uncertain of where they will end or how their direction will affect their players. You can't navigate a ship by studying the wind and the waves alone—you have to set your sights on a port, a lighthouse, some WHY—the purpose that keeps us centered and focused on honoring the high calling of being coaches.

My WHY: *"I coach to help boys become men of empathy and integrity who will lead, be responsible, and change the world for good."*

I began to see my WHY soon after Billy's death when I read Frankl's *Man's Search for Meaning.* As I mentioned in Chapter 1, it is one of the defining books in my life and it generated the foundation of my quest for meaning and purpose. This quest evolved into my coaching philosophy.

Frankl's internment in Nazi death camps led him to a startling observation: It was not the strongest, most vibrant, or even smartest inmates who survived. It was those who had meaning, purpose, or a WHY to live who survived. He saw that people who had hope of being reunited with loved ones or had projects they were impassioned to complete or those with great faith tended to have a better chance than those who had lost hope. Frankl concluded that humankind's search for meaning is the foundation for living a passion-filled, effective life.

He wrote: "It did not really matter what we expected from life but rather what life expected from us. We needed to stop asking about the meaning of life and instead to think of ourselves as those who were being questioned by life—daily and hourly. Our answer must consist, not in talk and meditation, but in right action and in right conduct."

I knew from the day I buried my brother that I wanted to find meaning in his suffering and the suffering of so many others on his on-cology floor. Building Baltimore's Ronald McDonald House taught me that meaning can be made out of suffering in other-centered advocacy and actions. In creating meaning from Billy's death, I created meaning in my own life. Spirituality, masculinity, advocacy, youth development, and sports all melded into my WHY.

As I've trained coaches over the years, I've come to believe that coaches burn out and quit not because of parents, difficult players, or money, but because they either lost sight of or didn't have a WHY worthy of the high calling of coaching. While the vast majority of coaches have no clearly articulated, written purpose statement, I've heard things like "I love the competition," or, "Coaching keeps me in the game." True, but these are transactional statements with little or no benefit to the players. Coaches are too often serving themselves at the expense of their players' needs.

I rejected this transactional thinking after years of running into its dead end. It may get a national champion each year in NCAA volleyball, an AAU basketball title, or a spot in state championships, but it retards the healthy development of our young people into productive and content adults. Winning and losing, in my coaching manifesto, is a consequence of a WHY, not a WHY in itself.

The cornerstone of my purpose statement is "to help boys become men." This became the focus of my coaching. I had been waylaid on my quest to become a man by false cultural messages and poor role models of manhood. I wanted to coach players in their transition from boyhood to manhood and redefine manhood. I wanted to develop a clear and compelling definition of masculinity that would guide and protect boys on their journey.

Once again, to move forward I had to go back. To go outward, I had to go in.

As I said earlier, the turning point in my life came when I was standing in the cemetery after my brother's death. At the end of the ceremony, the priest said the final "Amen." The moment when everyone walked away from the graveyard, that grave-site hole looked as deep as the hole in my heart. "What is the meaning of life?" I asked myself.

And more specifically, "What is the meaning of my life?"

I was twenty-nine years old, six years into my NFL career, and I had no concept of what life was about or who I really was. I had hit the long ball, according to the cultural concepts of masculinity: athletically, sexually, and economically. This crisis started a long inward journey as

I began to process my grief and ultimately ask the question, What does it mean to be a man?

In turn, this led me to study the social and cultural concepts that defined masculinity and femininity. I began to understand that most of us are imprisoned by false ideas and concepts of what it means to be a human being.

Eventually, I came to the conclusion that masculinity and femininity could be defined by two criteria and two criteria alone. And they are the same for men and women because they define our common humanity. I know this not only from my own journey in life but also from my twenty-five years in pastoral ministry. In my faith tradition, part of my job as a pastor has been to sit at the deathbed of dying people to help prepare them for their passing. And here's what I know to be true. I know it to be true for me and I know it to be true for everyone.

If you were on your deathbed today and you wanted to measure your success in life, if you wanted to measure the kind of man or woman you were, it would come down to two things and only two things.

First: Life is about relationships. It's about the capacity to love and to be loved. What does it mean to be a man? It means having the capacity to look somebody directly in the eyes and say, "I love you." And then being able to receive that love back.

The questions you ask at the end of your life are not what material things, awards, or applause you've acquired. Certainly the question is not how many wins you've had. The questions that will matter most on your deathbed are the questions related to your relationships. What kind of husband was I? What kind of wife? What kind of partner? What kind of mother? What kind of father? What kind of son? What kind of daughter? What kind of friend? What kind of member of the community? What kind of coach? Who did I love and who loved me?

Now, think about that. Think about how we raise boys in this country. We don't raise boys to be successful in their relationships. We tell them to be independent and be their own men, to take pride in individual accomplishments, compare and compete with other men, and earn their manhood.

All across America, seven- and eight-year-old boys, already saturated with false concepts of manhood, already ordered by adults to be men, begin policing each other and culling their playmates according to their understanding of manning up. Once he is identified, they pounce on the boy they consider too soft or too gentle or who cries a little too easily. Ganging up on that boy and shaming him has become a cultural habit. And the others teach that boy what they have already learned: If you're going to be a man you'd better separate your heart from your head. Then they all walk away from their victim thinking, "I hope that never happens to me!" So they start projecting a masculine façade to protect themselves from becoming the next victim. Like I did, many hide behind a façade for decades, repressing emotions in a way that hinders their ability to connect and form meaningful relationships. Yet it is not false bravado or claims to independence but the interplay of interdependence that teaches us how to connect to each other. In the end, it is the quality of our relationships that defines us.

On their deathbeds evaluating their lives, the second thing people want to know is what kind of difference they made in the lives of others, their community, and their country. People want to know that they lived for a reason, a cause, and a purpose that was bigger than themselves. I call this a transcendent cause; transcendent in the sense that it motivates one to get up every day with a vision that is bigger than one's own personal goals, desires, and ambitions, a vision that serves the needs of our teammates, community, and society and recognizes and enables a spirit of brotherhood, sisterhood, and the responsibility we have to each other. Life, I've learned, is a team sport and ultimately is unsatisfying if it is lived solely for self.

Imagine what would happen on a team, in a school, in a community, or in our country if all the coaches, athletic administrators, and parents came together and said we're going to use sports to help develop young men and women with the capacity to love and be loved. Imagine if we were united in our goal for them to be devoted citizens, friends, wives, husbands, or partners, committed mothers and fathers, good neighbors, and selfless teammates. And then imagine coaches giving their players permission to develop these skills and a vocabulary allowing them to express all of the emotions necessary to connect and bond with us and each other. Think what would happen if coaches chose to use their position to build and repair their players' hearts and minds.

Imagine if every player understood that he or she had a personal responsibility to contribute to the betterment of society by identifying his or her unique personal cause. Imagine that athletes walked in a world where whenever they saw racism, sexism, anti-Semitism, heterosexism, or any other "ism" that marginalizes and minimizes people, they could understand the need to demand that justice be done so that all could live with the dignity and status and maximum opportunity that every human being deserves.

In the same way we define authentic masculinity and femininity, a team is defined by the quality of its relationships and the commitment to its cause. Every team has a common purpose, performance goals, and objectives. In addition, every team has a mutually accountable work ethic and is built on the trust, respect, and integrity of every team member. It is the perfect venue to help boys and girls become men and women. Why do I coach? I coach to build my players' capacity and competency to build and maintain relationships. Why do I coach? I coach to teach my players how to commit their hearts, minds, bodies, and spirits to the cause of the team.

This is my WHY. It directs, drives, and determines my coaching. When any parent, principal, or person asks me why I coach I tell them: *I coach to help boys become men of empathy and integrity who will lead, be responsible, and change the world for good.*

WHY DO I COACH THE WAY I DO?

Coaches have one of the most powerful platforms in young people's lives, as I've emphasized.

Coaches spend an inordinate amount of time with our kids, but the platform does not result simply from a tallying of hours spent with one another. Within those hours the degree to which coaches can influence, teach, and penetrate a young person's psyche is phenomenal. Just recall the men in my breakfast club, who still vividly recall the coaches who scarred or inspired them.

With growing insight I came to realize that we tend to revert to coaching and parenting styles that we were exposed to growing up. I realized early on that my parenting style was a replica of my experiences with my own parents, primarily my father. Likewise, my impulses as a coach were almost genetically linked to Schwartzwalder, Dingboom, and the coaches I observed when I was playing.

The experiences we had with our coaches come back to illuminate us or bite us. I and many coaches I have spoken with often revert to habits and patterns from coaches of their youth.

Just as there is a Man Box and a Woman Box, there is also a Coach Box. And just as occurs with masculinity and femininity, there are stereotypical words and images that define coaches and box them into habits that dominate their technique. Once I blew up that false coach's box, I found a borderless land of possibilities for defining my role as coach. In my seminars, I ask coaches to put into a box words that stereotypically define coaching. Once coaches realize they can be defined by more than Xs and Os, their vision expands from the ground to the sky, the way mine did when I first encountered Coach Simmons. Change always begins with a new picture, and each coach in the room has to travel a different road. The vision for who a coach wants to become is what grounds his inside work.

I share with them how I built my coherent coaching narrative. I create a graph and plot out all the coaches I played for. I then grade these coaches. How positive was the experience? How negative? I then pose a series of questions regarding each experience I had with each coach: What did I learn? What did I learn that I wish I hadn't? What did I wish I had learned? What were my developmental needs at that age and how were they addressed, if at all? How did that coach make me feel about myself? Did the coach mold or shape my character in a positive or negative way? How did the coach treat my teammates? Was there a consistent moral or ethical dimension to the coaching? How do I feel about that coach now that I am a man? Much of what I shared in Chapter 1 is the result of this process.

My coaching narrative reveals that my father was my first coach, and my relationship with him is integrated in every aspect of why I coach the way I do. As I reflected on my relationship with Dah, I became cognizant of my lifelong hunger for his approval and the hunger so many young people have because of absent, dismissive, or abusive dads. America is becoming a fatherless society. About 40 percent of our children are living in homes without their biological fathers. And unfortunately, this has become a defining feature of childhood for far too many children. Too many dads have abdicated their roles as providers, protectors, and partners in parenting as well as moral role models for their children. This absence creates feelings of deep personal rejection and assaults children's sense of self-worth, self-respect, and personhood. Social scientists have produced a body of research conclusively showing that when children lack a healthy father-child relationship, they are at a higher risk for a host of negative emotional, educational, and psychological outcomes.

I coach the way I do to help players meet their needs for male mentoring, modeling, and acceptance. I want to contribute to their self-understanding, identity, character, and competence. Boys without dads need to know the role fathers can and should play in their children's lives. In the case of boys who have well-grounded relationships with their dads, I want them to understand what an incredible gift that is. It is a gift never to be taken for granted.

From my father I learned that being a sensitive little boy was not safe. My mother was left with few resources to raise four children, but she worked very hard to provide for us. There was always great food on the table and seldom did my mother miss a game or event. With few of her own personal needs met, my mother found her happiness in her children. Like many boys who grow up with absent fathers, my role became confused. My recognition in the community further confused this role and I grew into a man outside when I was still a boy inside. External physical strength often projects a false image of internal maturity and can create unrealistic expectations and opportunities for young athletes to be exploited. I coach mindful of the dynamic and the painful consequences when grown men continue to act out of their little-boy needs and fears. I understand that the size of the boy or the man has nothing to do with his internal, psychological age.

From my abuse, I became sensitive to children lying in bed at night, crying, feeling all alone with no one to share their fears, pain, or experiences. I am attentively aware of the humiliating and devaluing experiences many children endure and how these experiences shape their self-concept and behavior. Fifteen million children live in the shadow of domestic violence—many more in homes with drug- and alcohol-addicted parents. Approximately one in four girls and one in eight boys will be sexually abused by the time they reach adulthood. I coach knowing that children come onto my field every season carrying backpacks loaded with hurtful or harmful life experiences. When young people are "acting out," I don't just label, judge, and exile them. I know I can't judge them based on their current behavior or personality. Children behave the way they do for specific reasons. Part of my job is to try to understand and to help get them the appropriate support they need if I can't provide it. I coach the way I do because every young person needs a "confiding relationship" built on confidentiality and trust. I coach the way I do so players can confide and share what they need to, so that I can help them integrate their past with their present in an effort to shape and direct their future.

From my basketball coach who commanded I hurt another human being, I learned the first responsibility of every coach: Do no harm! The doctrine of winning at all costs is morally offensive and hurts the human development of players. I learned to denounce masculinity and coaching that promotes violence or disrespects or intentionally injures another person. I coach to be a positive influence, to respect the power of the position I have in the lives of my players.

From Ed Abramoski I learned the power of affirmation and resiliency a coach can provide to his players. I coach the way I do to affirm and help players discover and identify unique gifts and talents that too often go unnoticed and underdeveloped. I coach with affirmation to build my players' positive self-concepts and resiliency.

From Charlie Dingboom, my high school coach, I learned the lessons of team responsibility, rules, and respect for the game and my teammates. I coach the way I do with rules, boundaries, and appropriate discipline when needed.

From Ben Schwartzwalder I learned the difference between transactional and transformational coaching. I learned that when narcissism replaces other-centered coaching, teams can fracture into separate cliques. I also learned the consequences of remaining silent before injustices. I coach the way I do to promote teamwork, unity, justice—and reconciliation when needed.

From Coach Simmons I learned to look from the ground to the sky. I learned to appreciate the beauty, aesthetics, and spirituality of sports. I coach outside the box the way my mentor did, with dignity, integrity, and respect.

From my professional career, I learned that coaches need to see the warning signs in their players, not look the other way. Coaches should never put on blinders and overlook their players' personal problems and life issues. I coach the way I do with a desire to identify and remedy as many problems as possible in the lives of my players. I coach to not hinder or hurt them.

From my addiction, I learned players will self-medicate their insecurities, doubts, pain, and problems. When young men are hurt, confused, or don't feel they measure up to the false definitions of masculinity, they will medicate their sense of not being man enough. They will self-medicate on alcohol, drugs, sex, pornography, and a host of other meds, including playing sports. I coach the way I do to help them create their own life narratives to understand the source of their pain and find healthier solutions for their healing.

From my wife, Paula, I not only learned the process and power of healing but experienced her gift of healing as well. As a psychotherapist, she has spent thousands of hours listening to people's pain and problems. I've learned that healing means being honest with yourself and with others. Healing involves building trust based on confidentiality and heartfelt care and helping people make sense of their lives by integrating the good and the bad. I've learned more about being a man from her than from any other person in my life. She has modeled and coached me in developing other-centered relationships and helped me in becoming healthy enough to fulfill my true calling in life. I coach to help my players make sense of their lives and the lives of those around them. Paula, a wounded healer, has taught me to walk in a way that encourages my own healing and helps me to teach, encourage, and help heal my players.

From The Door I experienced firsthand the ravages of prejudice, racism, poverty, inadequate education, and dreams deferred and denied. I coach knowing that when good kids are faced with nothing but bad choices the outcome is often way too predictable. So I coach the way I do to teach critical thinking skills to help players understand how race, politics, and economics have affected their families and communities. I coach the way I do to educate all players on the unjust "isms" that marginalize and minimize other human beings.

So why do I coach the way I do? Because I have a working coherent narrative and am integrating my life experiences into my coaching. It took an InSideOut process to establish my WHY and it resulted in my understanding why I coach the way I do.

WHAT DOES IT FEEL LIKE TO BE COACHED BY ME?

I had developed my WHY to help boys become men. Once I understood the reasons I was coaching the way I was, I reframed the new and purposeful way I wanted to coach. Next I wanted to be aware of what it felt like to have me as a coach.

By building my coherent narrative, I got in touch with the feelings my coaches had generated in me as I passed through the developmental stages of my youth. I wanted to create an atmosphere in which I could connect with and transform my players. I thought about all the pressure young people battle every day. They get up early in the morning, grab something to eat, commute to school, endure full days of academic learning, competitive grading, SAT prep, parental pressures, and homework. Between classes they walk the halls dealing with peer pressure, social pressure, sexual pressure, and all the difficulties negotiating the uncertainty of adolescent development. At the end of the day they walk out on the athletic field and are coached by me. How does that feel to them? What feelings do my words, actions, and interactions create within my players?

To answer these questions, I had to begin with values. My values are those ideas and beliefs that I hold as essential to my character, constitution, and coaching. They are my most basic and deeply ingrained beliefs and personal ethics. Appropriate values provide the fuel and energy necessary to accomplish my purpose and provide a unique source of inspiration, insight, and motivation. So I started with my three highest values as a coach: empathy, kindness, and service to others. The absence of these values created the errant definition of masculinity and coaching that I repeatedly experienced.

Empathy is the standard bearer of my coaching values. Empathy literally means "feeling into another," to understand another person's feelings, thoughts, and desires. Empathy validates a boy's emotions even as the male socialization process encourages him to deny them. It is an absolute necessity for a transformative player-coach relationship, because it allows the coach to enter the internal world of a player. Empathy creates the foundation for a player to feel known, understood, and accepted for his or her authentic self. For young people to develop and learn empathy they must experience someone empathizing with them. Empathy is the building block of successful relationships. If boys and girls are to live an other-centered, cause-oriented life, empathy must be the guide. It is the antidote to injustice, apathy, and indifference to the pain and plight of others. It wasn't until I built my narrative that I had empathy for myself as a boy and the experiences I had endured. If I deny, repress, or ignore my own feelings, I will never be able to empathize with someone else's. Empathy allows me to see what my players see, feel what they feel, and walk in their shoes. It also lets me understand what it feels like to have me be their coach.

This is where I start to get resistance from many coaches. Most coaches do not yearn to be described as empathic. Especially male coaches. It is a word that doesn't fit into the traditional Man Box because it has a connotation of "softness." It gets pushed to the private domain of family or faith; it demands an awful lot of a person. Many coaches say that worrying about players' feelings is not why they signed up to be a coach.

In some of my smaller workshops, I have coaches introduce themselves, their school, and their sport. I will ask them to come up with one word essential to great coaching. As I record the words on the whiteboard, deep down my hope is that all of them will pick words like empathy, kindness, and service to others. Almost none do. I interpret this to mean that few coaches have done the coherent narrative work necessary to understand, encourage, and employ the development of empathy.

We can't be empathic toward others without grasping our own life stories, understanding our crises and failures, and using them as a way of putting ourselves in our players' shoes.

My second-highest value is kindness. Kindness encompasses a vast range of words and actions, and I often tell players that kindness has a ten-word vocabulary. One word—"please." Two words—"thank you." Three words—"I love you." Four words—"Can I help you?" I stand with the Dalai Lama, who said, "My religion is very simple—it is kindness." My coaching is very simple—it is kindness built on empathy.

Our high school football defense is predicated on three words: penetrate, pursue, and punish. Penetrate the line of scrimmage, pursue the ball carrier, and then get eleven helmets punishing the ball carrier every play. Before every game I reinforce these principles and exhort the team to fly around and play with reckless abandon. And I also tell them that if at any point during the game they doubt themselves, are uncertain, or are just plain getting beat by a better opponent, to come over to me and I will help. It is amazing to me the number of high-school-age boys who do come over to me on the sidelines and share their feelings. I help get them centered and focused and then whisper an affirmation into their ear about how much I believe in them.

Third, I value service to others. Service to others is empathy and kindness put into acts and actions. It gives meaning to life and helps sustain and dignify the lives of others. It is the opposite of self-service. Service to others is never a quid pro quo—doing a deed to receive an equal or similar deed in return. It means selflessly putting the best interests of my players and team first. It teaches them how to serve their teammates, school, and community and that service to others ennobles one's life. Service to their players gives coaches the moral authority and power to transform lives.

My values: empathy, kindness, and service to others. Easier said than done! Values have to be integral to a coach's character and integrated into his coaching. When values are authentic and flow out of a coach's character and self-awareness, they can be applied in practice consistently and with integrity. The reality is that players evaluate us and learn our values by watching us—watching how we treat them, their teammates, opponents, and other coaches. No matter how well we communicate, they gauge what we really value by our actions. This is why transformational coaches must coach from the InSideOut.

After determining my values and the character traits that I wanted to create, I was ready to implement them in my coaching. Once a value is actualized it becomes a virtue: a character trait of moral excellence. My value is empathy—the virtue is to empathically understand my players. My value is kindness—the virtue is showing kindness toward my players at every practice. My value is service—the virtue is serving others beyond myself.

The InSideOut process enabled me to develop a clear and compelling purpose for coaching. Although the way I was coaching grew out of my autobiographical sports story, the way I coach now is based more on how I believe players should be coached. Secure in my direction, I ventured into the vulnerable territory of exploring what it felt like to players to be coached by someone like me.

Was this enough to produce the transformational relationships and connection I desired to build with my players? To answer this question I defined my values and delivered them with their accompanying virtues. This led me to yet another question—and perhaps the most important one an InSideOut coach has to answer.

HOW DO I DEFINE SUCCESS?

Success has meant different things to me during different periods of my life. What I've come to learn is that success is often a journey. It has multiple peaks and valleys instead of one ultimate pinnacle. One success often builds on another. Success is not a one-dimensional tug-of-war between winning and losing. Setbacks, losses, and mistakes also help to build success.

I like John Wooden's definition: *"Success is peace of mind which is a direct result of self-satisfaction in knowing you made the effort to become the best of which you are capable."* Coach Wooden believed that true success comes when we simply do the best that we can do, no matter what the outcome. Between the lines of his definition, we can read that true competition lies within ourselves. We don't compete with the coach across the field. We compete with ourselves to be the best we are capable of being. In other words, we are successful when we give something our all. This concept never occurred to me as a player, when everything was measured by whether I won or lost, whether I beat my opponent or he beat me.

Defining competition this way challenges us to measure our own best efforts. The challenge involves learning how to compete with ourselves. How does someone know when he or she has given his or her best? It is much harder to give our best than we think. As coaches we are constantly seeking to achieve and produce success. The problem is that so few ever sit down and define what success is for them. We have to define success before we can measure it. If we measure ourselves against ourselves, we can determine if we are truly successful. This is especially important in our "win at all costs" sports culture where success is defined only by winning and, in the vast majority of situations, we are left to feel that we didn't measure up.

So how do I define success? Success can be measured only according to my stated purposes as a coach. I can't say my purpose is *to help boys become men of empathy and integrity who will lead, be responsible, and change the world for good* and then define success by my win-loss record. I must define success based on the masculine maturation of my players, the amount of empathy, kindness, and service to others they experience from me and internalize into their own lives. Success is defined and measured by the content of their character, their leadership, and their contribution to the betterment of their families, their communities, and the world.

The challenge presented with this definition is the amount of time it takes to determine success. I give myself a twenty-year window: I will assess the quality of the lives of the men I helped produce twenty years later to determine if I fulfilled my WHY as their coach. When my players come back and are committed husbands, partners, and friends, devoted fathers, empathic men of integrity, contributors and leaders on all levels in various communities—then I will know. People often ask what kind of success my team will have this season. I tell them I will let them know in twenty years.

Recently, a former player shared with me an email he received from a former teammate in a period of personal crisis. "You know . . . I never fully appreciated the building men for others thing that the coaches were talking about until now. Out here in the world, I have a much better idea what it all means." Ten years later, this young man is starting to understand and practice the lessons he was taught in high school. I know I need to be patient. My coaching philosophy is demanding. It takes time for it to settle into young people's consciousness.

Another player called me recently to tell me he had been selected for Teach for America. Another helped defuse a high-profile racial controversy at a school in Baltimore. A third essentially ministered a family back to life after they lost their son in a car accident. My players are out there doing well and I am eager to assess my success. I intend to do it player by player, name by name, truthfully judging my success.

I continue to wake up each morning visualizing and reciting my WHY, restating my values and virtues—some mornings robotically and others with new meaning and passion—and reading my affirmation:

I am a transformational coach who has the position, power, and platform to make a positive difference in the lives of my players. I coach to help boys become men of empathy and integrity who will lead, be responsible, and change the world for good. I allow for accountability and take responsibility for my actions.

And then I go out and execute my vision.

PART II

INTRODUCTION

The InSideOut Program

Being an InSideOut coach means dealing honestly and effectively with what's inside in order to be purposeful and transformational when coaching young people. In Part I, I wrote about how I put the jumbled pieces of my sports life into a coherent narrative. Doing this helped me understand the things—both good and bad—that drive me. I wrote with the intent of using my story as an example for coaches to help them develop their own sports autobiographies.

We all have a story, and it is the coherence of our story that helps guide us through the process of becoming better coaches. Simply put, we have to learn to become mindful of who we are and what we are doing. This development of mindfulness, the ability to perceive ourselves and others accurately, is the most profound journey a coach can take.

In Chapter 1, I wrote about how the struggle to make coherent sense of my life eventually led me to a new way of viewing the world of sports and coaching. Understanding myself helped me begin to change because I identified the triggers that prompted transactional coaching habits and impeded my efforts at being a transformational coach. To get where I wanted to go, I had to get myself out of the way. My journey started with this self-awareness. Once I made sense of my experiences, it became easier to help others make sense of theirs.

In Chapter 2, I identified three coaching archetypes and explained why Moses, Dorothy, and Coach Roy Simmons Jr. became and remain transformational coaching models for me. Moses, the defiant liberator/coach who understood the depths of the oppressive identities that were keeping his charges in bondage; Dorothy, a kindhearted visionary who saw the potential in her players; and most important, Coach Simmons, the man who gave me permission to step outside the traditional coaching mold. He modeled for me and taught me that sports and spirituality go hand in hand. Roy Simmons was the coach who brought dignity, integrity, and grace onto the field and into my field of vision.

In Chapter 3, I described a spectrum of transactional personalities, showing some of the bad habits we fall into as we hold this powerful coaching platform. We may be confused about what is acceptable behavior between coaches and athletes. Five transactional coaching styles, the dictator, bully, narcissist, saint, and misfit, help us to recognize destructive relationship patterns and can motivate us to establish guidelines for staying in the ballpark of healthy behavior and interaction.

Chapter 4 diagnosed some of the specific challenges, struggles, and toxic messages athletes receive and need to overcome. Our young people face overwhelming challenges today and many are searching for meaning in their own lives, just as I searched to find meaning in mine. Comprehending the complex world of our athletes is the best (and really the only) way to connect with them. Once I began comprehending myself, seeing what my players were up against was easier.

Finally, in Chapter 5, armed with all this previous work—my coherent narrative (a work in progress), a trilogy of model coaches (the dos), a list of the transactional coaches (the don'ts), and a deep sense of empathy for our youth—I doubled back and asked myself the mindsight questions: Why do I coach? Why do I coach the way I do? What does it feel like to be coached by me? How do I define success?

Going inside to improve my coaching on the outside, I arrived at the point where I could develop a program to fulfill my WHY statement and in various ways transform the lives of my players.

That coaching program constitutes the second half of this book. It is based on the same two-step paradigm—searching inside before coaching outside. But the primary focus of the program is the Ys—the Why questions of Chapter 5. Once I understood the why of my coaching, I felt the freedom to envision a program and team culture that would flow from and support my purpose statement: I coach to help boys become men of empathy and integrity who will lead, be responsible, and change the world for good.

In planning the program, I identified five pillars that support this purpose statement and ensure a transformative experience for players, on the field and in their lives. These pillars are community, cocurricular lesson plans that integrate our school's educational philosophy onto the playing field, collaborative communication, honorable competition, and ceremonies that emphasize the spirituality of sports and celebrate the player's transition into manhood. The authenticity and creativity of these pillars support and sustain the culture needed to deliver the virtues that are the foundation of healthy masculine development.

As a staff, we coached Xs and Os and we helped boys become men with an InSideOut coaching approach supported by these pillars. Winning was the by-product of teaching, nurturing, and prioritizing our players' developmental needs and honoring the sacred journey of each boy. With one hand we did our traditional game plans that helped us win games and with the other we defined, modeled, and integrated the virtues that helped us transform lives.

In a recent survey conducted by the U.S. Anti-Doping Agency and reported in the *Journal of Coaching Education*, it was estimated that

162 million Americans have some kind of relationship with sports. Of that 162 million, 25 percent have a direct relationship to sports as parents, players, or coaches. The study concluded several important findings including how coaches were ranked as the number one positive influence on today's youth playing sports, and how parents "overwhelmingly cite personal and social values when describing their hopes for their children in playing sports."

Parents falsely assume that their children are learning valuable character lessons through sports. Without assertively implementing a value-based curriculum into their program, sports seldom teach these lessons. In fact, the further up the competition chain we get, the less important integrity and character become.

I am convinced that one of the greatest venues in which to teach, model, and implement virtue is sports, because of the almost innate desire to associate virtue with sports. Despite the notorious moral failings of many coaches and athletes, we still wrap virtue and sports together precisely because the elements of cocurricular instruction, communication, community, competition, and ceremony are sports virtuous pillars.

My work on establishing a coherent narrative led me to analyze my behavior and relationships. I thought deeply about what sports have given me and could give others, and I settled on this virtue framework as the program, the playbook, to maximize the incredible power of the coaching platform.

We tend to think that only designated moral authorities can talk with integrity on the topic of virtue. I want to encourage and empower average Jimmys and Joes who need to know that coaching is more than Xs and Os. Coaches from T-ball on up are some of the most important and influential people in every community.

Coaches shouldn't be hesitant or embarrassed to use the words and lessons of virtue that fill the coming pages. The beauty of the position of the coach/mentor is that sports inherently allow us to leverage and relish the rhetoric of heroes and virtue.

While I wrote this book I watched the Vancouver Winter Olympics. The games have their deep flaws—commerce, global politics, and celebrity often trump their core message and mission. But as I watched the lugers and skaters and skiers and sledders, I felt the way I want sports to make my athletes feel. The virtuous origins, or at least ideals, of the Olympic Games have always spoken deeply to me. I realized as I watched that being an InSideOut coach means turning my struggles, errors, and misfortunes into lessons that will make me a coach who instills a sense of community; is a better classroom leader; is a clearer and more empathic communicator; is an advocate of healthy and constructive competition; and is a mentor who turns sports into a ceremony of celebration for young people.

Those are the five pillars of an InSideOut coaching program. In the next five chapters, I describe this program.

Most recently, I have been coaching coaches and missing my Friday nights on the Gilman sideline. Paula and I have made a commitment to remain available to our sons throughout their college journeys. Our youngest son, Joey, is a college linebacker now. We tell everyone that we gleefully chase after our boys—one in the spring, playing lacrosse, and one in the fall, playing football. We are thankful for the opportunity to spend more time watching them grow. Together, we created Coach for America to help train and teach coaches our InSideOut coaching process. (For more information, visit www.coachforamerica.com.)

I stay connected to Gilman, Biff, and our coaches as much as I can, but now I sit behind the sidelines with Paula and watch our boys develop under the guidance of other coaches who have the opportunity to transform them into men of character.

CHAPTER 6

Community

A TEAM WITHOUT WALLS

After determining my purpose for coaching, I wanted to create a community that could support the Sports Social Contract I envisioned. But I knew I couldn't accomplish this alone. Again the words of Dr. Martin Luther King Jr. came to mind: *"We are caught in an inescapable network of mutuality, tied in a single garment of destiny. Whatever affects one directly, affects all indirectly."* I would need a community of like-minded administrators, coaches, parents, and players to weave together this transformational vision. Dr. King's words fit an InSideOut coach's philosophy perfectly: It would take a "staff" of allied coaches to support the vision, values, and virtues of a transformative sports program.

So, I started with a community of two, Biff Poggi and I. We were two aspiring transformational coaches feeling our way through the creation of something radical: a community built on King's garment of "mutuality," a team in which school administrators, coaches, parents, and even the groundskeeper and trainers all committed themselves to one another for a common good. In 1994, we started meeting at the coffee shop, the deli, and our dining room tables (in retrospect we ate as much as we dreamed!). We recounted our lives and sports histories and were honest with ourselves and each other about the good, the bad, and the ugly parts of our lives and sports journeys.

As we communed, our coherent narratives meshed and a vision for transformative coaching became clear. We started this InSideOut journey a full two years before Biff was named head coach at Gilman—and they were two incredible years! We started two youth basketball teams and called them Building Men for Others. We coached them according to the virtues and values that we were making the core of our coaching philosophy. It was a great success, and the boys, their parents, and Biff and I enjoyed it immensely. We knew that if ten- and twelve-year-old boys were responding to our messages, we could achieve the same effect at the high school level.

Both age groups saw one thing clearly: I love Biff and he loves me. Our players got to see, feel, and witness authentic masculine relationships. My younger brother, Billy, would be Biff's age if he were alive, and I see a lot of Billy's boyish charm in Biff. Biff has an innate ability to connect with young people, mold them, and make them believe in themselves.

I remember Coach Simmons once posing the question, "If I gave an artist a block of granite and asked her to carve an elephant, how would she do it?" He soon answered the question himself by saying, "An artist with vision would take her chisel and hammer and chip away everything that did not look like an elephant." Biff, like Coach, has an eye to the inner landscape of boys and has been chiseling boys into men for a long time. He, too, is an artist.

We knew we had to chip away the previous concepts about sports and coaching to create a caring community where everyone was included, committed, and accepted. We had to chip away everything that didn't look like the community we were trying to build.

We envisioned creating a "team without walls"—a community in which there were no obstacles to becoming a team member and no separate rooms within the team. Though lacking walls, this team would still have a solid foundation: the principles of inclusiveness, authentic connectedness, and belonging. This new sort of team would stand in sharp contrast to what many teams have become: social ladders with position on higher or lower rungs based on old playground hierarchies of athletic ability, size, strength, past successes or failures, and a long list of socially accepted values based on race, class, or neighborhood. Our team would first and foremost be an accepting community.

I knew from my time on the pediatric oncology floor at Johns Hopkins Hospital and the Ronald McDonald House what authentic community looked and felt like. More than thirty-five thousand families from around the world have lived in this community, shared with each other, and drawn strength from the solidarity and mutual support of their suffering. Ronald McDonald House is architecturally designed so no one remains alone. Common eating areas, play areas for children, and activity rooms are all designed to build community. This was the architectural origin of our metaphor—a team without walls.

Biff and I sought to imitate this design on our team. Each player would live in a common space with no walls of separation. We didn't want insiders and outsiders or starters and scrubs. We wanted to include every boy who desired to be a member of the team and make him feel wanted, needed, and valuable. We felt that any player who wants to belong shouldn't be on the outside looking in. Why exclude when you can include? We have enough exclusion and elitism already in our culture—particularly in our sports culture. We knew that every boy could benefit from the warmth of belonging and contributing to community.

Belonging is especially critical to young people developing their sense of identity and self-worth. To be a part of a whole greater than one's self is crucial to a child's well-being and self-discovery. Paula had studied Erik Erikson's stages of social and emotional development in young people. His writings informed the five questions Biff and I agreed to strive to help each of our players answer during his time with us. Identity: Who am I? Integrity: What do I stand for? Intimacy: Who will love me and whom will I love? Interdependence: Whom will I stand with? Industry: What can I do with my life? Think of all the ways that a coach with power, platform, and position can help players discover the answers to those questions.

I often ask coaches to reflect back to their childhoods and remember times of personal exclusion when no one wanted to play with them. Maybe a time when they weren't invited to a party, or were picked on or bullied on the playground or cut from a team, a school play, or the band.

Biff and I recalled our personal experiences of exclusion and rejection as young men and reflected on every boy's and girl's deep need for compassionate acceptance and a place to belong. Belonging is essential to the healthy emotional and social development of young people. When we looked at the alarming increases in binge drinking, depression, anxiety, substance abuse, and sexual promiscuity among our youth, we knew we could make a difference by creating a caring community designed to build a web of supportive relationships. We didn't just want them to survive; we wanted them to thrive in such a community.

Our WHY, *to help boys become men of empathy and integrity who will lead, be responsible, and change the world for good,* provided us the inspiration to step out of the traditional coaching box to create our alternative model of thriving community. Our purpose not only provided the innovation to produce our program, but also attracted the kind of people we needed to build a caring community.

"Community" comes from the Latin word *communitas. Com* means "with" or "together" and the root word *munus* means "gift." Community literally means to gift to one another. A team without walls is a group of individuals who gift to one another with a mutual sense of authenticity, trust, care, and support. To be part of a nurturing, caring community is a tremendous gift in our individualistic society. Community provides the social and emotional nutrients every young person needs to grow, develop, connect, and contribute.

"Team" is a synonym for "community." It's a microcommunity of interdependent players, parents, and coaches that shares its gifts to one another's benefit. Team means every individual is inextricably bound to the others and to the success of the whole community. No player, no matter how talented, has ever won a game by playing alone.

But community does not just "happen" any more than great families just happen. No one has a great family by accident; it is the result of hard, diligent, and intentional work. In the same way, creating and sustaining a healthy team requires honest truth-telling, perseverance, and courage.

One of the great benefits of sports is that they give us permission, even encourage us, to think in terms of a type of community that few other endeavors offer. Community is implicit in sports—a team passes a season together, suffers and celebrates together, eats and hurts and excels and fails together. For boys, affection is even tolerated on the field. What a fertile ground to build an authentic community and not just one that pays lip service to communal values!

When Biff and I started to coach "out of the box" and use words of affection and love, it was the moms who got it first. Many of the dads struggled with our efforts to give boys permission to use words to identify and express their emotions. Some dads battled us to keep a narrow definition of "masculinity," one that fit their own culture, values, and experiences.

Moms were willing to join us and support us in changing the meaning that our culture attaches to their sons' masculinity. Boys are birthed and raised by women. Yet at some point in the socialization process, boys are conditioned to move away from anything considered soft, girly, or feminine. "Feminine" is thought to be "antimasculine," and boys dim their vision to exclude women. Moms have more to offer their sons than they realize. Too many women are forced to collaborate with the false definition of masculinity out of fear of feminizing their sons.

If manhood is about relationships, the capacity to love and be loved, and commitment to a cause, then moms are critical to the healthy development of boys into men. So when we initially talked about boys becoming men of empathy and integrity, the moms became the backbone of our program. The next challenge was to bring dads along.

The initial hurdle was helping dads understand their individual narratives and how they had developed their own concepts and definitions of masculinity. Many dads subconsciously prohibited their sons from expressing their emotions. I believe one of the most important roles dads play is to help their children identify, name, and verbalize their emotions and to consistently and continually validate them. To do so, dads need to understand their own version of the Man Box. Having emotions and the ability to express feelings doesn't feminize boys, it humanizes them. It enables them to have healthy relationships. Once fathers step out of the Man Box, they begin to help their sons break out as well. This big step allowed for the connections and communication necessary to build a nurturing community.

Three virtues form the core of community for me: liberty, respect, and moral courage. "Liberty" is a word with very patriotic overtones in this country, but it applies at the personal and team level, too. Liberty for young people means being released from imprisoning self-concepts and the cultural chains that impede young people's growth, fulfillment, and potential.

The second virtue on which we structured community is respect. Respect is internal as well as external; respect for one's self and respect for others. Respect can be summed up in the Golden Rule: Do unto others as you would have others do unto you. Respect is the virtue that cements a team. Respect on a communal team is not contingent on performance, success, or ranking; it is based on the fundamental rule of a coach that each player is valued because of who he or she is and not what he or she does.

Moral courage, our third virtue, sustains the integrity of authentic community. Moral courage is what enables us to stand up for what is right even if it means standing alone. This is courage because it not only maintains personal and communal values but at the same time risks personal rejection. Players, parents, fans, and coaches with moral courage stand up and speak out when faced with behavior, gossip, and criticism that defy the values of our team and community. There are no "free shots" at other community members in the stands, on the bench, or in the coach's room. Community demands the accountability that moral courage provides. As Martin Luther King Jr. said, "The ultimate measure of a man is not where he stands in moments of comfort and convenience but where he stands at times of challenge and controversy." We want to develop and measure our community by the yardstick of its moral courage.

LIBERTY

Inside

In Chapter 2, I wrote about how I came to identify with one of my coaching archetypes, Moses. I strongly identified with him as liberator of a people starved for freedom. To liberate, Moses created a well-defined community with rules and regulations, in which each member was coached on how to develop his full potential and how to grant others the same liberty.

The virtue of community-driven liberty is hard-won—it takes practice and structure and orchestration. In this sense sports are like music—organized notes, dynamics, and passions that yield an exquisite performance. InSideOut coaches are liberating conductors.

My InSideOut work provided me with one absolute certainty: I never felt freer than when I was on the practice field with my teammates. The locker room was my refuge. True, transactional coaches, commerce, and false goals muddied the overall experience. Nevertheless, I tasted moments of total liberation and they were always within community. Memorial Stadium rocking, playing for Coach Simmons, tobogganing in a Buffalo park—I never felt freer or more connected to myself than when I was working and playing with others.

Because of experiences like these, I tasted a sort of freedom that I believe only team members can know. The physicality, camaraderie, adrenaline, and challenge of organized athletics are unmatched. Liberty comes only in a community when others are free as well.

As a young man, I fancied myself the rebel—a long-haired Marlboro Man who needed no one and who heeded few rules. But sports are built on rules. I realized that the sensations of liberty need a structure in which to thrive. Sports were my refuge in large part because of the framework they provided. The rules of the game, the boundaries, the clock, the ref—they all establish the framework for liberating experiences.

This paradox is at the heart of sports—structure allows for freedom. And there is another factor: We need relationships, support, and community to be free. My best teams always felt like families. As an InSideOut coach, I was determined to put my players in a position to experience liberty as often as possible while helping them realize the importance of structure and rules in allowing for the expression of that liberty to occur.

Outside/Lesson

Realizing that liberty and community are inseparable, Biff and I set out to structure a liberating program around three basic realities of a great team: We belong to each other; we need each other; we affect each other.

1. We belong to each other.

Everyone on a team belongs on that team: stars, starters, substitute players, and managers alike. Regardless of race, religion, socioeconomic background, neighborhood, or family structure, each young person is a vital member of our community. All other categories are meaningless. Full acceptance is the rule.

One of the things we do before the freshmen's first practice is to have the varsity players take a moment for reflection and contemplation. I ask them to close their eyes, get connected to their breathing, and think about the night before their first practice as freshmen.

Think how nervous you were—wondering how you were going to be accepted—how you would perform—are you good enough? Who would you have to line up against? How would you fare? Think about having to go to the shower the first time with guys three and four years older than you. Think how you sat in the stands and watched the varsity players and dreamed your boyhood dreams of playing alongside them!

Once we help the varsity be mindful of the freshmen, Biff tells the seniors they have now earned the right to serve the freshmen. Servant leadership is the antithesis of self-promotion, of competing for positions of preeminence. It's the opposite of hazing. It's downward mobility based on the belief that if you want to be a leader you must first know how to serve.

Next, we invite the freshmen over and the varsity players give them an ovation. A couple of the captains will welcome them and let the frosh know how courageous it is for them to be here. They are admired and welcomed into our community.

As new community members, they, too, now have a responsibility to promote and honor our team's credo: Be a man for others.

2. We need each other.

A team is a complex organism. We are interdependent; no teammate can function without connection with other teammates. A sense of inferiority or a display of superiority is cancerous to a team. We start eliminating the potential for that cancer the first day of practice.

There is no greater impediment to a young person's sense of liberty than a sense of inferiority. Often players fail to fully engage because they feel unimportant, less talented, less gifted, less esteemed. There is an epidemic of low self-esteem among young people, among both the most talented and the least. I know that because I lived it. So as coaches, we try to identify these fellows. We develop a list of affirmations for them and then meet with our captains to design a game plan for making them feel more included, for mentoring them, for liberating them.

Another impediment to liberty is a sense of superiority, a sense of arrogance: I have no need for you or the team; the team needs me. This is a player who thinks the team is there for his self-aggrandizement. This is a player shackled by his distorted sense of self, one who keeps his teammates from the liberating possibilities of community. Biff and I identify these players as soon as possible. And then we love them into community. We call them on acts of selfishness, we have our captains call them out if they are acting superior, and we emphasize to them clearly the need to learn how to serve others with their talents.

3. We affect each other.

Oneness—a team is One. What more liberating experience is there than to feel whole, purposeful, and in sync? My most glorious moments as a player occurred when every moving part on the team worked together and I played my role in concert with my teammates.

On an InSideOut team, we practice together, we play together, and we win and lose together. We preach this—you don't give your all to the game, you give your all to the team. Emmitt Smith was recently inducted into the NFL Hall of Fame. With tears of gratitude, he thanked his family, former coaches, and teammates for helping him reach the pinnacle of achievement. But his most heartfelt thanks went to Daryl Johnston, the Cowboys fullback who cleared the path for many of Smith's great runs.

"You mean the world to me," the tearful Smith told Johnston, asking him to stand up and be recognized by the crowd, "not just because we shared the backfield, but because you sacrificed so much for me. You took care of me as though you were taking care of your little brother. Without you I know today would not have been possible. I love you from the bottom of my heart."

This epitomizes the transformative power of community. Johnston liberated Smith literally and figuratively on and off the field. And I am sure Johnston would say the same of Smith. African American Emmitt Smith from Pensacola, Florida, and the University of Florida pronouncing his love and affection for white Daryl Johnston from Youngstown, New York, and Syracuse University. We need each other, we belong to each other, we affect each other, and together we can liberate sports, players, coaches, schools, communities, and a whole country of young people.

RESPECT

Inside

My self-respect started to change with the intervention of Honest Abe. As I wrote in Chapter 1, his approach with me was to affirm my personhood. He tried to instill self-respect in a way that would initiate respect for my teammates and life itself.

Most of my life my self-respect was tied to my athletic performance. After the Ronald McDonald House opened in honor of my brother, I found people respecting me more for my contributions to society and my character than for any of my accomplishments on the field. The respect I received off the field started to change how I felt about myself and how I treated myself. It meant far more to me than any athletic accolades. The supporters of the Ronald McDonald House willed me to respect community, other-centered living, and myself, too.

My wife cemented this transformation over time. She taught me to believe the hype, if you will: I had touched the people of Baltimore with my effort and determination, with my personality and generosity. She set me on the InSideOut path and then I set out to make respect—how young athletes feel about themselves, their teammates, and the game—a core goal of my coaching. She taught me that the inside journey usually produces a sustainable external change. Peace with ourselves and our story begets a respect and empathy for our players. It is hard work with a simple, profound result. One yields the other. InSideOut coaches respect themselves, their team, and the game; their players follow suit.

Outside/Lesson

My track record shows I'm not a big believer in rigid rules—but rules are necessary, and the Golden Rule of respect is essential. Biff and I insist on respect, for one's self and each other. We enforce it. We demand that team members be as deeply committed to one another's growth and success as they are to their own. We want them to go beyond themselves in terms of their athletic performance but also in terms of their commitment to a higher good for their teammates.

We set out to create and implement a "no cut" policy. Every player who tried out for the high school team would either make the frosh-soph, junior varsity, or varsity. A junior would automatically make the varsity regardless of athletic ability or past experience. We wanted to eliminate young people's fear of being rejected and having to risk one more dismissal or "failure" at an early age. We had seen so many young people coming to high school scarred by youth league coaches and policies that sent the wrong message for their self-esteem and healthy development.

We practiced the wisdom of Phil Knight, CEO of Nike: "If you have a body, you're an athlete." He knew that if Nike outfitted individuals with athletic gear and inspired them to "Just do it," a new generation of athletes would participate and that would increase his market share. We decided to increase our share of student-athletes trying out for football because if they came, we knew we could equip them to become men built for others. "Just love 'em" became our mantra. You can't do this in every sport, but in football you can carry as many players as you have uniforms for. Biff made sure we had plenty of uniforms.

One of my favorite results of the team-without-walls approach is an English paper written by one of our players in his junior year after making the varsity team. He stood about five foot five and weighed about

185 pounds, not particularly well suited for football physically, but he was one of the most popular players and best leaders we ever had. By the time he was a senior his teammates honored him by voting him captain for his character and commitment.

MY TROPHIES

I walk into my room and see lots of things: my schoolbooks, my TV, my stereo, my desk, and my bed. But the most significant things that I see when I enter my room are my trophies. They stand tall on my shelves with pride and dignity, as if to say, "We are the owners of this room. Gaze upon our glory." They are arranged very precisely, positioned from shortest to tallest and back down again, like the outline of a mountain. Medals draped down from the trophy pedestals and plaques stand proudly behind them. Turn on the light and the trophies glisten and gleam.

Those trophies have always been a great source of pride for me. They symbolize all of my sports achievements when I overcame adversity and succeeded. They represent all of the times that I returned victorious from the athletic field of battle. They define the successes and achievements of my middle school years. I look at the bronze medal hanging from its purple ribbon that I won as the most valuable player of my seventh grade basketball team. I look just to the left of that medal and see the big gold and blue lacrosse trophy from my days on my rec league lacrosse team. I remember the day I received it very clearly. We won the tournament and I could not have been happier winning the Super Bowl or the NBA title.

I look below and see the Unsung Hero Medal that I received for my hard work on the middle school cross country team. This award, in particular, meant a lot to me. I despised running cross country. I was never very fast, but I worked hard every day because I knew that running would be very important in all my other sports. I felt an enormous sense of satisfaction when I won this award, because getting through the cross country season was such a struggle, and it was nice to be recognized for my hard work.

I am no longer the star of any team now. When I entered high school, I learned the valuable lesson that there are always going to be players that are bigger, stronger, and faster than I. This was a sudden and upsetting realization, but one that was necessary to my development as an athlete and a human being. What used to represent my accomplishments on the athletic field now symbolize my hard work and dedication. My trophies used to mean that I was the great athlete, the star. Now they mean that I can accomplish things because I work very hard.

So far in high school I have not received any sports trophies or awards. Last year, I even got cut from the JV basketball and lacrosse teams. However, I made the varsity football team. I am just as satisfied working hard on the third string as I was when I was the star in middle school. It is the hard work and the camaraderie of being on the team that mean something special to me now, not my individual accomplishments.

Still when I enter my room and gaze upon all those symbols of my past glory, for just a brief moment, I am overcome by an incredible sense of sadness. But that moment passes quickly. I look at those trophies again, and I light up as I take hope from the thought that occurs to every Jewish kid who is too short and too slow: "I might not be able to play on an NFL team, but by God, one day I'm going to own one."

Can you imagine cutting this player because of athletic ability? His senior year we made this young man our blitzing middle linebacker. Every time he went into the game our huddle, sidelines, and fans erupted in encouragement and excitement. It was a wonderful example of a community benefiting everyone. The starting middle linebacker understood why he was coming out of the game at crucial moments; his teammates learned community wasn't just designed for the "best" but that everyone can contribute and has something to offer. The parents learned to appreciate that every player is a critical part of the community and therefore deserving of full support. This is why Biff and I coach the way we coach.

Our notion of the virtue of respect also came in part from our co-parenting of each other's sons. Biff has three sons and I have two. They have grown up together and love each other.

When they were very young, four of our five sons tried out for the school choir. Three were unceremoniously "cut." Now to me, when young boys want to sing together with their peers, that is a beautiful thing. Does it really matter at that age if a boy is off tune? Why are prepubescent boys being judged by the tone or pitch of their voice rather than the desires and longings of their heart? Music has much to teach beyond singing in chorus. How many little boys are steered away from discovering the magic of harmony because their voices aren't suitable? How important is performance at such a young age that you would cut boys from choir? Or any artistic or athletic venture at that age? Every time we sing in church, I notice my sons barely lip-synching the hymns. I, on the other hand, with terrible pitch and tone, bellow songs from deep within my soul. I love to sing. We tend to walk in the beliefs about ourselves based on the messages we receive as children.

Jimmy Poggi, our one son who made the "cut" for choir, went on to play in a band all through high school and is now playing football at the University of Iowa. I'm sure he is singing in the locker room after every win. Somebody told him he could and he did. Others were told they couldn't and they didn't.

Even within our own community, it has been a struggle to get other coaches on board to stop cutting players and rethinking old coaching philosophies. The use of cuts stood in sharp contrast to our philosophy. It created a lot of work on our part to "convince" players who were cut in grade school that they could be on the high school team, contribute to the varsity, and have fun. Socrates said the two most important venues in which to create a just society are the gymnasium and the music hall. Both are about the integration of individual mind, body, and spirit into symphonic relationships. I suspect that if Biff and I were pianists or thespians we'd be doing the same thing with the orchestra or drama club.

I appreciate how difficult it is for coaches when they have to make final cuts. Most sports are not conducive to carrying large rosters and many coaches say this is the single most difficult day of the season. My problem is with the way too many coaches cut players. To publicly post a list of players who did and didn't make the team on a wall outside the locker room adds insult to injury. Players who are cut deserve a constructive conversation and affirmation of their value and worth. That is how a caring community treats every member.

A transformational coach has to be fixated on the virtue of respect. It constitutes the crux of a coach's game plan. Each player deserves a coach's specific focus as we plan for the next practice or game.

That is the key to helping develop each young athlete's self-respect. Interact with them, converse with them, praise them, correct them, and support them. It is not complicated; an equal devotion to each and every team member can help transform each life.

Outside/Lesson

For the past several years, I have participated in the NFL's Player Development Program. Every team has to have a mandatory ninety-minute session on player-conduct issues, and I have led this session for many NFL teams. I share my perspective that the reason men go from the sports page to the crime page usually has to do with false concepts of masculinity. When these men feel disrespected or devalued, anger and rage are often triggered, which can lead to personal and legal problems. I give them my definition of masculinity: relationships and a commitment to a cause. I then define team: a set of relationships for a cause. Every team has a common purpose, performance goals, and objectives. A mutually accountable work ethic and successful teams are always built on the trust, respect, and integrity of each member toward the others. I ask the players to define what being a great teammate means. On the field? In the locker room? Off the field?

Then I take them through an exercise titled "Being on the Team vs. Being a Teammate":

Being on the team benefits your personal goals and ambitions. Being a teammate benefits the goals and ambitions of your team and your teammates.

Being on the team can make you a bystander. Teammates intervene in the lives and actions of their teammates.

Being on the team involves personal effort. Being a teammate involves the efforts of every player.

Being on the team means doing what is asked of you. Being a teammate is doing whatever is needed for the team to succeed.

Being on the team can involve blaming others and making excuses. Being a teammate involves accepting responsibility, accountability, and ownership of the team's problems.

Being on the team makes you "me-optic," asking what's in it for me? Being a teammate makes you "we-optic," asking what's in it for us?

Sometimes players on the team are drawn together by common interests; teammates are drawn together by a common mission.

Sometimes players on a team like one another; teammates respect one another.

Sometimes players on a team bond together because of a shared background or compatible personalities; teammates bond together because they recognize every player is needed to accomplish the goal of the team.

Sometimes players on a team are energized by emotions; teammates energize one another out of commitment.

I am always impressed by the players' responses and have never left an NFL locker room without being grateful for such a wonderful group of young men. It is a shame the media focus on the two or three guys on the team who get into legal trouble while ignoring the fifty others trying to become the men they are capable of becoming and using their position for the betterment of their families and communities. They need each other. They affect each other. They belong to each other.

As InSideOut coaches, we focus on respect for a variety of people in the athletes' lives: parents, girlfriends, brothers and sisters, those less fortunate. All these weekly themes focus on respecting others. We game-plan for each player, for his play on the field and his struggles and growth off it. We also plan weekly lessons of respect that demonstrate how we want self-respect and respect for others to become completely interwoven. In time a culture of respect takes hold, and respect becomes reflexive—instinctive.

MORAL COURAGE

Inside

It takes courage to build and maintain community: going against the cultural grain, defying the messages we are almost forced to ingest as coaches, standing up against a powerful system of misguided values that we reject. All these are courageous efforts.

And yet, to try to build a program that strives to instill moral courage in our young people is really not an option as a coach. *Webster's* defines "courage" as "the attitude of facing and dealing with anything recognized as dangerous, difficult, or painful instead of withdrawing from it; quality of being fearless or brave; valor."

Courage can be divided into two types: physical and moral. Of the two, physical courage is a well-recognized virtue held in high esteem in the world of sports. Coaches constantly talk about it, encourage it, and hold up examples to the team. It ranges from the noble acts of facing physical challenges and playing through and rehabbing injuries to overcoming fears and limitations. Any young person who is willing to commit the time, energy, and discipline of playing a sport and being part of a team is displaying courage. Often physical and moral courage go hand in hand, as evidenced in the lives of Mahatma Gandhi, Nelson Mandela, and Martin Luther King Jr. Without the physical courage to overcome fear of bodily harm, their moral courage would have been quieted and they would have quit before seeing the fruit of their labors.

Biff and I liken moral courage to a muscle: It can be strengthened and developed through consistent training and proper nourishment. We define moral courage as doing what you believe is right, even if others disagree; doing what is morally right even in the face of criticism, ridicule, rejection, or retaliation. This means standing up and speaking out on behalf of your moral and ethical values and showing up to put them into action while encouraging others to do the same.

To help boys become men who will lead, be responsible, and change the world for good demands moral courage. As coaches, we see that as part of being an InSideOut coach. We know that all of our players face daily pressures and situations that challenge and test their moral courage. They are tempted to lie about a missing homework assignment, stretch the truth about postgame activities, engage in gossip, or boast about the sexual proclivities of themselves or others, and the myriad other academic, peer, and social pressures to conform to social norms.

Moral courage is the third leg of our tripod of community. It helps support liberty and respect. The best way to develop moral courage is through modeling, teaching, and providing opportunities to make moral choices. It is in face-to-face encounters that you gain the courage not to turn away and to fight for the rights of others. I believe InSideOut coaches have to be morally courageous. Gandhi said that moral courage is not necessarily knowing the correct answers but seeing the suffering of the world and taking action. To buck the cultural coaching messages, to step outside the cultural coaching box, and to teach a different paradigm are morally courageous. Quite simply, teaching moral courage as a coach requires moral courage of a coach.

Outside/Lesson

Biff and I had an outstanding player and young man who was being recruited by just about every college in America. One day Biff heard that one of the college coaches recruiting him had given him money to entice him to his college. Biff knew this was a teachable moment.

He immediately called that player and asked if the rumor was true. Our player confirmed the story and said the coach had left a couple of one-hundred-dollar bills in the cleats he was carrying. The player said he hadn't spent the money but didn't know what to do. He did not know how to give the money back without embarrassing the coach or making it more awkward than it already was for a seventeen-year-old kid.

Biff called the boy's parents. They were disappointed in their son but even more disappointed that a college coach would put him in such an unethical situation, potentially corrupting their son's character. Biff suggested they take the money back to the coach, which the parents and player did, while Biff called the university's head coach. The coach decided to self-report the situation to the NCAA. Needless to say, Biff was not held in high esteem by the staff at the university. Biff did the right thing in the right way and displayed and modeled moral courage to his player.

As I write this I can't help but think of Reggie Bush and the penalties imposed on the University of Southern California for Bush's illegally taking money from an agent. Reggie might have made an entirely different decision had someone taught, modeled, and coached the moral courage he needed to just say no.

Outside/Lesson

We had a player a few years back who asked to speak to the team. He said he had repeatedly overheard his teammates in the locker room using the term "that's so gay" and referring to other teammates and students as "gay," "homo," "faggot," and "queer." While he knew his teammates were trying to be funny or slinging insults at others, he also knew how disparaging and hurtful those words are. So he stood before his peers and called them out on their lack of empathy and understanding toward other human beings. He challenged us as players and coaches to have the courage and conviction to defy the cultural acceptance and use of such words. Our coaching code of conduct disallows swearing; we certainly never condone the n-word and a host of other words. This player said it was hypocritical to talk about social justice and the inherent value and worth of every human being and then exclude gays, lesbians, and transgendered people. Then he paused and his voice cracked. Biff and I looked at him to see if he was okay. We knew that one of his family members had just come out of the closet, and we knew how much the young man loved his family member.

Biff and I were moved by the moral courage it took to correct and challenge his teammates. The young man didn't even come and ask me or another coach to address the issue! He had a moral conviction and the courage to act upon it. Among the many courageous players I've coached, he was truly remarkable!

Outside/Lesson

I decided to leverage his moral courage into a teaching moment that now is a regular part of my coaching. The next day I took the opportunity to speak to the team regarding my own history with homophobia and the pain caused by such remarks. I told them about my uncle Artie, who was gay. Growing up in the 1940s, he suffered terribly in a culture that demonized and dehumanized him. At the end of his life he was under psychiatric care, dealing with depression and alcoholism. A psychiatrist encouraged him to write his daily thoughts and activities in a journal. After my uncle Artie died, my mother and sisters came upon his journals while cleaning out his apartment. I loved my uncle and knew that his life was sad. I reluctantly read his journals and discovered a world I had never imagined. He wrote about getting up every day as a seventy-three-year-old man just looking for a hug or a sign of acceptance from the world.

One of his most significant relationships was with a blind nun who befriended him. He took her grocery shopping and helped her. She went to AA meetings with him, encouraged him, and provided the hugs, warmth, and acceptance he so desperately craved. In his journal he also recounted a recurring dream he had had since he was a child. In that dream people were standing over him ripping the flesh off his body. As he screamed in agony, the mob chanted, "Faggots must die! Faggots must die!" As I read those words, my heart broke.

As an InSideOut coach, I knew how many of my players were suffering similar pain—be it because of sexual orientation or some other perceived shortcoming that leads to self-hatred and shame. My empathy for my uncle Artie and for my player and his family member challenged me to live up to the moral courage displayed by a seventeen-year-old. As a coach, with my power, platform, and position, I need to speak up and stand up for all people. I've learned that students who regularly experience verbal and nonverbal harassment suffer from emotional turmoil, low self-esteem, loneliness, depression, poor academic achievement, and high rates of absenteeism. As a coach I try to model, teach, and help develop moral courage in my players.

When a coach explicitly prioritizes moral courage over physical courage, or at the least emphasizes the value of both, something transformative happens. The young people start to play better, more in unison, more supportively. They sacrifice more and start to take great satisfaction in sacrifice. They recognize common humanity and they regard their morally courageous teammates with awe. And then moral courage becomes contagious.

I played professionally for thirteen years and what I enjoyed most about my career was the sense of community I experienced. Every year fifty-three men came together from all four corners of our nation, black men and white men. Men from the inner cities, suburbs, and farmlands of America. Each season we created a community called team.

We learned quickly that to be an asset to the team we had to set aside our own personal goals, wants, and ambitions and find our welfare in the well-being of the team. We were, as Dr. King said, caught in a web of community where what affected one affected all. Our mutuality was based on the communal virtues of liberty, respect, and moral courage.

CHAPTER 7

The Classroom after Class

SPORTS AS COCURRICULAR

In the eyes of most observers my title is "Coach"
Wooden, but this is not what I would list first on my
résumé or business card. From my earliest years I have
viewed my primary job as one of educating others:
I am a teacher.

—John Wooden, Hall of Fame basketball teacher-coach

During the final semester of my senior year of high school, I stopped acting like a dumb jock and became one. I had accepted a full athletic scholarship to Syracuse and was coasting. I figured that all I needed to graduate were passing grades in English and history, so I decided not to show up for any of my other final exams. I failed to realize that overall GPA was a factor, too, and that the zeroes in these exams would pull down my GPA. One day in early summer, my mother got a call from Syracuse saying my admission application had been rejected.

My high school principal, a compassionate man and also a big football fan, pleaded with Syracuse, but the Admissions Department would not bend. The SU football coaches settled on an alternative plan. They enrolled me at Manlius Military Academy. What a perfect name for what I needed!

That year at Manlius was a rude awakening for an undisciplined knucklehead like me. From getting up before daylight for reveille and white-glove room inspections, to spit-shining my shoes for full-dress parades on Sundays, it was not a life I was used to. But this school was one of the best things that could have happened to me. They drilled some of the ignorance out of me, taught me some discipline, and taught me to commit to my studies—at least for the time being.

Looking back, I realized how stupid it was to act like a dumb jock. I wanted to learn; I craved learning. Books were my refuge all through my bumpy adolescent years. But I never found a classroom situation in which I could learn in the way that suited and excited me. I needed imagination, stories, excitement, interaction, physicality, and connection. I loved the Greek heroes, and I think Homer could have filled an entire year of classes for me if a stirring teacher-coach had taught me Homer.

My regrets regarding my education are numerous. I could have learned so much more, expanded my brain, enjoyed the world of knowledge in a much richer way. I take responsibility for much of this failure, but there was a systemic breakdown, too. With my InSideOut work, I realize now that I had needed teachers who cared about me, inspired me, brought the material alive and made it relevant to my life.

I didn't come across a teacher I really wanted to "play" for until I met Coach Simmons. My brain craved his "classroom" like food. From Native American religion, to art museum visits, to American history, Coach Simmons integrated coaching with all sorts of learning. Knowledge is knowledge, education is education, and the motivation for both can come from coaches just as easily as from teachers. A great coach is a great teacher and a great teacher is a great coach. There is no better proof than legendary coach John Wooden. Both teacher-coach Simmons and teacher-coach Wooden understand that sports can be an essential part of a student-athlete's education. Sports need not be seen as separate from academics; rather, they can work hand in hand with academics to educate and equip the whole person.

Sports should be viewed as cocurricular, not extracurricular. The term "extracurricular" implies that sports and coaching take place after the end of the academic day. The term "cocurricular" designates sports as an educational activity with the potential to develop the academic, social, emotional, moral, and civic competency of every player. This makes practice the last classroom of the day. Extracurricular sports merely need players and a coach: Cocurricular sports demand student-athletes and a teacher-coach.

I hold that sports merit this sort of educational status for three reasons. First, sports offer thousands of kids the opportunity to learn in a different and potentially more holistic way. We all learn differently, psychologists tell us, and sports and teams offer a very active, physical, and practical way to instruct and guide. Sports develop the brain and in particular the reasoning capacity of the brains of young athletes as they learn and master plays, techniques, and formations and learn to make split-second decisions.

There is a clear if-then logic in most sports. If I angle my hand in a different way during my stroke, I will push more water and go faster as a swimmer. If I keep my weight on my back leg a split second longer, I will have more bat speed when I decide to swing and will have more power, too. If I memorize the playbook more diligently, I will ultimately reach a point where I don't have to think as much on the field, I will simply react and my level of play will improve.

Second, as I emphasized in Chapters 1 and 2, sports are built on stories. By the water cooler, at the lunch table, on the radio, or in the coffee shop, sports stories are a classic way to bond. I grew up in ethnic

Buffalo where people told all kinds of stories all day long, and I learned a great deal about life from them. Our brains are wired to learn through anecdotes, and sports offer an endless supply of them.

Imagine if, instead of tightening his jaw and parsing his words, Schwartzwalder had related some of his World War II adventures as a commando to us. I might have connected to him and might even have taken a course on World War II history as a result, just to satisfy my curiosity. Storytelling could have made my football experience more educational and could have brought us closer together.

Third, in a much more socially acceptable and direct way, sports offer an opportunity for connection that can help many kids embrace learning. I know they did for me. Coach Simmons's lessons about historical injustice to Native Americans constitute one of the most long-lasting instructions I received in college in large part because of the way in which I related to him. Or, better said, the way in which he allowed and encouraged me to connect. His demeanor, personality, and D-I-G (dignity, integrity, grace) approach to lacrosse all combined to make a very fertile and comfortable environment in which I could learn.

Vince Lombardi seemed to bless the anti-intellectualism of sports when he said: "A school without football is in danger of deteriorating into a medieval study hall." But I say that football programs or any team without virtuous coaching and a classroom-based approach dangerously resemble medieval torture chambers. The existence of anti-intellectualism in sports, or for that matter the very tension between sports and the classroom, is fundamentally illogical. Success in sports usually requires a high degree of cognitive development and functioning.

I try to imagine what would happen to standardized test scores, dropout rates, and school learning environments if sports became cocurricular and were seen as part of the holistic development of student-athletes. What would happen if teacher-coaches were held accountable to deliver lesson plans on responsible decision-making and self-management? What if coaches taught the virtue of community?

What would happen if coaches all across America caught hold of a vision of transforming sports as we know them, so sports could transform young men and women who could then transform society?

Biff and I imagined this glorious scenario. And then we acted.

We decided to lay out our season according to the topics and lesson plans that would support our WHY as coaches: *to help boys become men of empathy and integrity who will lead, be responsible, and change the world for good.* Since we define masculinity (and femininity) in terms of relationships and commitment to a cause, we broke the season into two semesters. In the first half, we engaged our players in the process of becoming good and involved men; we taught empathy, character, leadership, and responsibility. The second semester we devoted to helping players discover a cause in their lives that was greater than themselves—being men built for others.

We took a topic a week and for the first ten minutes of every practice Biff taught the lesson plan. On game day, we took twenty minutes to summarize the lesson of the week. We were also committed to creating and using as many teachable moments as possible. Teachable moments were everywhere for us as coaches. They naturally presented themselves during practice, at school, and in the community. When one of these moments occurred during practice, we stopped everything and took advantage of the opportunity to teach a life lesson. We went out of our way to make a point.

We also incorporated "Moments of Greatness," periodically asking players, on a voluntary basis, to describe something they or one of their teammates had done that day, week, or game that demonstrated a positive impact on another person—for example, acting with empathy and friendship; speaking out or intervening against some form of injustice, such as bullying, hazing, sexism, or racism; or behaving in a way that contributed to the team, school, or community. We awarded decals to be worn on their helmets that symbolized these moments of greatness. The starters selected scout team players whose work ethic and commitment had helped prepare them and the team for the upcoming game.

The helmet decals carried more honor than decals based on touch-downs, sacks, or fumble recoveries.

"Coach" and "teacher" are really synonymous words for me, as they were for my hero, John Wooden. When Biff and I described ourselves, the term we used was "teacher-coach." And the educational dimension of our program—the classroom part—focused on instruction in the virtues of justice, reason, and contemplation.

To help boys become men who would lead, be responsible, and change the world for good demanded these three pillars. The recent history of sports mirrors America's quest for justice regarding civil rights, women's rights, and human rights. Athletes such as Jackie Robinson, Muhammad Ali, Arthur Ashe, Billie Jean King, Magic Johnson, and John Carlos and Tommie Smith dared to fight for social justice on and off the field. Sports develop the reasoning skills needed for active contemplation skills and responsible leadership; skills that are agents of change.

JUSTICE

Inside

Doing my InSideOut work, I realized that I was walking through life with a nagging sense of injustice as a result of how I was treated by adults and authority figures. I looked back and realized I was walking around blindly craving the sort of support and acceptance I had rarely received.

I learned early that life was not just.

Trying to draw meaning from my experiences led me to try to turn the playing field into a classroom in which the virtue of justice would be one of the key teaching points. Biff and I decided to see if a coach could become an agent of social change. We set out to emulate the great liberators like Moses, Nelson Mandela, Mahatma Gandhi, and Dr. Martin Luther King Jr.

A sense of justice also drove my parenting—and my parenting has inevitably influenced my coaching. My children have been some of my greatest teachers. Of the many upending events at the Ehrmann household, one has strongly influenced how we teach gender justice. Joey was an Under Armor All American lacrosse player in high school and was recruited for lacrosse and football. One day during his junior year of high school, I came home and my daughter Esther was irate.

"Dad," she said, "you're not going to believe the recruiting letter Joey got in the mail today. I am furious!"

Barely able to contain herself, she showed me a letter written by a Division I assistant coach. At the top of the letter was a picture of a young woman in bra and panties lying on her back in a bed. The photo was shot from the neck down, straight through her cleavage.

Underneath the picture the first paragraph of the letter read:

> *Joey, did I get your attention? If you come to our university you will meet many females that look like this which will make it hard for you to concentrate on school and lacrosse. As the saying goes—to the victor goes the spoils. Our spoils are pretty unmatched anywhere else in college lacrosse. At [X] University we are experiencing our share of victories and our players are walking around with smiles on their faces more often than frowns!*

I, too, was irate. Add to that his mother's response! I immediately called this coach and left a message letting him know how I felt about sending letters like this to teenage boys' homes. This primitive and sexist thinking and abusive display, inflicted on both boys and girls, was shocking and disrespectful to the profession of coaching. When the coach and I eventually talked, I saw he was ignorant, not evil. He was young, new to coaching, and unfortunately had succumbed to the false masculine correlation of athletic ability with sexual conquest. I wanted him to know that when a coach promotes, encourages, and models such demeaning attitudes and behavior, he not only hurts females, but also hurts his players and all men. Finally, I gave him one of my favorite quotations from the late Hall of Fame coach Eddie Robinson of Grambling University, who said: "You ought to coach each player like they are going to become your son-in-law."

He immediately sent out a letter of retraction to every player and family, apologizing for his remarks and the error of his message. Not long after our exchange, I led a half-day InSideOut coaching seminar for this university's entire athletic department. I watched him out of the corner of my eye as he contemplated the collective responsibility all coaches have in ending violence against women. I believe I saw the lights of justice and reason go on.

Why, I wondered, am I so driven to teach justice? It always goes back to my coherent narrative and the injustices I witnessed and experienced growing up. Because of my past, I've identified with the poor, the marginalized, and the hurting. As a teacher-coach I have an incredible opportunity to show players that I am willing to fight for what is right. What better place to teach the virtue of justice?

Outside/Lesson

In 2007, the Rutgers University women's basketball team lost to the University of Tennessee in the NCAA national championship game. The next morning they found themselves embroiled in a national controversy unrelated to their successful season. Don Imus, host of *Imus in the Morning*, and his cohosts made disparaging comments about the predominantly African American team. Imus, who had watched part of the game, opined that the Rutgers team was composed of "some rough girls." His cohost chimed in that the Rutgers players were "some hardcore hos," to which Imus immediately said, "That's some nappy-headed hos." The conversation continued with statements that the Rutgers team physically resembled the NBA's Toronto Raptors, to which Imus's producer suggested the Memphis Grizzlies would be a more appropriate comparison.

These remarks triggered a national protest calling for cancellation of *Imus in the Morning* and a censuring of Imus and his cohosts. The public outrage centered on Imus's "nappy-headed hos" comment. Imus claimed it was all good fun and just part of his morning routine. Critics responded that there was nothing funny or innocent in his insults. The remarks denigrated women, especially black women and female athletes, by turning their physical appearance into targets for racist and sexist humor. The word "nappy" is often used to disparage the form, texture, and style of some black people's hair. "Ho" is short for "whore" and a slang word for "prostitute." Together they reflect the denigration and marginalization of women in general, black women specifically, and disrespect toward all female athletes.

Several days after the incident Rutgers women's basketball head coach Vivian Stringer and the Rutgers team held a press conference to voice their emotional pain and outrage over Imus's disturbing remarks. Coach Stringer, no stranger to the fight for sexual and racial equity, spoke from personal experience, paraphrasing Eleanor Roosevelt's famous statement: "No one can make you feel inferior unless you allow them." One of her first battles for justice came when she sued her high school in the 1950s for not allowing her to be a cheerleader because of her race. She won the case and was given a spot on her school's cheerleading squad, becoming the first black cheerleader in her town. Stringer also managed to turn this incident into an opportunity to teach her players how to engage the nation in a provocative discussion about justice and about why gender stereotypes and racial prejudices still linger today. Her message was clear: "We all need to make changes, all of us, beyond Imus. We need to serve as examples of how to be winners on the basketball court and we need to serve as examples of how to be winners in life." Then teacher-coach-advocate Stringer let the young women speak. Identifying themselves by name, hometown, and year in college, they spoke of the pride they felt as they won a spot in the Final Four. They spoke of the hurt they felt when Imus caused their pride to dissolve into embarrassment and of their decision not to ignore his insult.

Essence Carson, the team captain, said, "I know we're at a young age, but we definitely understand what is right and what should be done."

In the spirit of my transformational coaching model Moses, Coach Stringer critiqued American culture, helped her players embrace and articulate the pain caused by Imus's racist and sexist remarks, and then coached them in speaking out against injustice. She is not just a basketball coach—she is an advocate for justice who uses basketball to liberate her players from demeaning stereotypes.

Coach Stringer coaches her player's souls. She used a teachable moment to enlighten her team and engage a nation. Talk about "Moments of Greatness"!

Inside/Lesson

When Biff and I sat in the school cafeteria developing our lesson plans for our first season, we decided to aim high. We made justice a core curriculum course for our classroom. A constant awareness of and emphasis on justice would dictate how we interacted with our players. But more important, we made social issues components of each weekly lesson plan. Our goal was to educate our young men about current social injustices and help them to develop their own sense of social justice. We didn't want to preach but rather to teach our players how to contemplate, reason, and develop their own convictions.

Biff and I spent weeks drafting the core principles that would support our classroom. We scribbled them down, and over the years they have become clearer and more concise:

Defining humanity, both masculinity and femininity based on the strength of your relationships and the contributions you make to society.

Developing relational skills with teammates, parents, siblings, teachers, and friends and learning to maintain and sustain strong positive friendships.

Developing empathy toward others so that you can be supportive and understanding.

Practicing good sportsmanship before, during, and after practices, games, and events, and in life.

Defining success in life as being relationally successful and having a cause bigger than yourself.

Acting with integrity in every area of your life.

Contributing to society by taking it upon yourself to get involved in actions and projects that make the world better in some way.

Becoming an advocate of justice and an ally with others by speaking up on behalf of others and against injustice.

Refraining from committing acts of injustice, including bullying, harassment, racism, sexism, homophobia, and other forms of hurtful behavior and not accepting or tolerating this kind of behavior in others.

Refraining from violent behavior and learning how to resolve conflict in a positive and productive manner.

Developing a coherent narrative by making sense of your life experiences, good, bad, and ugly.

At the beginning of each season, we lay out our weekly classroom schedule and define "justice" for our athletes. Justice is personal (how we treat ourselves), relational (how we treat others), and economic (making sure everyone has the basic necessities of life). We teach all three components. As the Chinese proverb says, "Give a man a fish and you feed him for a day. Teach him to fish and you feed him for a lifetime." But once he learns how to use the rod and reel you have to make sure he has access to the pond.

We explain how justice can bind a team and how it is the foundation on which the team is built. Justice, we teach, begins on the practice field and carries over into all parts of life—at home, in the cafeteria, in the locker room, and beyond. Biff gives coaching "status" to the people who come in at night and clean the building and to those who drive the bus we take to the games. Coach Tyrone, who is a custodian, is asked to come into team meetings and report on how well the players are doing cleaning up the locker room and hallways. He is to be treated with the same respect offered to Biff and me. Our players hold each other accountable when we ride buses to away games. The bus is to be just as clean when we exit it as when we entered it. Do justice, we tell them.

We developed weekly topics centered on helping our players discover causes bigger than themselves. These include such topics as:

Prejudice and racism
Dating abuse, sexual violence, and successful bystander
    intervention
Poverty: its causes, effects, impact, and solutions
Educational inequalities, the achievement gap and educational
    equity
Current hot or controversial issues in the news

Gilman is a top academic school and our players know it is a privilege to have one of its four hundred seats. With that privilege, they are repeatedly told, comes a responsibility to give back and make a difference in our society. So educational inequality and the consequent achievement gap is an especially illuminating topic for our athletes. The gap in academic achievement between minority and disadvantaged students and their white and Asian counterparts is one of the most pressing issues in America. This "achievement gap" is seen in the differences between standardized test scores, grade-point averages, dropout rates, and college enrollment and completion rates for poor children and children of color.

There is a unique middle school in Baltimore called KIPP Umoja that orients its whole curriculum toward addressing and closing the achievement gap. It is part of KIPP's national network of open enrollment, college preparatory schools dedicated to preparing students in underserved communities. KIPP serves fifth- through eighth-grade boys and girls from one of the poorest census tracts in Baltimore. Baltimore City has close to a 60 percent high school dropout rate, and Biff and I preface the week with a recitation of this and other startling, unfortunate statistics and their consequences.

For the past couple of years, we've invited the KIPP seventh- and eighth-grade male students to come to one of our practices. Before practice begins, our captains welcome the KIPP students and talk with them. They encourage them to keep their eyes on college, work hard, and be mindful of the rewards of studying. The experience transforms our athletes as much as the young students from KIPP. Many of our players have eye-opening experiences. They see the human face of educational injustice and begin to grasp how families have to struggle just to get their children adequate education. They start to see education as a civil rights issue and justice as a virtue.

The personal, relational, and economic teaching points of justice often become lifelong lessons for our athletes. Players leave our program with a sense of a larger world. They embrace what Mahatma Gandhi said: "Be the change you want to see in the world." InSideOut coaching and the sports venue make these lessons in justice all the more accessible and effective. In our sports classroom the virtue of justice is as vivid and tangible as a screen pass or a blitz. Our goal is to make one as clear as the other by the end of the season.

And a funny thing happens along the way. A program that teaches justice comes to embody it, too. Our young athletes sense their own value and worth and respect the value and worth of everyone else. Justice fills our program and interactions as much as our lesson plans.

Now what really makes this process work is when as coaches we live it, not just teach it. It only works from the InSideOut. One day we had a scrimmage, and Biff was doing his half-hour teaching before the game on the week's message about the process of becoming good men. As he got up in front of the team he shared an experience that he had driving into school that morning.

There was a young boy in a white shirt and tie at the intersection where he was stopped holding a sign that said, "My dad needs help getting back-to-school supplies." His father stood beside him in the same white shirt and tie. The light turned green and Biff drove off thinking how unusual the scene was. By the time he got to our meeting, his highly developed sense of empathy and justice had kicked in and he told the team what he had just witnessed. He shared the story and then told the team it was not enough just to be good men—it was important to become involved men.

Then he said, "I am going to leave now and go and see if that boy is still there."

When he returned, he called the team together and said he had found the boy and asked about his circumstances. He asked the boy how he, Biff, and the team could help. The boy stood there, and Biff told the team how he could sense the father's shame and embarrassment. The man had lost his job, his wife was sick, but he swallowed his pride to try to help his son realize his talents as an artist at one of Baltimore's premier schools. They had exhausted every other method of securing the necessary funds and had resorted to panhandling on the corner. Biff then called the boy's school to describe the situation to them and see how our team could help. Biff illustrated our quest to do justice by using an experience from his day as a lesson. Justice in action, not just in theory, becomes the transformational coach's objective.

REASON

Inside

Coach Simmons used to tease me about applying a smash-mouth football mentality to what he believed to be the more graceful game of lacrosse. Indeed, I was an overly aggressive defenseman who relished the power of my long wooden stick. I clobbered people with it. For me, it was like football with a weapon. But Coach's teaching and inspiration motivated me to learn the nuances of lacrosse quickly. Scooping, cradling, passing, and catching—these were the stick skills I had to learn.

The purpose of the long pole is to throw checks and to strip the ball with uncanny maneuverings—it is a tool of finesse not unlike a paintbrush. Coach talked about using it like an artist. I never got quite that far, but I did learn to use it in a way more in line with its original intent.

Many years later, I sat in the bleachers at Georgetown University and watched my son Barney and his lacrosse teammates play top-ranked Syracuse University on a chilly spring day. And suddenly, an even colder spring day back at my alma mater came rushing back to me. Barney is as easygoing a young man as you will meet and, unlike his old man, he plays the game without anger. He is six foot six and 230 pounds, and he just glides out there. I saw in his play the elegance and grace I could only begin to imagine with Coach Simmons. And most vividly, I watched him use his stick to make precise checks and pick pockets, and push back intruders on his goal. He had mastered the artistry of lacrosse, using an appropriate level of aggressiveness without the excessive anger that characterized my way of playing the game.

After the game I was talking with Coach Simmons. He still travels with the Syracuse team on away games and it was no small thrill to have him see my son play the game that he had taught me to love. He commented on Barney's athleticism, artistry with his lacrosse pole, and ability to dissect offensive plays, and then he said: "What a thinker you've got out there!"

And I realized that Barney's elegant use of the stick arose as much from his mental capacity for the game as from his physical prowess. He had learned proper angle, approach, and position through years of practice and repetition. If there was one adjective to describe his play it would be "reasonable." His economy of movement and precision were all logical, full of reason.

That day reinforced for me why reason must be a core virtue for instruction in our classroom. The brain of the athlete receives far less attention than his brawn, yet it is the fundamental athletic organ. Those are developing brains out there on the fields and they require the integration of emotional, physical, and cognitive skills.

My wife is very interested in brain research. She spends her life helping people deal with their emotional problems and her philosophy and treatment are based on an amazing concept: the neuroplasticity of the brain. Neuroplasticity refers to the brain's capacity to change and adapt as a result of a person's experiences and relationships. Brain plasticity enables us to accommodate new thoughts and patterns of reasoning. Ultimately, this rewiring manifests itself in new reasoning processes and actions. As I stated before, this is a critical part of the InSideOut process and the role transformational coaches play in their players' self-concepts.

Making sense of our past by developing a coherent narrative helps us to restructure neural connections and rewire our brains. It is never too late to change who we think we are. We needn't be chained to who we have become. We can change our minds and thereby transform ourselves and our lives. We can teach old dogs new tricks!

I am living proof of this. My InSideOut work helped me identify those life experiences that literally altered my brain and changed my behavior. It also helped me to realize why I lacked Barney's self-control and reasoning skills on the field when I was his age. I learned the process of understanding my own narrative and now use my rewired mind to rewire the brains of the hundreds of athletes who pass through our program.

The most startling fact about our cocurricular platform as coaches is that we literally affect our athletes' brains! Teacher-coaches who are relationally connected to their players can change the form and function of a young person's mind. Knowing this elevates the awesome potential and power I have as a relationally centered teacher-coach.

Another key realization from my InSideOut work was how the

age-old rivalry between reason and emotion plays out in each athlete every day. I was an emotional ballplayer in large part because of all the confusion of my youth. I lacked the emotional management skills needed to traverse my journey into manhood. Coach Simmons's developing of reason in me and his encouragement of my pride in those reasoning skills helped me harness my emotions and play, shall I say, more scientifically. With better balancing of emotion and logic I arrived in the NFL a more complete defensive tackle than I had ever been, thanks to my lacrosse coach's classroom.

Logical reasoning and the harnessing of destructive emotions became a sturdy plank in our cocurricular platform.

Outside/Lesson

Biff and I set out to create what we call an optimal brain environment. While sports are played in the physical realm, they are much more intellectual, relational, and emotional than most coaches think. School takes place indoors and sports on fields or in gymnasiums. One uses textbooks and language and the other playbooks and choreography. But both can develop reasoning abilities, both can develop the imagination, and both can help a young person grow in a way that encourages proper moral decisions. In short, both develop a young person's precious mind and reasoning ability.

As an InSideOut coach, I am regularly and powerfully aware of my athletes' brains as much as their ankles, knees, and elbows. Some days I imagine seeing through their helmets to track their brains' wiring.

Our defensive cocoordinator, Stan White, is a former Colts teammate and roommate, and has been a friend for more than thirty-five years. Stan was a great player at Ohio State and we played together professionally for twelve of my thirteen years. Almost all of those years we played in the same defensive scheme, developed by NFL Hall of Fame coach George Allen.

Stan has the best football mind of anyone I have ever met and has taken Coach Allen's defense and applied it to our high school team. Players are taught how to break down films by formations, down, and distances and then to recognize opposing teams' passing and running tendencies. Based on these tendencies, players call audibles on almost every play to try to win the "chess match" with the opposing offense. Our players have to be able to read the offensive formation, check the stances and splits of the offensive linemen, switch the defense, communicate audibles to all eleven players on the field, and realign themselves in unison. All this takes place in a matter of seconds under tremendous pressure. It is a very complicated scheme, and it takes a player on average about two years to really grasp the system.

As a staff, we have often debated whether the results are worth the amount of time, energy, and effort needed to master this defense. Could we just dog, blitz, and slant on every play and be successful in high school football? Our response always comes back to the cocurricular argument. Reasoning is critical to educational attainment: It is central to SAT scores and to college entrance and acceptance requirements. Reasoning is critical to the moral, ethical, and relational decisions players make to determine which actions or attitudes are the right ones in any given situation. We don't put everything we know about football into the playbook but add just enough to stretch and strengthen their minds.

Our cocurricular approach each season tries to get student-athletes to see how this development of their reasoning on the field applies to the difficult choices they have to make off the field. Decisions regarding the use of tobacco, drugs and alcohol, sex, dating abuse, and pornography all require complex reasoning skills. Young people need to be able to reason, not rationalize. InSideOut coaches know they should link sports reasoning with life reasoning—the same skill set based on the same virtue.

Another example of a reason-based program comes during what Biff and I call Race Week, when we teach about systemic racism and prejudice. We begin by teaching about Dred Scott, the runaway slave who was repeatedly caught in a free state and returned to his master, as the law then required. Abolitionists took his case to the Supreme Court. Chief Justice Roger Taney issued a decision in 1857 saying people of African descent were "beings of an inferior order and altogether unfit to associate with the white race." The Dred Scott decision helped to institutionalize racism within U.S. government, law, and society.

We use a skit to get the point across. Three of our black players go out into the hall where they put on some do-rags and bling. Then we tell the team to pretend they don't know these guys we are about to bring into the room. When the players come back into the room we ask the team to verbalize all the assumptions they make about these three players based on race, dress, posture, and so forth. We use reason to think about all the biases and assumptions we make about people we don't even know. Then we take three of our white lacrosse players, who usually have some kind of flow (long hair) and wear high tops and board shorts and repeat the same process.

The virtue of reason cannot be taught in a day or a week of lesson plans. Our teachings need to be woven into the traditional school curriculum. We want our players to grow up to be champions of reason and logic. We want them to thrive in school, to be the best students they are capable of being, to go to great colleges, and to become consummate professionals in the fields of their choosing. But, that is all secondary. When our seniors graduate, we watch them walk up to receive their diplomas. We can assess the degree to which our program contributed to the expansion and enhancement of their brains as reasoning organs—capable of making split-second decisions on the field and the proper moral judgments in life.

CONTEMPLATION

Inside

Contemplation is a key virtue and is absolutely essential to an InSideOut coach. During the coaching season, our hectic lifestyle ramps up to warp sped with almost no time left for self-care, rest, renewal, or recovery. Coaching demands and drains the physical, mental, emotional, and spiritual energy needed to connect with our players and stay aligned with our purpose statement as coaches.

I see too many coaches who violate almost everything they know about rest, recovery, and performance. We all know muscles exposed to strenuous work need rest and recovery to repair and increase muscle fiber and mass. We practice players hard early in the week and then make sure they have time to recover and rest to get their legs back for peak performance on game day.

Yet most coaches build no time into their schedules for their own rest and recovery to meet all the demands of life and coaching. Coaching seems to either create or draw people who are obsessive-compulsive or overindulge in their work and can't seem to regulate their hours. Unfortunately this "coachaholism" is often admired, encouraged, and rewarded in the coaching ranks. I see this in the NFL and college ranks all the time where seventy-hour weeks are more the norm than the exception. Some coaches become addicted to their work and self-medicate, acquire stress-related illnesses, and end up divorced. The pressure to win undermines any effort at pulling back or getting off the strenuous and relentless treadmill.

So what's a coach to do? I think the practice of spiritual disciplines (in almost every religion they include silence, prayer, fasting, solitude, and contemplation) helps us find and keep balance in our lives. Spiritual disciplines are tools in the quest for self-transcendence and connection. They are a source of positive energy and motivation. They can fuel our passions and keep us connected to our purpose as coaches. We become rejuvenated when we step out of the business of coaching and take time to reflect on the values and virtues that inspire and motivate us to coach.

Contemplation, silence, solitude, and centeredness are critical to the InSideOut work required of a transformational coach. We can't construct our coherent narratives without contemplating our personal lives methodically and rigorously. If we don't contemplate our own lives and the lives of our players, we stand little chance of becoming InSideOut coaches.

Unfortunately, our coaching culture discourages contemplation. Part of the problem is the pace of our seasons. The excessive demands we put on ourselves and allow others to put on us leave little time to just sit, think, and be with ourselves. In sports' masculinity formula, contemplation is seen as weak, too intellectual, too soft. Another part of the problem is our own internal resistance to facing the scary stuff inside that we either don't want to see or are afraid to see.

I was always a thinker, but it took the contemplation of InSide-Out work to focus my thinking, to give it a method, and to remove the masculine taboo against becoming a contemplative athlete and coach.

Contemplation is the conscious and methodical analysis of the experiences we have as people, and then the integration of that analysis into a larger, comprehensive understanding or story. For inside work, it is the contemplation of a coach's formative experiences in sports that helps him understand how he coaches. For the outside work it is the linking of that coach's self-awareness with his players' behavior, needs, and growth that translates into a coach's methodical contemplation of each young life on his team.

I had a lifetime of collected experiences, emotions, memories, and beliefs stored in my subconscious mind. We all do. But few of us are taught a method for accessing them and collating them into a coherent narrative. I loved the Greeks and contemplation. According to Coach Aristotle, contemplation is essential to becoming a virtuous person. Coach A said the three components of a virtuous person are justice, friendship, and contemplation. Think about that! Without contemplating injustice and the wasted human potential and suffering it causes, it is impossible to understand justice. Developing and deepening relationships also requires contemplating the needs of others as well as your own. It is a skill that demands hard work. It requires a method, a focus, a discipline to be used effectively.

The writings of the Catholic theologian Thomas Merton also influenced my development as a coach. Merton wrote about spiritual discipline: how silence, meditation, fasting, and solitude make you better able to identify, analyze, and understand key issues in life. As I devoured Merton, it also struck me how a cloistered monk could also be a leader in the civil rights and antiwar movements of the 1960s. He was the epitome of the contemplative activist, balancing justice, reason, and contemplation with action. That was what I longed to become.

At the time that I was working at The Door on housing issues, I was invited to go on a spiritual retreat with the founder of Habitat for Humanity, Millard Fuller. The retreat was built around silence and contemplation. After Fuller spoke, we entered into silence and contemplation, reflecting on his message. My wife warned me that it would be a tough weekend for me—I was a talker and a doer, not a silent sitter. But I knew I could learn from him and I figured we would be able to get some time to talk. I was confident I could sway the event a bit my way!

Wrong! It was a silent retreat straight through; he spoke and we listened, but his speeches were only guides for our meditations. There were only brief moments for Q and As!

I went home frustrated. I barged into the kitchen and, without even saying hello after a weekend away, complained to Paula about the lack of discussion and conversation at the retreat.

And she turned to me and smiled.

"But didn't you discuss and converse with yourself?"

I paused, grew even more frustrated for a moment, then smiled. I did. I had. And I realized that contemplation is tough stuff—something unnatural to me, but a virtue I could develop and from which I could benefit.

I realized that the weekend spent in silence helped me develop an understanding of myself I hadn't seen before. It showed me how much I was avoiding myself through busyness and how I was finding all kinds of reasons to justify this avoidance.

Contemplation, the inside work, generates self-understanding. Self-understanding leads to understanding others, which can lead to life-changing transformation. InSideOut coaching contemplation boils down to regular reviewing and updating of the answers to the four questions I posed in Chapter 5. Why do I coach? Why do I coach the way I do? What does it feel like to be coached by me? How do I define success? That sort of contemplation is demanding and rigorous. But what it reveals and our reaction to those revelations can transform how we are viewed by our athletes and how we affect their lives. Those big questions generate the contemplative habit, which then becomes the basis for daily, purpose-driven thoughts and actions directed toward each athlete.

Outside/Lesson

Socrates said, "The unexamined life is not worth living." Yet, life seems too busy to allow one to slow down for self-reflection. It has almost become a radical act to stop and contemplate life. But according to Socrates, it's the only game that really matters. Contemplation is not easy to build into the already jam-packed busyness of a high school football season. If I were the secretary of education, I'd emphasize a fourth R to supplement reading, 'riting, and 'rithmetic: reflection.

Reflect on the busy life of young people. With school, sports, social life, iPods, cellphones, Facebook, video games, music, and television, there is almost no time to sit, be still, and think about the things that really matter. To offset all the noise, we incorporate short times of contemplation in our daily lesson plans.

Every October, during the week of the Homecoming Dance, we teach lessons on dating abuse and gender violence. On Monday, we begin by asking our players to think about the girls they are taking to the dance. Dates are not to be misused or conquered, but are to be treated kindly and respectfully, the way you would want your mother or sister to be treated. We ask them to put their heads down and consider this. This can be uncomfortable for many boys, but the exercise leads them to engage in conversations regarding the behavior they would desire for the women in their lives whom they love.

The next day is a guided meditation. We ask them to remember the last time someone called them a name and hurt them. We challenge them to think about the words that were used and how those words made them feel. What was the intent of the person using those words? Once they are connected to their experience, I ask them to think about what it might mean to a high school girl to be called fat, ugly, or promiscuous? I ask them to consider how those words might make their sisters or their mothers feel and how they would feel if anyone used those words to describe their sisters or mothers.

And then I tell them to grasp the power of their words to either hurt or be kind to girls.

The next day we give them case scenarios. Imagine you're at a party and some girl is drinking. One of your classmates is trying to coerce her into a behavior or activity that you know she wouldn't be comfortable with if she were sober. What do you do at that moment—as a friend, a classmate, a teammate, a man? Are you going to be a bystander or will you intervene? Do you think your teammate is going to get lucky? Do you think that it's none of your business? Or, as a man, do you intervene on behalf of both the girl and your classmate?

Another example: You walk into the locker room and one of your teammates is talking about having sex with some girl in school. What do you do at that moment?

As coaches, we want to challenge our young men to stop, sit, think, and contemplate these situations, to visualize and feel their responses. It never ceases to amaze me how teenage boys engage in the process.

We conclude the contemplation parts of our lessons with a reflective writing exercise.

On Thursday of Homecoming week, we ask the players to visualize picking up their dates, taking them to the dance, and bringing them home. They are required to write a couple of paragraphs describing how they will treat their dates. These assignments are turned in the next day and a selected number of players read them to the team. They meditate, contemplate, and reflect as they examine their thoughts, attitudes, and beliefs.

Imagine the transformation of fields and courts and pools and gyms into classrooms, into authentic cocurricular experiences that build on the school experience and focus on instruction in virtue! Imagine what would happen to a nation if coaches taught young athletes the true essence of being men and women! Imagine if athletes learned that justice and reason were more critical to their success as human beings than winning and losing. If sports can transform young men and women, can't they transform society? It's not just logical, it's possible. A cocurricular approach can feed a revolution in which we all help boys become men and girls become women built for others.

Cocurricular sports enhance, enrich, and expand the regular curriculum schools provide during the school day. When coached by men and women who have a clear understanding of who they are and why they coach, sports can foster school pride, establish positive relationships with the school and classmates, and further develop student-athletes' social and emotional awareness.

The virtues of justice, reason, and contemplation offer a unique opportunity for service-oriented learning and unifying diverse school populations. Students who develop these skills perform better and feel better about themselves and their peers. A solid relationship with an InSideOut coach can also help to develop student-athletes in ways that can carry into other arenas of their lives. The opportunity to belong, to be known, and to be accepted for who they are can be the first rung on the ladder to success for these young adults.

CHAPTER 8

Contact, Communicate, Connect

For many years, Tom Pecore has led a winning soccer program at Putnam City North High School in Oklahoma. But in 2003 his team became successful in a new way. It was the year Tom began the InSideOut process. The change in Tom, and consequently in his team, came as a result of a tragedy, which ultimately became a redemptive story that teaches coaches a critical lesson about the importance of mindful communication with their athletes.

Tom was having a rough start that December day. His students were acting up in class, seemingly in concert with the rising barometric pressure. He kept one student after class to discuss his behavior, making Tom late for a parent conference. He was meeting the mother of one of his students. She was upset and blaming him for her daughter's suspension. They sat in the guidance counselor's office and, despite the closed door, the secretary and kids found it difficult to ignore the increasing volume of the discussion.

Tom admits he lost his cool. He took the mother's anger personally and raised his voice to match hers. The meeting ended abruptly and Tom got up and walked away without shaking her hand. He was right in his diagnosis—the girl needed stronger supervision at home and wasn't getting it. But Tom admits that he was wrong in his approach: He let the mother's anger dictate his response.

As he walked out of the office, he felt his blood pulsing through the veins in his reddening neck. One of his star players was sitting in the lobby. Tom caught sight of the ice bag on his knee, and his eyes locked on to the knee and the knee only. He never made eye contact with the young man. Instead, he engaged in a conversation with the leg—a critical piece of his soccer team's success.

"How is it today?" Tom asked.

"Better," the young man said.

"Get down to the trainer a half hour before practice."

Those were the last words Tom ever spoke to his athlete. A few hours later the young man went home and shot himself. Tom rushed to the emergency room to console the boy's mother and father. He held his player's hand and kissed him on the forehead before he died. There were no last words to supplant the previous transactional exchange; no final good-bye to replace his conversation with a leg cast. The unfinished, uncorrected conversation haunts Tom to this day.

But Tom soon did do something to honor the young man: He transformed his communication with his players and thereby transformed his coaching. Tom took the courageous InSideOut journey and identified his own experiences as a young athlete that shaped his communication skills as a coach. He recognized his transactional tendencies and decided he wanted to be a transformational coach instead. Tom defined the WHY of his coaching and he learned to listen and to be mindful of his words. He decided to converse with his players instead of talk to them. He studied history's great communicators and learned from them. The result was an accessible coach with whom players could talk and connect.

Tom's program was humming along just fine. The team was winning games and kids were getting scholarships and acclaim, but he admits he had not done the work to become the kind of coach who might have transformed a lost soul's life. He was more or less a transactional coach—goodhearted but dedicated first and foremost to winning, monitoring injuries, and rallying school and team pride.

Typically, Tom admits, his coaching communication was limited to informing and instructing—practical and critical things, no doubt.

InSideOut communication, however, is collaborative; it involves the exchange of information, ideas, questions, and concerns. It entails give-and-take. At every practice players are sending us verbal and nonverbal messages. The challenge is to be mindful enough to receive, interpret, and respond in an appropriate and timely manner to their needs or uncertainties—be they about instruction on the field or problems off the field. With each of our communications, we convey acceptance and affirmation or rejection and lack of interest. Our communication is both verbal and nonverbal: Eye contact, facial expressions, tone of voice, body language, all contribute powerfully to a coach's communication. A coach has to be a mindful communicator who is aware of how his words and nonverbal signals are interpreted and understood in the context of his athletes' developmental needs and capacities.

For me, the two virtues of mindful communication are clarity and discipline. Clarity in verbal communication means conveying intentions, plans, and requirements as precisely as possible. Discipline in communication is required if we are going to remain mindful of the effects of our words, deeds, and demeanor. InSideOut coaches are always aware of their words and gestures as well as their players' needs and sensitivities, and of the potential damaging collision of the two. Communication discipline entails coaches constantly weighing the effect of their words and body language and the importance of placing players' needs above their own.

Coaches may not necessarily be telling players what they want to hear, but it can be transformative when we tell them what they need to hear in a way that causes them to learn and grow from our instruction.

Transformational coaching demands personal contact and connection. Communication is a contact sport. To be able to communicate across the generational, gender, and cultural divides requires a connection that helps players understand what we are saying and why we are saying it. Contact can occur with a look, a kind word, a question, or a pat on the shoulder. The connection can be verbal or nonverbal. And both, contact and connection, set the stage for collaborative communication.

Our culture discourages the sort of communication that transformational coaches practice. In fact it seems set up to obstruct it. I learned this the hard way. My notion of traditional masculinity muddled any chance of clear, authentic, and heartfelt communication. That was not what men did. We remained tight-lipped, uttered harsh appraisals or minimal compliments, and moved on down the road. I think of the cartoon showing two men sitting at a bar. One man looks at his friend and says; "You know we've been sitting on these same stools for twenty years. All we've ever talked about are our jobs, the news, and sports. We never talk about feelings, our relationships, or the meaning of life." And then he pauses and adds, "You know, I've been meaning to thank you for that."

Our practices often begin with a clear and disciplined refrain. Not a rah-rah pep talk, or a macho challenge or even technical jargon. This is our refrain:

"What's the coaches' job?"

The players respond: "To love us!"

"What's your job?"

And the players shout: "To love each other."

This might come across as trite or mushy in the wrong tone or situation, but we thought long and hard about crafting a refrain that would cut to the core of what we wanted to communicate: *to help boys become men of empathy and integrity who will lead, be responsible, and change the world for good.* We wanted to give boys permission to use and develop words that define and express their emotions. We wanted simple words that cut through the athletic stereotypes of masculinity, individuality, and achievement. We wanted words that encourage camaraderie. We wanted words that ring out and remind us of our jobs as much as they encourage our athletes. We wanted words that communicate a clear break in the rhythm and expectations of their eight hours in the classroom.

America's common coaching vocabulary may be culturally entrenched, but that doesn't mean it has to be heeded. Biff and I thought of ourselves as Don Quixotes at first, battling against a system of communication that the false notions of masculinity and sports demand of male coaches.

Two communication virtues, clarity and discipline, can transform coaches' interactions with young people and help them fulfill their purposes as coaches. Mindful communication is a critical tool we use to fulfill our WHY. These virtues are the foundation of a system of communication that spreads from hours on the field into young athletes' daily lives. They begin to sense the lifelong value of the clear and disciplined exchange of ideas, sentiments, and support.

CLARITY

Inside

Clarity is an art form. One might say it has something to do with transparency, but I think clarity has more to do with authenticity in communication. Clarity is precision—using words and inflections in as precise a fashion as possible. But clarity is more than that. Clarity in coaching revolves around the communication of mutual expectations, desires, and needs. Clarity is a by-product of purpose-driven coaching, of knowing where you and the team are going. Coaches need to ask themselves: What messages do I need to send to my athletes today at practice? What do I expect from them this week and how will I design our lesson plans to deliver the message? What sort of behavior do I expect from them off the field when they interact with their friends and families and in the community? What do I need to communicate to empower them and prepare them to flourish as fathers, friends, and citizens of a community, country, and world?

And likewise, what are their clear needs from me? What can I do for them to help them develop as athletes and thrive as people? How can I connect with them? How can I help them connect to me and others?

We must communicate to them what we expect of ourselves as coaches: to love them and to help them become involved, responsible, and devoted men and women for others. It is only fair to turn the expectation game back on ourselves as coaches once we have laid out what we expect of our players. I do not hesitate to call clarity a virtue, because emotional clarity is all too often missing in coaches. Virtues are hard to practice and clarity is a rigorous tenet of the InSideOut coaching platform. Looking back at the absence or presence of clarity in our own lives and sports careers is the best starting point.

A short time after *Season of Life* came out, a gentleman in San Diego named Brian Buffini invited Jeffrey Marx and me to come to San Diego and speak to five thousand Realtors. I sure didn't know anything about Realtors but I figured if this guy read the book and liked it, he knew what he wanted.

The date was set and Jeffrey Marx and I spoke to Brian's group. The book hadn't been out too long but Brian had read it, liked it, and wanted to hear what we had to say. After we spoke to the enthusiastic crowd, we were amazed at the standing ovation. We walked off the stage, astonished at the response, and I whispered to Jeff, "What did we say?"

Apparently Brian thought we said something significant, because later that fall we had a visit from him. I told Paula that Brian was flying

out on his personal jet and we were going to take him out to dinner. We
had a football game that day and Brian sat in on our pregame meetings
and lesson plan. At the game, Paula spotted him and introduced herself.
She mentioned to him that she understood we'd be going out to dinner
later.

"Oh, no," Brian said, "we'll be going to your house! I'm here to see
if you're the real deal!"

"But my house is messy and I wasn't planning on cooking . . ." Paula
stammered.

"No problem!" Brian smiled. "We'll get pizza!"

So pizza it was. We ended up at our house after the game with our
sons and a few other scattered players. After eating and the initial small
talk, Brian pulled out his eighteen-by-twenty-four sticky note pad and
started dissecting our lives. While Paula and I are usually up for a good
challenge, we really weren't prepared for the sudden critique that landed
in our living room that night.

Brian, we learned, built and ran the largest real estate coaching business in the world, Buffini and Company. He seemed to be an upstand-
ing and very accomplished fellow, so we weren't going to throw him out.
But a sort of obscure threat hovered over his visit. It revolved around
that bold statement of his: "I am coming to see if you are for real!"

He is a private jet type of guy, so we understood how he could move
around the country so easily. And the hype surrounding *Season of Life*
was buzzing. So the whole premise of his visit seemed legitimate. What
really threatened me, I think, was that I knew what was coming. He
was going to study me and our program up and down, comment on it,
evaluate it, and in the process probably question the fundamental tenets
of my life and work. So I girded myself for this bold inquisitor's visit and
his demand that I instill even more clarity in my life and in the communication of my message about sports and young people.

"What's your ultimate goal?" he asked.

"I want to change the world." I quickly responded. "And, I believe, sports are the way to do it." He didn't laugh or roll his eyes at my answer, but he did pause and stare.

He then taught us something profound. He said that there is an appropriate sequence for people to follow in life, one we had apparently missed. He said that the true path to significance came as a result of stability and success. Success, he said, is building value for you. Significance is creating value in and for others. But significance is unsustainable without stability. You have made significant contributions, but at the expense of your and your family's stability.

Ouch.

He looked at us and looked at our lives. Some things were very clear to him that apparently weren't clear to us, at least on a conscious level. We were working very hard and affecting lives, but we were exhausted and only becoming more exhausted. We were impassioned by significance, but short on stability. The success of *Season of Life* only increased the demand—it didn't increase our stability.

Brian made Paula cry when he suggested that all my good works, speaking, and coaching were detrimental to my family. He said while we were accomplishing significant feats in our lives, we needed security and sustainability built into them if we were going to finish the race strong. He pointed out where I was unclear with my family and where I was unclear with myself. He cut straight to my lack of clarity in my personal life. Tough stuff to hear! But he was spot on and we knew it.

He then offered to coach us in clarifying our needs and not the needs of everyone else. I had done significant things I was proud of, but I saw that they were at the expense of my family. "Messiah complex . . ." I thought I heard Paula whispering in her head.

We thanked him, said good-bye, and closed the front door. Drained and admittedly wigged out, we looked at each other, smiled, and, at the same time, asked the rhetorical question, "Who *was* that guy?"

Later that night, Paula said: "We have been out of sequence our whole lives. We've never had that sort of clarity before. What a gift!"

This whirlwind visitor cut to the core of my life message and my means of delivering it. He didn't question its content, but rather the lack of framework supporting it. We set about clarifying what we needed to build stability in our lives and for our children. Brian had us write out our family objectives and create a budget and taught us how to ask for help when we needed it. He knew, and soon we learned, that the many speaking opportunities resulting from *Season of Life* would demand clarity. To seize the opportunity to change the world through sports demanded clear, consistent communication that flowed from a stable and secure heart, mind, and life. I recognized clarity as a virtue, a rare and harmony-promoting trait that could enrich others' lives and sustain mine.

An InSideOut process made this leap from confusion to clarity possible. Because of the clarity of his own vision, Brian could see what was fogging up mine. If a game plan or technique is not communicated clearly it can lead to failure—losing the game. If interpersonal expectations, codes of conduct, and a dedication to transformation over transaction are communicated clearly, the positive impact on an athlete's development not only can win a game, it can change a life. An unexpected and providential visitor taught me the power and importance of crystal-clear communication. Brian and I continue to be great friends today.

Outside/Lesson

Clear communication requires explicit expectations for how we will treat each other, stand by each other, and care for each other.

As I undertook these commitments to work on the clarity of my communication, I realized that clarity enhances the relationship between the technical and the virtuous. Clarity defines a program so that we all know where we stand, what our roles are, and how we are going to act and care for one another.

In that light, Biff and I developed three contracts: one for us and our coaches, one for our students' parents, and one for our athletes, documents that prioritized and emphasized clarity as essential to stating our purpose and implementing it effectively in our program.

For our coaches we developed a Coaches' Code of Conduct that specifically outlined our behavioral standards for interacting with our athletes, administrators, parents, referees, and opposing coaches and their teams. As I travel the country speaking and training coaches, my estimate is that less than 2 percent of coaches have a written code of conduct. Astounding! Coaches are some of the most influential adults in the lives of young people and yet most have no rules or guidelines for how to behave. Too many coaches are put in this position of power and authority because of their athletic backgrounds or hired because schools and leagues are often desperate to fill positions and settle for "warm bodies." Many coaches are hired for technical skills and fired for lack of character. Coaches should be hired for their character and the clarity in their answers to the big questions I posed in Chapter 5. Why do you coach? Why do you coach the way you do? What does it feel like to be coached by you? How do you define success as a coach? These questions might come in handy for administrators during interviews.

COACHES' CODE OF CONDUCT

The purpose of our coaching is to help boys become men of empathy and integrity who will lead, be responsible, and change the world for good.

Be mindful never to shame a player, but to correct him in an uplifting way. Affirmation!

Believe in every player. Remember, "In youth is where miracles are made."

Protect our players. Be big enough to build up, not tear down. Our kids are getting attacked from many places that we don't often see and of which we are not aware.

Remember our job is to put our players in a position where they can develop to their fullest potential through proper teaching and nurturing.

Each player is part of our family, deserves every chance to succeed, and deserves the utmost respect.

Coaches can disagree in meetings but never in front of our players or anyone else outside our family. Disagreements are saved for private meetings.

Our players are student-athletes and we are teacher-coaches. We hold ourselves accountable as teachers of young men and the lessons they need in order to navigate masculinity and life.

If you do not know, say so and get appropriate information. Don't bluff our kids! They know the difference.

Remember that parents are our partners. We strive to work with each family in helping their sons to succeed. "Every boy is a son to his mother and father."

Love your players and the other coaches.

No profanity!

Know the difference between shaming and coaching. No screaming, shaming, swearing, or sarcasm.

Don't be afraid to apologize! We all make mistakes. When mistakes are made publicly, apologize publicly; when mistakes are made personally, apologize personally.

We are nurturing successful people, not just successful athletes.

Treat all opposing coaches and their teams with the honor true competitors deserve.

Respect all referees, officials, and timekeepers. They are imperfect and trying their best just as we are.

Regardless of our wins and losses, we will be successful if we carry out the above items.

Because I am a role model who has the power, position, and platform to make a positive difference in the lives of my players, I commit to this code of conduct. When failing to live up to our standards I will allow for accountability and take responsibility for my actions.

Signature   Date

For parents, we always strive for clear and open lines of communication to ensure that we are working out of the same playbook. We meet twice before each season and make sure parents understand the WHY of our program as well as the commitment and expectations of parents and players to one another, the team, and coaches. I love to tell parents the story of the coach who pulled one of his players aside and asked, "Do you understand what cooperation is? What a team is?" The player nodded in affirmation that he knew. "Do you understand that what matters is not whether we win or lose but that we play together as a team and do the best we can individually and collectively?" Again, the player nodded yes. "So," the coach continued, "I'm sure you know that when a coach makes a bad call or the referee drops a penalty flag you shouldn't argue, curse, or call them a peckerhead. Do you understand all that?" The player again said he did. Coach continued, "And when I take you out of the game so another player gets an opportunity to play, it's not good to call your coach an idiot, is it?" The player shook his head. "Good," said the coach, "now go over there and explain all that to your mother and father."

We developed a Parents' Code of Conduct that explicitly communicates our expectations of them and of their children. As I have said before, the most competitive sport in America today is parenting. Parents in stands are often competing with each other, seeking validation and status through their child's performance and success. I have seen far too many athletic programs, coaches, and players sink under the weight of parental competition, innuendo, nitpicking, and gossiping. We knew we had to address and include parents specifically and pointedly. By the time some parents get to us, having spent enormous amounts of time, energy, and money on travel teams, sports camps, personal trainers, and skewed information about college scholarships and recruiting, they are caught in a riptide of unhealthy expectations for their children.

Our Parents' Code of Conduct offers a lifeline to help them get back to the shore of realistic expectations and healthy investment in their children. In order for the team to function at its absolute best, there must be trust between parents and coaches.

PARENTS' CODE OF CONDUCT

Understand and endorse the purpose of our program: *to help boys become men of empathy and integrity who will lead, be responsible, and change the world for good.*

Support the coaches by applauding behavior in your child and his teammates that demonstrates characteristics of integrity, empathy, sacrifice, and responsibility.

Acknowledge and appreciate players' growth toward maturity and their effort toward establishing stronger relationships with teammates, coaches, and themselves.

Affirm your son and his teammates when good character, healthy sportsmanship, and other-centered behavior are displayed. Do not affirm only his athletic performance or a victory.

Serve as role models for our players, talking politely and acting courteously toward coaches, officials, other parents, visiting team parents, and spectators at practices, games, and meetings.

Model good sportsmanship. Acknowledge and applaud the efforts of team members and opponents. Accept defeat graciously by congratulating the members of the opposing team on a game well played. Support the team regardless of how much or how little your son plays or what the win-loss record is.

Encourage your child and his teammates with positive statements, even when they make mistakes. At every practice they are growing physically and emotionally. At every practice they are learning moral and ethical lessons. At every practice they are developing character.

Refrain from boasting about your child's accomplishments.

When problems or questions arise, please have your son present the problem to his position coach. We want players to develop self-advocacy. After meeting with his position coach, if the issue requires more clarity, contact the head coach.

Because I am a parent with the power and platform to make a positive difference in the life of every player, I commit to this code of conduct. When failing to live up to these standards, I will allow for accountability and take responsibility for my actions.

_____

Signature   Date

Our Parents' Code of Conduct communicates precise expectations and sets an explicit framework for our relationship with parents and parents' relationships with other parents. But, perhaps as important, it explicitly demonstrates our insistence on and respect for clear communication.

Some people look bewildered when I say I consider clarity a virtue. Some parents still have trouble understanding, or at least agreeing with, the items in this contract. But the tone and intent are undeniable: We lay it out there. Our athletes and most parents understand that clarity is a fundamental tenet of our program and the communal conversation takes on the clarity that we cherish.

Most of our athletes and parents are grateful for this explicitness. We live in a world in which insinuation, suggestion, and consequently misunderstanding all too often characterize our communication. This is all the more true in coaching culture. So when we establish at the outset that clarity is a virtue, communication becomes a tool that lessens chaos, minimizes misunderstandings, and helps build patience as well as collective peace.

Our players sign a contract, too, and this becomes the guidepost for our communication with each other.

PLAYERS' CODE OF CONDUCT

I accept responsibility for my behavior on and off the field. I understand that what I do and say affects my teammates, my school, and other people either positively or negatively.

I lead courageously and live with integrity by speaking up against injustice and on behalf of others even when it is hard or unpopular.

I act with respect toward myself and the people and things around me, including my parents, my coaches, my teammates, my teachers, my opponents, and the spectators.

I do not put people in boxes according to their race, sex, religion, neighborhood, sexual orientation, or abilities. I judge people by the content of their character.

I act with empathy. I try to understand what is going on in the hearts and minds of others and what is causing those feelings so that I can be supportive and encouraging. I ask, "How can I help *you*?"

I serve as a role model at all times by talking politely and acting courteously toward coaches, teammates, opponents, officials, and spectators. I understand that it is a privilege to represent my family, school, and community as a student-athlete.

I give 100 percent effort to practices, games, and events. I understand that that effort demonstrates my commitment to the team and my respect for my coaches and teammates.

I display good sportsmanship. I acknowledge and applaud the efforts of others. I encourage my teammates with positive statements. I refrain from boasting to my teammates and "trash-talking" to members of other teams. I accept defeat graciously by congratulating my opponents on a game well played.

Because I represent my family, school, and team, I abide by the policies, rules, and guidelines of the school, team, and coaches.

_____

Signature   Date

These ground rules for our expectations allow us to focus on our key communication step, which is to engage each player every day, both before practice and during practice. I read a survey conducted by the Gallup organization that said 74 percent of all employees are either indifferent to their work or actively disengaged. I thought about the average high school team. How many players are fully engaged and how many disengaged?

We carry approximately sixty players on our varsity team. During the course of any practice, that usually means eleven varsity players are practicing against eleven players on the "scout team." What are the rest doing? Are they engaged or disengaged? Coaches walking around, making eye contact, connecting, and conversing with all players is the difference between engaging and disengaging players. So Biff and I make an effort to engage all of the team members each and every practice.

This personal extra effort code of conduct we have for ourselves is something I learned from playing for NFL Hall of Fame coach George Allen. He was masterful at making each of his players feel wanted and significant. I've often suspected that Ken Blanchard had George in mind when he wrote *The One Minute Manager*.

According to Blanchard, and as exemplified by Coach Allen, the secret to one-minute managing is one-minute praising. It involves being open with people about their performance as players and as people. When someone is doing something right, the goal of the one-minute manager is to tell that person so and praise him or her immediately.

George Allen could look his players in the eye and communicate messages of great value in brief moments. These moments with George allowed his players to feel positive and encouraged regarding their importance to the team and their teammates.

One-minute managing also involves a one-minute reprimand. Being honest with those around you involves reprimanding people for mistakes. When critiquing players, it is important to remind them of their value, tell them that their behavior needs correcting, and maintain a positive connection. Praise and reprimand enable players to understand their responsibilities and how to complete them correctly. Coach Allen was a master of one-minute managing, and I try to imitate him in my coaching.

Here are three habits we strive to develop to ensure that contact, connection, and communication take place every practice with every player.

- Welcome each and every player onto the field, letting them know we value and appreciate their presence, contribution, and commitment to the team.
- Commit to making sure every player is personally addressed at every practice. (People often ask about the proper number of coaches to have on a staff. I say you need enough to let every player feel a personal connection.)
- Engage the student-athletes with questions related to the players' interests and problems off the field and develop conversations that affirm the worth of each student-athlete.

Think about what young people have just gone through before arriving on the practice field. They got up at 6:00 or 7:00 A.M., grabbed something to eat, commuted to school, and went from class to class, teacher to teacher, who piled all sorts of information, homework, and tests on them. Think of all the performance pressures they have, of the parental, academic, social, peer, and sexual pressure that they are confronted with every day. Many students can go through an entire day without having a single moment of personal communication with an adult. As coaches who are mindful of this, we want to set a transition to a new space—one in which fun, learning, and communication intermingle and provide a sense of relief and respite from the stress of young adult lives.

We also want to demonstrate how well we communicate with each other. Biff and I are not ashamed of or afraid to show our love for each other as people or coaches. As large men (both of our mothers called us "big-boned" when others called us fat), we break many of our players' stereotypical ideas about how men act. We know boys need modeling and permission to accept and acknowledge their feelings, and I think we do a great job granting them permission, mainly by granting ourselves permission in front of them. I often express my love for Biff and he for me.

Almost every program faces a tragic moment each season. Be it an ill family member, a car accident, or, in Tom's case, the loss of a team member, the odds are that a coach will have to address an issue far more challenging than sports at a certain point each season. Bound up within the lies of masculinity is a culture of silence. We coaches sometimes put on blinders and cordon off life's tragedies from our games. We too often enforce silence or ignore the problems that our athletes face.

So Biff and I decided to do the opposite. We wanted to embrace each of our athletes in the same way we had wanted to be embraced as kids. We realized the only way to do this, to communicate authentically with our young men as human beings and not just as athletes, was to embrace the totality of their lives. So whenever a young man encounters struggle or tragedy, we gather with him as coaches and ask him what he needs. We ask this clearly and try to deliver support—specifically and with clarity. We offer the support of the team and ask him how best the team can help him.

In the case of a young man whose mother was recently diagnosed with breast cancer, it meant having a prepractice meeting and talking about how scary the "c" word is and all the emotions and fears it creates, especially when it is your mom who is the patient. Because of our philosophy that parents are our partners, we often call or visit with families in times of crisis. With the parents' and players' permissions, we gathered the team, explained to them the situation that their teammate faced, and discussed what that must feel like. Biff had asked the player if he was willing or able to talk about it and share some of his emotions and concerns. The sixteen-year-old shared his fear and distress, and it seemed to be cathartic for him. Biff asked the players to imagine it being their mom. How would they feel? How would they want their teammates to act around them and support them? It was wonderful to see, hear, and feel the compassion and desire to support their teammate in his and his family's needs. We then contacted a couple of moms who arranged to take dinners to his home to support the family.

Boys need permission to openly express and share their emotions as well as opportunities to put compassion into action. I always ask my players: "What is one thing I don't know about you that you'd like me to know?" It is always amazing to me what players will share once you build a relationship based on clear communication with them. They carry so much weight and pressure, often looking for a safe person with whom they can vocalize their deepest anxieties, fears, and worries. I have had players tell me of pending divorces; drug and alcohol problems in their homes; girlfriend and dating problems; economic woes; verbal, physical, and sexual abuse; and a host of other shame-related issues. This kind of dialogue allows me to coach them in a way that communicates concern and empathy. I ask parents the same question I ask their sons: "What is one thing I should know about your son that will help me coach him?" Parents often tell me about their son's emotional makeup, learning differences, relational problems at home, the impact their divorce has had on their sons, and a host of other issues.

In addition, one clarity-generating gesture a coach can make is to tell his own story. Too often we hide our lives and our struggles from our athletes. We tend to think we need to maintain a certain aura or, at least, distance when it comes to our own humanness. One day, I witnessed Biff communicate his own story, and it opened new doors for players to connect with him.

Biff assembled the team and began by saying, "I am going to tell you a story about someone among you. He is a good athlete. A darn good one who might garner Division I interest. He is big and strong and sharp. But he hates his coach. His coach bullies him, embarrasses him, and shows him up in front of his teammates." I could tell our team was stirring and beginning to wonder who the subject of the story might be. Biff started to walk among them, and he modulated his voice as he got to the next part.

"One day," Biff continued, "this person among you made a mistake on a blocking assignment. It was a hot September day and he missed an audible call at the line of scrimmage. The coach blew the whistle and everyone stopped. 'HOW STUPID ARE YOU?' the coach screamed. Well, that man among you took off his helmet and started to walk,"

Biff continued. "He walked off the field and off the campus and walked about two miles straight into the woods behind his house. And he sat there as darkness fell and he wondered what life would be like without him. He knew his coach wouldn't miss him, he knew he wasn't happy, and he wondered whether he was really stupid or not. And worst of all, he thought about just checking out. Maybe taking off for a while; maybe even taking his own life."

There wasn't a sound in the room as Biff paused, for what seemed like an eternity, before he continued his story.

"This person among you finally got up and walked back to his house. When he got there, his parents told him his coach had called to apologize and ask where he was. Everyone was worried about him. So he went back to practice the next day, stuck with the team, and went on to play Division I football."

The room remained silent. The boys, avoiding each other's gaze, just waited for Biff to go on.

And he did. He said: "Today, I am standing right in front of you and that is the defining story of my athletic career."

From that day forward, I saw how certain members of our team changed when they were around Biff. They could connect to him like never before. They knew what he had gone through and why he coached the way he does. Some of them, I suppose, had had similar experiences with coaches or teachers or parents. The clarity of his own life allowed him to communicate in a way that gave them hope and solace. The good news for coaches is that clear communication grows out of a coherent life story. It is an almost unavoidable result. It worked for Biff, it worked for me, and it works for most of the coaches who are willing to risk it. Self-aware coaches are empathic communicators because they understand how their words sound and how their actions come across to their players. "I am who you see." "I mean what I say." "My interest in you is sincere and deep-seated." This is the crux of coaching communication between a coach and a player. I want my players to know I love them and I am very clear about this. I do not love them in the way their parents or siblings or friends do. But I love them in a way that results from the sharing of a common goal, communal space, and lots of time together. I love what we do together. We engage in a common goal striving toward something greater than ourselves—together.

DISCIPLINE

"Discipline" is a word that really trips coaches up. When we hear the word "discipline" we think of the old Lombardi, militant, my-way-or-the-highway approach to coaching. Some parents love this word because it means to them that their children will learn to conform, work hard, or simply behave themselves.

But what I am referring to here is specifically discipline in communication. It is the intentional act of being disciplined about the mindfulness of our communications. Discipline is the virtue that a coach develops when he learns how to be mindful about what comes out of his mouth. It also involves being aware of triggers from the past that affect what he says and does to his players in the present. Disciplined communication requires constant awareness and intentional effort.

If a coach cannot be disciplined with how he uses his words and gestures, should players be expected to be disciplined in executing blocking assignments? I realize now, going inside and looking back, that some of my behavior was specific rebellion against the double standard and hypocrisy often associated with the concept of discipline. A coach who could not discipline his words, who did not have the mindfulness to predetermine his impact on me, did not merit my respect.

Many of my coaches suffered deficiencies in this virtue. Schwartzwalder and many others were known as strict disciplinarians. Disciplinarians abound at all levels of sports. But here is the irony: Most disciplinarians lack self-discipline. As communicators they are not always mindful of the irony in their messages. They do not take time to contemplate their athletes' needs and effective ways to truly engage them. They lack the discipline to do the InSideOut work required for transformational coaching.

Inside

One day during my freshman year at Syracuse, my academic advisor summoned me to discuss my plans for my major. He brought me and a teammate into his office and asked us why we both declared business as our intended majors. (My teammate also was an esteemed veteran of the military school postgrad year and, like me, a prolific reader—we just never read any of the assigned books!) That first meeting with our new coach-advisor set the tone for my academic career. He explained the advantages of being a recreation major. "A recreation major?" we both asked, wondering what in the world a recreation major was. Coach-advisor proceeded to tell us that it was a great degree that enabled you to work for major corporations setting up their bowling parties and other fun events! "Put in your thirty years and walk away with a great pension."

Neither of us had stellar high school academic credentials—so being steered into certain majors best ensured our eligibility to play.

We received classic transactional, quid-pro-quo coaching—meet the coaches' needs and you get praise, playing time, and publicity. So we took classes like Theory and Practice of Rhythm and Dance (our final exam was performing a Polish folk dance called a mazurka) and a white-water canoeing class where we never actually went into the water, but sat at our desks in Slocum Hall with canoe paddles making J-strokes. I took the low road academically throughout my time at Syracuse with an unofficial double major in football and pinochle. Not because I wasn't intelligent enough or because I couldn't do the work, not because a coach suggested that I wasn't smart enough to be in the business school. Coach's remarks were just one more interaction that supported my self-definition. I took the low road because I saw myself as a man's man, and academics weren't part of my masculine self-concept.

The realization I came to through my InSideOut work is that discipline is a two-way street. For a coach to demand it of his players, a coach has to demand it of himself. Otherwise young athletes lose respect, interest, and discipline.

Sick of the talk that was lacking the walk, I set out to walk the talk. If I was going to demand discipline from my athletes—in their practices, games, and behavior—I had to demand it of myself. I realized that this boiled down to developing the mindful discipline I was lacking. As a coach, I had to discipline each word, gesture, instruction, and command. I had to be mindful of my words, of my coaching vocabulary. I had to apply the virtue of discipline to that passageway between my brain and my mouth.

I love giving this list to coaches at my seminars:

NINE REASONS I SWEAR

It pleases my mom so much
It is a display of my manliness
It proves I have great self-control
It indicates how clearly my mind functions
It makes conversation so pleasant
It leaves no doubt in anyone's mind as to my upbringing
It impresses people
It makes me a very desirable personality to women and children
It is an unmistakable sign of my culture and refinement

This list invariably generates plenty of laughter. But swearing is merely the easiest example of undisciplined communication. The list also drives home the whole concept of disciplined communication in a way that makes it an exercise that challenges many coaches' vocabulary. Discipline in communication is an infectious virtue—once we harness certain words, we usually begin to realize the effect all our words and gestures have on our players.

Outside/Lesson

As I tried to discipline my communication skills, I realized that acronyms were the best way to keep me mindful about what and how I communicate to and with my players. From a wonderful book called *Teens Who Hurt,* I appropriated what the authors call a VCR approach to interaction with young people—Validate, Challenge, and Request.* Young people seek validation from their coaches. They crave it. Whether ultimately agreeing with the players' point of view or not, coaches need to validate their players' views and perceptions, otherwise it is a one-way conversation leading nowhere. No matter what they tell me, I validate their point of view. I may say, "I can see how you might think or feel that way." Once I validate their perspective, I have earned the right to challenge them on their thoughts and perspectives and can suggest an alternative way of looking at the issue.

An InSideOut coach realizes that confronting, criticizing, or critiquing a troubled player is useless until that player has been adequately validated. Affirmation should always precede criticism. I discipline myself to recognize that all young people, no matter what they look like, have experienced some form of devaluation, rejection, or ridicule. I word my challenge as clearly and directly as possible. "Have you thought about this angle or perspective?" I lay out the challenge and help them process why a different attitude, point of view, or thought might be more appropriate. Then I make my request. "Well, will you try this for me and see what happens?" And my request brings the discipline into the communication. I word it politely but firmly, calmly but authoritatively, and young athletes usually understand that there might be another way to respond or behave. The VCR approach is always centered on my purpose: *to help boys become men.*

---

* Hardy, K., and Laszloffy, T. *Teens Who Hurt: Clinical Interventions to Break the Cycle of Adolescent Violence* (New York: Guilford Press, 2005).

As a coach, I turned the tables on myself. Walk the talk. If I was going to criticize my former coaches for their damaging words and lack of disciplined communication, I had to adhere to a standard of total linguistic discipline. I had to watch each word, be on guard for stray thoughts or triggered responses that I would make without calculating their effect on players, and I had to be mindful of how a seemingly random but sarcastic comment could turn itself into a lifelong memory for another human being.

I established my InSideOut Communication Rules:

- Modeling is the most important part of coaching. If you can't model civil, empathic, reflective, effective communication, why should you expect your players to be able to? On the other hand, if you always communicate civilly, empathically, reflectively, and effectively, your players are much more likely to learn to do the same.

- Research shows most communication is nonverbal; only a small percentage is based on spoken words. We communicate with facial expressions, gestures, eye contact, posture, and especially the tone of our voice. Anyone who is married knows this to be the case! Good communication is the foundation of good coaching and we need to be mindful of our verbal and nonverbal messages.

- Our duty as coaches is to create an environment in which our players feel that it is safe to communicate. If we don't allow players to talk and are quick to shoot down ideas or make fun of serious comments, they will not learn to be better communicators. They will shut down and tune us out.

- Remember that if we ask a player for his honest opinion we must respect the opinion that he or she gives.

- We also subscribe to the acronym ROARS to remind us of the discipline necessary to achieve the kind of communication we strive for. "R" stands for reflective communication—

communication that engages the thoughts, feelings, memories, and experiences of our athletes. "O" stands for open-ended questions—we want to engage players in communication that forces them to converse and not just respond. "A" stands for affirmation—as they share their thoughts and perspectives we affirm their responses. We don't have to agree, but we honor their willingness to engage with us. "R" stands for reflective responses—we respond in a way that pushes them to reflect even further in the seesaw of collaborative communication. "S" stands for summation—we try to always summarize the conversation so our athletes can hear what we think we heard them say and clarify our understanding of what they shared.

Over the years Biff and I have collected a list of ROARS questions that we continue to toss to our players. They are simply conversation starters that help us to communicate and connect with our athletes. A few of them are: If a rhinoceros fought a hippopotamus, who would win? Do you think it is more important to be kind or rich? What is the ideal number of children to have? If you could trade places for one week with any person in the world, whom would you choose and why? Who is the most influential person in your life and how has that person affected your life? If you could have a date with any woman in the world, whom would you choose and why?

I am constantly surprised, moved, and motivated by the power we have through simply communicating with our players in a clear, authentic way. The words, "Thanks, Coach. I've never told anyone that before," signify the beginning of change in that player's life. I may not be the person who can solve all of my players' problems, but I can sure make it safe for them to verbalize what is on their minds.

So it turns out that discipline is a demanding word. InSideOut communication requires discipline. Discipline has always been considered a great sports virtue. Announcers praise disciplined players; the label defines many coaches and it goes hand in hand with success. But it also goes hand in hand with hypocrisy. Our tongues and our lips are objects to be disciplined as much as our athletes' muscle memory and training habits.

Transformative coaching depends on clear, concise communication. It begins with clarity about WHY I coach and then it must be verbally and nonverbally communicated to my players. Effective communication begins only when the message is sent, received, and understood the way it was intended. Communication builds trust, sustains relationships, and fosters learning and community.

I know there was a time I focused only on the information I intended to send. But sending a message and communicating are two entirely different things. Coach-to-player communication needs player-to-coach communication to be effective. I've learned over the years that there are three things going on in any communication: the message we intend to send, the message we actually send, and the message our players hear. Even then, some players interpret what they hear differently and others miss the message altogether. It is not enough to send a message—the message must be clearly and coherently acknowledged for communication to be successful.

Clarity and discipline are the stabilizing virtues of communication. We all too often communicate to players in an emotionally charged environment. There is plenty of external noise, and the chatter and static inside a player's mind can make hearing and understanding a challenge. Clarity and discipline are critical tools in life-changing and life-affirming communication.

CHAPTER 9

"Just Win, Baby"

Sports Illustrated called John Hannah the greatest offensive lineman in NFL history. I already knew that because I lined up against him twice a year for eight years. We were both drafted in the first round of the NFL draft—I was picked tenth and John fourth. Our teams were in the AFC East—the Colts for me, the Patriots for him—and most years we competed for the division title. After my first game against Hannah, I realized I had a problem. John was a little more than I could handle. In the NFL, you can't just raise your hand and ask to be excused from superior competition. You learn that to compete you sometimes have to compensate for your deficiency in ability with desire, toughness, and even deceit.

Between the first and second time we played against each other, I broke the first three metacarpals in my left hand. The team doctor put me in a cast that extended from my knuckles to my elbow. To play with a cast, players are required by the NFL to wear three inches of padding bound in a few rolls of athletic tape. The cast was so heavy that if I didn't pay attention, I walked in a large looping circle.

Fortunately for me, the head slap was legal at that time, so I decided to use my encumbered hand to help me compete. The second time we met, I was prepared. I got in my left-handed stance and at the snap of the ball reached back my arm and hit John in the head as hard as I could. I could hear the plaster cast hit the plastic of his helmet and he let out a little groan. I did this for the entire game—pounding John Hannah in the head. In the end, I didn't do any better against him, but I sure felt better while I was doing it.

When my hand finally healed I had the doctor bivalve the cast and for the next couple of years, every time I played against John, I slipped into that cast and tried to head slap my way around him. Looking back, I don't think we ever talked during or after a game, but I always admired the way he handled himself on the field as a player and competitor.

The year following my brother's death, I woke up the Sunday of the Patriots game with good energy. I had a hunch that this time against Hannah might be different, even though the head slap was now illegal. I was ready for him and I knew it. I felt it. For some uncanny reason, I felt like today my game would match his.

"Pancake," when you're knocked flat on your back by an opponent, is the word defensive linemen hate most. As embarrassing as it is, you know the play will serve as a highlight in the film room on Mondays in front of the whole team. If you lose, the coaches point it out as a reason we lost the game. If you win, the coaches use the pancake play as a humorous moment, playing it in slow motion or at fast speed over and over again, making sure everyone has a big laugh at your expense. Players avoid getting pancaked at all costs.

John Hannah led the league in pancake blocks. On a third-and-long passing down I used my patented fake, slap, and swim move. I faked like I was going inside, slapped him on the outside, and should have then been able to throw my arm over his body to swim past him, make the sack, and be a hero of the game. I had meditated on it all week, visualized it, and felt the sensation of my patented move. The problem was he didn't go for the fake: My slap hardly moved him, and just as I was bringing my arm over his head to swim past him, he uncoiled with both fists and launched them into my sternum. Immediately, I found myself suspended in midair, horizontal to the field. As I was floating back to earth the first thing I thought about, even before I hit the ground, was, "Films on Monday!"

And as I lay there looking up at the sky, John Hannah, big number 73, came up to me, grabbed my hand, and helped me back on my feet.

"I am so sorry to hear about the loss of your brother," he said.

It was the first time in seven years he had ever spoken a word to me. I was so stunned I didn't know what to do or say. Had he turned to psychological warfare? I asked myself.

After the game, I realized he had been sincere. John Hannah was one of the greatest competitors I ever played against, and this moment explains why. It wasn't because he was so darn good, which he was. Rather, with almost every collision after the snap of the ball, I felt we weren't so much attacking each other as trying to achieve something together. He was challenging me to raise my game to a new level, to practice harder than I ever practiced in the week before facing him, to try to beat him with every move and all the will I could summon. And after each game, we shook hands and looked each other in the eye, and I felt uncannily as if I was becoming a better player and a better person. One of the things I realized is that when we have a win-lose concept of competition, we tend to demonize the other player or team. This sort of traditional competition produces unethical, hostile, and demeaning actions toward opponents: Steroids, pine tar, or cheap shots are justified in the name of competition.

Once upon a time, I built my "case" against John with hostility, aggression, and violence. But the more I reflected on true competition, the more I learned how distorted my thinking was. He was such a professional that he disregarded my behavior. He forced me to collaborate with him. We competed in a way that helped me grow as a player and person. He not only brought out the best in me, but in retrospect, I realized that I enjoyed competing with him more than with any other opponent.

The root word of "competition" is the Latin word "petere," meaning to search or strive for. Most often it is used in the context of striving or searching for something of value or excellence. The preposition "com" means together. So, literally, competition can be defined as a "mutual quest or striving for excellence." It is more process oriented than out-come oriented, whereby competitors strive together or with each other to bring out the best by presenting a worthy challenge. Competition, therefore, is not defined by winning or losing, but by the degree to which all competitors realize their fullest potential. Since true competition is a "mutual quest for excellence," there are no winners and losers; everyone who competes wins. This cooperative sense of competition is a value-driven process that leads to respect for others, personal and team integrity, and justice and fairness.

Once I understood the proper concept of competition, I realized that John brought out the best in me, and I'd like to think I brought out the best in him. While I might not have had my "best" games against him in terms of tackles or sacks, I played some of my best football with him. I regret the unethical use of my head-slapping cast, but I understand it as part of the collateral damage of a "just win" philosophy devoid of any morals, ethical rules, or consideration. The results of this just-win mentality are evidenced daily on sports pages as players are fined, suspended, or subpoenaed for illegally and immorally trying to "compete."

If coaches could embody true competition and teach their players how to honor competition and their competitors, imagine how much the satisfaction, pleasure, and participation in sports would increase. Imagine the social impact of all athletes learning to compete with themselves and others and learning to apply these concepts to their everyday lives. Imagine "Be the best you are capable of becoming" replacing "Do whatever it takes to get ahead and win."

In retrospect, it seems too many of my coaches thought that winning games was so critical and life-affirming that losing was a form of dying. They taught this, believed it, modeled it, and took it out on players following a loss. To them competition was a zero-sum game. Enjoyment and excellence were found only in winning. And competitors were valued and validated only by coming out on top.

"Winning isn't everything; it's the only thing," has become an American sports cliché. I prefer former Buffalo Bills coach Marv Levy's retort: "The only must win was World War Two."

The credo of American coaching seems to be that competition exists to prove superiority, to project a greater mastery or strength, and to celebrate dominance, power, and control over others. Too many coaches see competition as a way to compensate for their own insecurities and inadequacies. Their team's performance is tied to the hope that winning will produce the self-worth and validation for which they've longed. Players' needs and welfare are placed at the end of the bench, seldom seen or thought of. When a coach's self-esteem is tied to performance and victory, winning becomes the most important thing and, indeed, the only thing. There is a great deal of difference between the need to win and the desire to win. "Winning is everything" coaches steal the joy from sports and ignore the edifying life lessons that can be taught from competing with others, instead of competing against them.

Second to the "winning is everything" philosophy is another destructive saying that has stuck: "Show me a good loser and I'll show you a loser." This one is a whopper, a competition where there is no value in having done your best and losing the contest. Losing with honor and winning with humility should be deemed virtuous. The line "second place is first loser" is a fitting reminder that all of us who have power and authority over young people must teach a definition of competition that not only brings out the best in players but also allows us to celebrate all the accomplishments that competition can bring. Barring sports that permit ties, there is a 100 percent chance that when any two teams play, one will lose.

I know from working on issues of gender and sexuality for two decades that this winning-versus-losing attitude is tied to the socialization of men. Men are taught that having power "over" another is more masculine than having power "with" a competitor. Men are taught to dominate, be in control, and, above all, win. Winning is masculine and losing is emasculating. Men compare and compete with each other—be it the size of their biceps or their bank accounts or the beautiful women on their arms. This comparison and competition destroys the opportunity to enter community and find compassion in competition.

Most of the coaches throughout my athletic career lived according to this win-at-all-costs credo. It is so ingrained in our sports culture that the reformation of the notion of competition is one of the most challenging parts of being a transformative coach. I have seen coaches so driven by their fear of failure and need to succeed that their modus operandi is pounding wins out of their players. I have had coaches who were so afraid of rejection and so sensitive to criticism that they threw their players under the bus every time something went wrong in order to make themselves look better or less at fault. Every season players are physically and emotionally abused by win-at-all-costs coaches. Too many players are scarred, hospitalized, and even die as a result of this pathetic form of competition.

Probably the most dangerous coaches are the ones driven by shame. I know this because of my own toxic bouts with shame and the need to be on top, proving my value, worth, and identity. Shame is what lingers at the core of most triggers. When we find ourselves ashamed or embarrassed by losing, we risk behaving in regressive and destructive ways.

In constructing my coaching narrative, I saw my own insecurities and self-doubts that generated a need to play and win regardless of the negative social, ethical, and emotional costs. Too many coaches use competition as a legitimate way to medicate the nagging questions of their competency as human beings. They vent their aggression through competition and use it to establish themselves as smarter, stronger, tougher, and more manly. This often creates an unhealthy drive to win at all costs, because their sense of value and worth are tied to the scoreboard.

It is pathological behavior because these coaches coach in a way that is detrimental not only to their players, but also to their spouses, their children, and their own health. "I am going to win so many games that I will prove my worth." The ultimate irony is that no number of wins is ever enough to fill the hole in that coach's soul.

The InSideOut journey helps us realize that a coach's self-worth is never determined by winning or losing. Our desire to dominate or destroy an opponent is a result of insecurity, a sense of insignificance, and shame. Competitors can be after the same goal—excellence—but they cannot find it alone. The relationship among opposing coaches and teams should be built upon respect for each other, the game, the rules, and the honor of competition.

One of my favorite sports anecdotes captures this vision of competition. It comes from the Special Olympics.

Nine athletes, all mentally or physically challenged, were standing on the starting line for the one-hundred-meter dash. Their "huggers" were at the finish line yelling words of encouragement to their sprinters. Huggers are the standard bearers of true competition. Each is assigned a special athlete to validate, affirm, and honor for competing, not winning. The starter gun fired and the race began. Almost as soon as it started, a boy tripped and fell, did a couple of somersaults, and started to cry. The eight other runners saw the boy fall and they all slowed down and looked behind them. They stopped and went back to where the boy was lying and crying. A girl with Down syndrome sat down next to him, hugged him, and asked, "Are you feeling better now?" Then all nine held hands and skipped to the finish line. The whole crowd stood and applauded.

This story is known as one of the great moments in sports. It profoundly moves us because deep down we know that there is something more important in life than just competing to win.

The ritual of the postgame handshake has become a mainstay of our sports culture. Young athletes line up, often grudgingly, and many halfheartedly slap hands with their opponents without even making eye contact. This is a noble idea, but its implementation has become hollow and lackadaisical. The "winners" often go through the line smug in their superiority while the "losers" endure feelings of inferiority. Most players have never been taught the purpose of this ritual: to honor your competitors for setting the bar of excellence. In contrast with the legendary sense of competition demonstrated by those Special Olympians, the postgame handshake has become perfunctory, a farce to many.

The team handshake is a ritual that has lost its meaning. Restoring the meaning of the team handshake is a critical symbolic step in the restoration of a proper notion of competition. President Teddy Roosevelt summed up the honor of true competition in a speech titled *The Man in the Arena.*

> It is not the critic who counts, not the man who points out how the strong man stumbled, or where the doer of deeds could have done better. The credit belongs to the man who is actually in the arena; whose face is marred by the dust and sweat and blood; who strives valiantly; who errs and comes short again and again; who knows the great enthusiasms, the great devotions and spends himself in a worthy cause; who at the best, knows in the end the triumph of high achievement, and who, at worst, if he fails, at least fails while daring greatly; so that his place shall never be with those cold and timid souls who know neither victory or defeat.

My errant sense of masculinity prohibited me from "striving valiantly" in the face of competition. Rather, it had me seething whenever I lost to the "enemy." The shame of losing emanated from associating losing with concepts of personal failure as a man—I wasn't good enough, man enough, or tough enough. Once I came to know myself, I saw that the "enemy" was within me and my memories.

Virtuous competitors honor and respect opponents who present them with the opportunity to play to their fullest potential. They also honor and respect opponents who did the best they could regardless of their ability or the outcome of the game.

EMPATHY

I have used the word "empathy" repeatedly in this book. I use it repeatedly in my life. It is the one word that, were I forced to pick, I would select as the quintessential virtue for coaches who are trying to help boys become men. It is the broadest and boldest virtue that a coach can exercise. Empathy is the foundation upon which morality is built. The virtue of empathy, the understanding that what hurts others hurts us, is also part of the foundation for competition.

On the surface, empathy runs contrary to our sports culture. It is a radical concept, flying in the face of the dominant impulses in contemporary sports. It defies machismo standards and is thought to undermine competitiveness. Contrary to this primitive thinking, a civil and functioning society requires empathy, and sports are a great venue in which to develop, model, and teach it.

Empathy is hard to fake. It's not a hat or an act that you can pick up and put on. Empathy requires the inside journey. It requires an understanding of our own experiences so we can develop compassion and forgiveness for ourselves. Once you have empathy for yourself, you are then able to be empathic toward others. We simply cannot connect with others in an authentic and effective way when we cannot imagine what it is like to stand in their shoes.

Inside

I was sitting in my office in Baltimore just before Christmas in 2009 when the UPS guy arrived with a large box from a stranger named Fred Spytek. Taking out a pair of scissors and cutting it open, I was stunned to find my Syracuse football helmet from 1969. It looked like an antique, an artifact: faded coloring, no padding inside save for a few pet-rified leather straps, and a minimalist face mask. Inside the box was a note from the sender. It took about five seconds before the memory of this particular orange helmet came rushing back.

My sophomore year at Syracuse, we beat the Wisconsin Badgers be-fore forty-five thousand people at Camp Randall Stadium in Madison. With two minutes left, our running back Greg Allen ran sixty-three yards for a touchdown to make the score 41–7. Then, suddenly, we saw our coaches signaling for a two-point conversion. There was less than two minutes left; we were up by thirty-four, and we were going for two more points? Not something I thought Schwartzwalder would do un-less we were playing Penn State.

After the game, we found out that the Wisconsin athletic director and Hall of Fame player Elroy "Crazy Legs" Hirsch had called down to the bench earlier and asked Ben to go for two points in the event we scored again. He was concerned about losing so many balls into the stands on PATs after our five touchdowns. This was before they had nets behind the goalposts.

There was one problem. Hirsch neglected to inform the Wisconsin coaches and players about his request.

So we scored on the two-point conversion and then all hell broke loose. Our going for the extra two put the Wisconsin players and fans over the edge. The fight was on. The players left their sidelines and rushed onto the field. Our team ran into the end zone to support our teammates. Dozens of students jumped the restraining fence to enter the melee. Fred Spytek, a freshman baseball player for the Badgers, got his licks in as well. Before I knew it, I was brawling with players and fans while my teammates were similarly engaged.

In the midst of the chaos, I felt someone grab my face mask, twist my neck, and yank my helmet off my head. Not exactly something you wanted to lose at such a time! As I continued fighting, I saw a guy bran-dishing my helmet like a trophy with people cheering as he paraded it around. That was Spytek.

Security guards and the coaches somehow managed to break up the fight and we were escorted to the locker room. As I sat there in front of my locker wondering about the fate of my helmet, I felt as if I had been scalped. Losing it was humiliating. But the Orangemen had won a lopsided victory and we had held our own in an equally lopsided skirmish.

Later, as I integrated this memory into my sports narrative, I couldn't help but think that the athletic director hadn't given a second thought to the young men proudly wearing Badger uniforms that day. Had budgets overcome any thought of empathy for his players? Or had losing been so frustrating that he just stopped thinking about the emotional temperature of the Badger team and fans rising as a result of the score? Either way it seemed like the worth of a bag of balls was the biggest concern at the time.

We have all made regrettable decisions in the midst of competition when our empathy circuits get overloaded by the scoreboard, decisions made without taking the time to understand their emotional consequences.

My helmet, a symbol of conquest, sat in Fred Spytek's attic for forty years. The event gnawed at him enough that he wrote me a letter of apology that accompanied his surprise shipment.

I wrote him back, accepting both and thanking him with a copy of *Season of Life*. He had provided me with another part of my sports journey, forgotten and unexamined. In working through the memory of that game, I was reminded of the power and importance of demonstrating empathy for players, fans, and even for a college athletic director.

As radical as it seems, empathy is an organic virtue. We are born with empathy; it is life that muddles and confuses it for us. Empathy must be nurtured, coached, modeled, and affirmed. In our journey to become InSideOut coaches, finding our coherent narrative entails purposeful self-examination and yields powerful insights into our own feelings and the circumstances causing those feelings. Self-understanding allows us to understand the feelings of others as well. Our capacity for empathy—once blocked by shameful events, defenses, and distorted beliefs—is regained. The very process of making sense of our lives increases our capacity for empathy. An InSideOut coach will become more aware of his players' experiences, needs, limitations, and strengths. Sports tend to provide the milestones for coaches as we structure our life stories, and these recollections make it very easy to put ourselves in the shoes of our young athletes. Despite some generational differences, the experiences of togetherness, achievement, pride, and oneness are the same.

I felt empathy from Coach Simmons. I knew he got me. He cared about me and he told me so with his eyes. He knew players sensed it when someone understood and cared about them. He was real, genuine, and empathic. My connection to him grew because of this. An InSideOut coach recognizes that most young athletes, regardless of their skill set or genetic gifts, are seeking an empathic connection to their coach. Every coach who examines his life in sports realizes that he sought connection and affirmation from coaches in the same way that young people still do today. They are not so different from us and we are not so different from them. Empathy is the backbone of true competition.

Outside/Lesson

A few years back, we had a player at Gilman who was a very gifted athlete. But being young and talented, he got the idea that his athletic performance somehow reflected his superiority as a human being. He watched the highlights and lowlights of ESPN *SportsCenter* and he had mastered the showboating of his favorite stars.

One day we were playing a game in Baltimore. He ran a great pattern and beat the covering cornerback so badly that the kid twisted in his shoes and fell down. This was back when NFL receivers were allowed to make throat-slashing gestures whenever they scored a touchdown or made a big catch. Well, my guy didn't do that, but after he scored he went back, stood over the fallen corner, and spiked the ball near his head.

The referee didn't see his unsportsman-like conduct, but our coaches did, and I think every coach on our team admonished him as he came to the sideline—some more gently than others. He was a great kid, but in a split second he had reverted to cultural concepts of shaming and humiliating an opponent to boost his own ego. But it was in the film room that we really coached him up.

During film sessions on Mondays, we reviewed game tapes with the objective of correcting and teaching. We tried never to shame or embarrass a player and to speak one on one when a player needed substantial correction. However, we always highlighted moral mistakes together so every player could benefit from the corrections.

When we came to this play, Biff asked everyone to watch it and then turned off the projector and turned on the lights. "Imagine that young man's family in the stands. Imagine how he felt—getting beat, giving up a touchdown, and feeling like he let his teammates down. Imagine lying there, feeling all these emotions, and you add humiliation by your actions. What do you think that feels like? Now, imagine yourself in his place. You're competing, doing the best you can on behalf of your team and yourself. Your family and friends are in the stands supporting you on every play. Now tell me how you would feel if that was done to you? If that was done to your brother? Your teammate?"

While the player sat there stunned, feeling the suggested consequences of his action, Biff had him verbalize how he would feel. He paused, stammered, and finally said in an emotionally packed way, "Awful."

Then Biff spoke quietly: "That is not how you were brought up. That is not how you were coached. That is not how you treat a competitor and that is not how you play as a member of this team." A teachable moment, powerfully taught to help boys become men of empathy.

The irony is that many coaches are good people who unfortunately act like my star receiver. They don't typically embarrass opposing coaches or players, but they see competition in the same way as this teenager. This is where lopsided scores come from, when coaches keep their first-string players in the game despite being way ahead on the scoreboard. It shows a lack of empathy for the other team, its players, its coach, and its extended family. Competition, true competition, is about maintaining the honor of the opponent. Sure we want to prepare to win and play to win, but never at the expense of our opponents' well-being. As a coach, I want to make sure opposing teams have a good experience. I am not competing with the other coaches; I am trying to complement their coaching as they, too, strive to help boys become men.

Unfortunately, not all coaches comprehend this. When I was coaching my ten- to twelve-year-old Men for Others basketball team, we played a team far superior to mine. They ran a full-court press against us and by the third period we were down thirty points and the opposing coach kept the press on. I finally called a time-out and had my team sit on the bench while I walked across the court and asked the coach if I could speak to him. I complimented him on his team's performance and then asked him to consider how my players were feeling about themselves. He looked at me like I was from Mars. You mean not annihilate and destroy your opponents? Not run up the score and win by the largest margin possible? He didn't know what to say, but he put his team back on the court without a press. Afterward I thanked him on behalf of my players and affirmed him as a coach and a person. I like to think he learned something then about connecting empathy with coaching for all players.

That is one way to approach coaches who lose empathic connections to opponents. Here is an example of how not to do it. We had a football player at Gilman who was the most talented player I ever coached. We were playing a team that built its offensive game plan around neutralizing our star player. Since he was a defensive end, the offense outflanked him with a wingback and a tight end. Even though they ran away from him on most plays, they still cut blocked, chopped blocked, and clipped him on most plays. I talked to the official and got one or two calls, but since most of the action was taking place away from our player's side of the field, it mostly went unnoticed. The risk of injury triggered my sense of fairness. I called a time-out and went to the middle of the field and started yelling across the field at the opposing coach. In retrospect I am sure he could not hear me and just saw an angry coach screaming at him. At halftime I ran over to him and started yelling at him about the way they were treating my player. He immediately got defensive and a shouting match ensued with coaches from both teams joining in the fracas, resolving nothing. We ended up taking our player out of the lopsided game for the second half. Monday morning our athletic director received a call from the opposing coach apologizing for the illegal blocks. While watching the game films Sunday night, they realized their game plan had morphed into tactics they had not taught or desired. Our staff accepted his apology and a coaching relationship was strengthened.

What I've learned is that it is critical to develop relationships with opposing coaches before the competition starts. Film-swap conversations and pregame warm-ups should be used by InSideOut coaches to communicate what true competition means and your commitment to honor the opposing team as competitors. Nothing is more powerful than a pregame conversation and handshake followed by a note or phone call afterward thanking the coach for the privilege of competing with him.

Empathy is the antidote for narcissistic coaching. Yet, sadly, I think some coaches suffer from an empathy-deficit disorder. A big part of the problem, particularly among men, is that in the name of masculinity, boys are not allowed to name, feel, or share their emotions. When we created our program, Biff and I made empathy one of its foundations.

Our starting outline looked like this:

Coach empathy—We will talk to players about their feelings and emotions and also about paying attention to their teammates' feelings. We want to make sure that our players have permission, set by our example, to use and develop a complete vocabulary to name and express their feelings. We will ask questions about how certain situations feel to them and how they think others may be feeling, and teach them how to read signals or displays of emotion during the season.

Model empathy—As coaches, we will share our own emotions and feelings. Whenever a player shares or displays an emotion we will validate that emotion, evaluate the circumstances, and seek to understand.

Empathize with our players—We will empathize with our players and let them know that we understand the pressures that go along with being their age. Their actions and reactions are often produced by feelings and emotions of which they are unaware.

I adapted a well-known poem titled "Children Learn What They Live" by Dorothy Law Nolte to drive home to coaches the power they have to model and shape our youth:

PLAYERS LEARN BY *HOW I COACH*

If I coach with hostility—my players learn to be hostile.
If I coach with ridicule—my players learn to disengage.
If I coach with shame—my players learn to be ashamed.
If I coach with sarcasm—my players learn to hide.
If I coach with love—my players learn how to be loved.
If I coach with tolerance—my players learn to be patient.
If I coach with encouragement—my players learn to encourage.
If I coach with empathy—my players learn to express their
feelings.
If I coach with compassion—my players learn to care about
others.
If I coach with praise—my players learn to value themselves.
If I coach with fairness—my players learn justice.

*If I coach with affirmation—my players discover their full
    potential.*
*If I coach with acceptance and friendship—my players learn how
    to find and give love in their relationships.*

Football is a tough game. Most sports are grueling physically and
mentally these days. Years ago, while I was coaching at The Door, a
young linebacker got his leg tangled up with a lineman's leg as he tried
to fight off his block. Many of us have seen this sort of injury—the leg
gets twisted at an angle that makes the onlookers gasp and cringe. I was
standing about ten feet from the tackle when I heard the dreadful sound
of that young man's bone breaking. I shiver even now as I remember the
snap and his scream.

As the boy writhed on the ground, I froze for a moment. And then
I immediately went InSideOut. I remembered the pain and anguish of
my own injuries, the shame at wanting to cry, and the embarrassment
at being the object of everyone's attention. I went out to the linebacker,
held his hand, beckoned some of his teammates to stand with us, and
I said this to him: "That must really hurt. I'll stay right here with you,
don't be afraid."

That was a breakthrough day for me—a day I coached with true
empathy. Before that day I would have tried to deny the player his pain,
minimize it by telling him he was fine, or tell him I knew how he felt
because I also once broke my leg. I empathized with him because I allowed myself to be mindful of his pain, mindful that he hurt and didn't
have to hide it because of the false sense of manhood that I had once
followed. I combined instantaneous internal reflection with external action as a coach. The result was an empathic encounter that provided a
young man with a healing connection in the midst of a frightening and
painful experience.

The oddest thing happened—the tense and frightened boy started
to cry, but his pain seemed to suddenly ease, too. The comfort that my
empathy provided for him quickly took effect and his whole demeanor

changed. He grew less tense, the EMTs could more easily examine his injury, and we calmly got him to the hospital for the appropriate treatment. There may have been trauma to his leg, but by supporting him empathically, we averted emotional trauma that would have taken much longer to heal.

If athletes leave our program with a competitive and empathic spirit, their capacity to fulfill their human potential and transform lives increases. Don't get me wrong: We want to produce warriors—virtuous warriors in the Greek model who go forth from our program and do good.

I think coaches can startle young people today with empathy. They expect pep talks and exhortations from us, demands and discipline, competitive drills and insistent competition, but they are not accustomed to receiving empathy. But empathy is the lifeblood of a virtuous coach and the core of a virtuous program.

EXCELLENCE

The late Bill Walsh, former 49ers head coach, said, "In the football arena, competition involves not only winners and losers; it also serves as a meaningful opportunity for the development, exercise, and expression of human excellence. In other words, your focus should be on attempting to demonstrate excellence in all the ways the game calls for."

Competition when defined as a mutual quest for excellence and when immersed in empathy is a pathway to human excellence. Aristotle wrote: "We are what we repeatedly do. Excellence then is not an act but a habit." We designed our program and every practice to help players acquire excellence: athletically, educationally, morally, relationally, and in everyday choices on and off the field.

For us as InSideOut coaches, competition is also the communal habit of searching for excellence together. There are no losers in this truest and most virtuous sense of competition. I make you better, you make your teammates and your team better. The notion of total effort and total commitment to the goal of excellence is produced in an environment with a virtuous view of competition.

Every year our players learn our version of the Parable of the Talents, a biblical parable that teaches the importance of recognizing, using, and investing the players' unique abilities. In the biblical story, three servants are randomly given talents. Ultimately, each servant is held accountable for what he does with the talents he is given. The one who was given five talents invested them and returned ten talents to his master. For this return on investment, he received a "Well done, my good and faithful servant!" The servant given two talents also doubled his and he too received praise and a promotion with far greater responsibility. The servant given one talent buried his in the ground for fear of losing it and was chastised. His talent was taken from him and given to the one with ten talents. The moral of the story is that excellence is not measured by the number of talents we have but by what we do with the talents we are given. One player's excellence is different from another's. It doesn't take great athletic ability to give an excellent effort. Each player's responsibility is to pursue the excellence within him or her. Transformational coaches ensure that each player strives to identify his or her talents and works toward maximizing them to achieve personal and team excellence.

Inside/Lesson

As I reflect on that milestone moment with Honest Abe that I wrote about in Chapter 1, I realize that during our encounter in the school gymnasium that day, he was trying to give me a vision of excellence. He realized I was competitive in an unhealthy way. He saw my skills, but he wanted me to see that sports were about the full realization of talents, not necessarily the victories—be it kickball or professional football. Honest Abe was trying to tell me: Be the best you can be, not just in sports but in life! This may be a cliché, but it is one of great value. Abe saw more in me than I saw in myself and encouraged me to strive for excellence in every aspect of my life—as a person, as a leader, and as a student.

It wasn't until my brother's death that I started to understand Abe, started to understand that there was more to life than just striving to excel at sports. With the construction of the Ronald McDonald House, I realized that I had done something excellent and that there was more to me and my capabilities than knocking heads and facilitating wins. My life had been so myopic—"me-opic" is a better term—and based on the conviction that excellence in sports was the epitome of excellence in life. At that point in my life my definition of excellence was based on my performance on the field and how coaches, fans, friends, and reporters perceived how I played. When one's definition of excellence is based on performance and other people's opinions, the fear of failure restricts excellence to areas where we know we can excel. The fear of failure and disapproval drove me to limit myself to walking in well-worn grooves rather than risk stepping out of my comfort zone.

I try to teach that lesson to my players. We play these games. We strive and succeed and we strive and fail, and then we strive again. That is what doing one's best means—surpassing our limits. That is what defines the habit of excellence in competition.

Outside/Lesson

One of our young assistant coaches, Chris Dawson, teaches English at Gilman. Chris spent one year at Wofford College before transferring to Tulane University, where he was invited to join the football team as a walk-on. Impressed with him as a quarterback, the school gave him a scholarship.

In 2005, I spoke at Louisiana Tech. Tech happened to be housing the Tulane football team, which had been displaced by Hurricane Katrina. Chris heard me speak, and the message resonated with his coaching instincts. He wrote me a letter expressing his desire to coach from the InSideOut. Gilman hired him in 2006 and he has been an incredible addition to our team and staff. He is an outstanding teacher-coach who hopes to develop and integrate the cocurricular structure combining the academic and athletic classrooms.

As a staff, we always look for ways to reframe competitive excellence for our athletes. Chris designed a lesson related to a classic text that is mandatory reading at Gilman, Ernest Hemingway's *The Old Man and the Sea*.

We assembled the team and Chris artfully recounted the story of virtuous competition between the Old Man (a player named Santiago) and his competitor, the noble fish. The sea was the arena that hosted the competition. He turned on the PowerPoint, put up some slides, and told them the story. I recall the power of his teaching and how it captivated our student-athletes—classic cocurricular coaching.

Chris explained that the younger fishermen on the ship thought of the sea as *el mar*, which is masculine. The sea, he explained, was an enemy combatant they fought against and for which they held no respect or admiration. To Santiago, the sea was *la mar*, which is feminine, signifying his love and respect for her. Chris taught about competition and explained how the contemporary definition uses the preposition *against* instead of the more constructive concept of competing *with* opponents to bring out their best. Two prepositions make all the difference.

Far out at sea, Santiago hooked a thousand-pound fish on his hand line and the competition began. It was the responsibility of the fish, as a competitor, to present the greatest obstacle possible for Santiago to master his skills and pursue excellence. Over the ensuing days and nights, Santiago and the fish engaged in relational competition with each other. Santiago acknowledged the necessity of a worthy opponent to achieve excellence and said, "Fish, I love you and respect you very much."

Chris made it clear that this relational competition is characterized by friendship and a sense of striving together for excellence. In relational competition, competitors respect each other and the game. They realize that without each other, they will not be pushed to reach their

CHAPTER 10

Ceremony

Dear Coach,

I realized today is the Gilman vs. McDonogh game and figured I had to say something. It occurred to me that after the game today my teammates and buddies will be huddled around the 50 yard line physically and emotionally spent with many in tears. I will always remember the feelings that go with the last game of the season and for most seniors the last game of their careers. I remember hugging the guys that had become my brothers realizing that we had become something more than just a football team, recognizing that what we had accomplished as a team was bigger than any of our individual accomplishments on or off the field.

I, as you are well aware, had a different experience than my teammates. Injuries hampered most of my career and I spent most of my time rehabbing and standing on the sidelines with you. I was miserable (nothing personal), there is no question about that.

I realized then, but more so now that I was as much a part of that team as any "star" we had. I got to watch and experience the growth of what is and will always be a phenomenal group of guys, come together and become men. I was never treated differently by the coaches or the kids on the team. I feel what was great about that season was not the 9–1 record, not the Championship nor beating McDonogh, but the time we spent together in the locker room, at meetings and learning that "we play like we practice." It was all the eating together with meatball bombers, crab cakes, Papa John's, and bagel bonding and growing close with every member of the team. It was the time spent in our football "class-room" learning about real masculinity and discovering our own personal cause in life. It was preparing our obituaries that the guys will be sharing this morning before the game. I learned more about manhood, character, and morality listening to the coaches speak than anywhere else. If you step back and think about it for a moment I don't know where other boys get that experience. I don't know where they learn that kind of stuff. But I feel lucky to have been taught it and I am a better person because of it. Those are my memories of Gilman Football. I try to explain to my college friends what it is like but they obviously don't understand.

Although it's cliché now, I am going to say it anyway. I miss being a part of something, I miss the spirit, the camaraderie, the coaches, the environment, but more than all of that I miss being a part of the team. Gilman Football means more to me than I could ever explain. This becomes painfully obvious when you try to tell people about it and you literally can't find the words to explain it. I legitimately feel bad for athletes who don't get to go through the experience I went through. Knowing that you were a part of something great and that you were becoming a better person made the pain worthwhile. This is not to say that when I was lying on the ground with two stingers and a strained neck, I was thinking, "Oh, at least I am a better person now," but you know what I mean. Gilman Football is something special. It is bigger than the guys know right now, but they will know it soon. Give the coaches and the guys my love and wish them the best of luck today and the rest of the school year. Go Gilman! Beat McDonogh!

Love, Alex

P.S. I don't really know what the point of this letter was. I just woke up and felt like I needed to write.

I know why Alex wrote this email and why so many of our players continue to call or send emails and texts on this day. Alex is affirming his continued identification with the band of brothers who have gone through the same physical and moral testing, virtue-based teachings, and rituals that cemented this phase of his passage into manhood. He is communicating that he hasn't forgotten the lessons he learned. He endured his rite of passage and knows he worked for, invested in, and paid the price to belong to our community of men for others. He wants his coaches to know he is still on the path we set before him. He values his membership and desires to stay connected to the community that helped guide and nurture him and give meaning to his life journey. Alex knows that he has acquired the wisdom, experience, and perspective to help guide the next generation of players who will take the path he took. So he wrote. He wrote because he understands that players don't leave our program once they graduate. Once they are initiated and validated, we commission them and send them into the world to fulfill their own unique purpose and cause. Alex has accepted the responsibility that comes with belonging to a community of heroic men: to be a man for others.

But the process doesn't end there: Creating meaning is a lifelong challenge, one that involves forming healthy relationships, communication skills, empathy, and the ability to cooperate with others as a team.

Alex's letter shows that he has negotiated this stage of the hero's journey and is competent to confront life's next call to adventure.

When I hear from players like Alex, I often reflect on the genesis of our ceremonial approach to coaching boys. While ministering at The Door, I realized that boys often lack a clear rite of passage into manhood. As I reflected on my past, it became even clearer that my own journey followed the paths of athletic ability, sexual conquest, alcohol, drugs, and material things to prove my masculinity. They were all dead ends. I set out to create a path that leads boys toward an authentic form of masculinity.

In reading mythologist Joseph Campbell's classic, *The Hero with a Thousand Faces*, I realized that sports could provide a contemporary and ceremonial version of what he calls the hero's journey, which begins when a young person leaves the familiarity and comfort of his home and endures extraordinary testing and challenges that transform him into a better person. The hero's journey is a time-tested rite of passage symbolic of the transition from childhood to adulthood. It involves the quest for identity, validation, and belonging. Throughout human history, before Judaism, Christianity, and Islam, every culture invoked rites of passage to initiate boys into manhood to help them become contributing members of their communities. There is something about masculine coding that necessitates this rite.

Campbell's rite of passage involves a five-step process: a call to adventure, a separation from family, time of testing, instruction from a mentor-coach, and reentry into family and community with an acknowledgment of the adolescent's changed status. The initiate is then ceremonially brought into a community of heroes who have also completed the quest. Ceremonies personally and publicly acknowledge the changed social status of the hero and his new adult identity.

ANSWERING THE CALL TO ADVENTURE

The acceptance of the call to adventure begins with an internal recognition of the need to change, grow, or answer nagging questions about

self. Millions of young people respond to the *call to adventure* by playing sports. Sports have the potential to increase or resolve self-doubt
about their identity, potential, and worth. Throughout the journey athletes struggle with insecurities, injuries, fear, and uncertainty. Every
day young athletes all over the world answer the "call" by trying out
for some team, risking failure, rejection, and physical hardships. I often
watch our less talented or undersized players and see how much more
courage it takes to try out and practice every day against more gifted
or accomplished athletes.

It was much easier for someone like me, who was always the star or
the starter, than for many of my teammates and friends. Many players
were treated by coaches in a far less respectful way than I was and still
they courageously stayed the course. I had much to learn from them, although I didn't recognize it at the time. While all boys want to be heroes,
they need to know that heroes come in all shapes, sizes, and strengths,
contrary to the images presented by the macho heroics of media and
movies. As a transformational coach, I mindfully honor every player's
heroic and sacred journey into adulthood.

SEPARATION

Having decided to answer the call to adventure, the hero-in-development
must separate from the world of the known to venture into the unknown. This step represents times of separation from home, childhood
identity, and sources of comfort. The hero will encounter a new set of
rules, community, and way of being. This separation is often viewed by
parents as a time of challenge and potential physical, emotional, and
social danger. Partnerships must be established between parents and
mentor-coaches to ensure the successful accomplishment of each player's passage.

Parents must be our partners in creating the community necessary
to support the hero on his quest. Every year we hold parent meetings to
welcome the returning parents and those new to our program. We want

them to understand our purpose-centered and value-based approach to coaching. Problems arise when a parent's expectations and objectives for their child's participation aren't in alignment with our objectives. At the first meeting we ask them to list their five areas of greatest concern as their sons begin the separation process from them into their new adolescent world. Often the responses are related to drug and alcohol use, negative peer pressure, sexual activities, and the ability to balance academics with athletics. We ask them to list five reasons they want their child to play sports. The list usually runs the gamut from fun and physical activity to college admittance and scholarships. We help them make the connection between their greatest fears and seeing our program as an antidote to those fears. We align their children's purpose for playing sports with our purpose as coaches. The journey from boyhood to manhood is seldom linear. It takes all of us working together to support the heroic steps their sons are taking.

TIME OF TESTING

When we meet with the parents we also explain the physical, relational, and ethical testing that lies ahead for their sons. We want them to understand that these trials are all designed with one purpose in mind: *to help their sons become men of empathy and integrity who will lead, be responsible and, change the world for good.* The ensuing trials and tests will help "slay the dragons" that question their manhood, value, and valor.

WISE MENTOR-COACH

As the hero enters the field of adventure and faces various trials, he meets the wise mentor-coach who trains and equips him and provides wisdom that will support him on his quest. To help slay the dragons of self-doubt, the hero must be validated by an older, wiser mentor-coach. The mentor-coach is someone who has taken his own InSideOut journey, been tried and tested, and can empathically steer players through the minefields of adolescence. Biff and I envision ourselves as mentor-coaches called to assist these heroic players in their quest for self-discovery, providing the insights that help them to know themselves and to be able to honestly assess their strengths, weaknesses, and potential.

And when we fulfill our proper role we are creating heroes who will be devoted husbands, friends, partners, committed fathers, and conscientious contributors to society.

I often tell the following story to various groups of wise teacher-mentor-coach types who support young people on the hero's journey. It is an adaptation of a poem written in 1999 by Taylor Mali. I want to remind them of the important role that mentor-coaches play in a society that often diminishes that role.

The dinner guests were sitting around the table discussing sports, education, and life. A successful businessman decided to explain the problem with education. He argued, "What's a kid going to learn from someone who decided his best option in life was to become a teacher-coach?" He reminded the other dinner guests what is often said about teachers: Those who can, do. Those who can't, teach. To stress his point he said to another guest, "You're a teacher and a coach, Bob. Be honest. What do you make?" Bob, who had a reputation for honesty and frankness, replied, "You want to know what I make? I make kids work harder than they ever thought they could. I make them push through self-imposed limitations, athletically and academically. I make them strive together and for each other. You want to know what I make? I make boys into men. I make them question. I make them self-critique. I make them aware of their social responsibility to build a better world. I make them competitive and teach them how to win with humility and lose with honor. I make them understand that if you follow your heart and someone ever tries to judge you by what you make, you must pay no attention because they just don't get it." Bob paused and then continued. "You want to know what I make? I MAKE A DIFFERENCE. What do you make?"

REENTRANCE TO FAMILY AND COMMUNITY

Having answered the call and having completed this season of the hero's journey, the hero is ready to reenter society with a new identity and a new sense of self. To celebrate, honor, and cement this transition, we created ceremonies to personally and publicly affirm his heroic feats. Ceremonies not only seal this passage in the hearts of players but keep parents, coaches, and community members in touch with their own natural life cycles. We want every player and family to recognize them as heroes who have accepted this quest, for they are truly heroes in our eyes. We created our own ceremonies to signify and honor the sacred journey of boys becoming men.

THE LONG WALK

For the past ninety-five years, Gilman has competed with the McDonogh School. It is one of the great high school rivalries in Maryland. Every year our team's goal is "to win the league and beat McDonogh." This was true long before Biff and I ever came to Gilman and I'm sure it will be the case long after we're gone. If our players were forced to choose between winning the league and beating McDonogh, they would choose beating McDonogh. Regardless of each team's season record, the game is always hard fought.

The Friday before the game our captains go to the McDonogh School's pep rally and speak to their entire school. The McDonogh captains come and do the same at Gilman. Both sets of captains speak of the respect they have for each other's team and school and the wonderful tradition of the game. It is a moving and unique representation of true competition: the mutual quest for excellence. McDonogh always brings out the best in our players, our coaches, our school, and our fans, and we want to honor McDonogh for making us better. We always play this game on the last Saturday of the season.

As evidenced by Alex's letter, last games provide lasting memories, and this game creates an added sense of importance and significance to our players. For our seniors, their families, and coaches it is an exceptionally bittersweet time, as it marks the end of one journey and the beginning of another.

THE LAST PRACTICE

Immediately after the season's final practice, we send our team off to shower and get dressed. They exit the locker room in pairs, seniors first, holding hands in total silence. We begin by leading them through the school buildings. We pause at the portraits and plaques they have walked past for four years without ever knowing the names or why they were honored. Biff, a Gilman alum, discusses the people memorialized and their contribution to our school and to society.

As we leave the building, we solemnly pause at the tree the team planted in commemoration of the 9/11 attacks and we reflect on all the police, fire personnel, and EMTs who sacrificed their lives serving others. Then we silently walk in the dark toward the lights of the practice field.

We tell the underclassmen to remain in silence and circle the playing field. Then we instruct the seniors to go and make peace with the field on which they battled, were tested, succeeded, and failed. Some grab pieces of sod, some jog or even do sprints, others walk alone in solitary contemplation as they reflect. Then the seniors come together and have their last huddle break on the practice field. The underclassmen always honor the sacredness of the ceremony and watch and wait, knowing they too will have a last huddle break. This nighttime ceremony is a ritual that we intend to be transcendent. And it is. We want our players to cherish these moments as much as the victories. And they do.

THE LAST DAY

The following morning, we conduct another ceremony that symbolizes the hero's passage into manhood. Every year we set the same ceremonial table and re-create the same scenario. And every year we get the same transformative results. The seniors sit in our meeting room facing their teammates. The first of our seniors nervously stands up and unfolds a piece of paper on which he has written his own obituary. His teammates sit in silent respect, looking up at him as if they are waiting to hear the greatest pregame pep talks of all time. He looks around the room and the hush is churchlike.

He clears his throat and fights back the emotions. He holds the paper up, looks at it quietly for a moment, and reads:

> We are gathered together today in memory of Anthony Jones, a loving father, a faithful husband, and a devoted friend. It is fitting that he should be remembered in such a way as he believed that the value of one's life can only truly be measured through its impact on others. He believed that life is to be lived through relationships and that reality is found not in the physical world, composed of wealth, accomplishments, and possessions, but rather in the minds of our fellow men. As a result he lived his life for others. . . . Through the relationships he built in life, he shall live on forever in death.

Another player prefaces his remarks by stating his obituary is being read by his firstborn child.

> We are gathered here today to remember the life of my father, Andrew Smith. . . . When talking about his life, I think that it is appropriate to start with the foundation, Gilman. My dad always spoke most emphatically about Gilman, especially about his time playing Gilman football. It was at Gilman that he met

his closest lifelong friends, many of whom are in attendance today, as it was on the Gilman football team that he formed a foundation for the way he should live his life.

And another:

Today we are gathered to celebrate the life of my father, Bryan Kowalski. He was truly a great man who was not the wealthiest, strongest, or most powerful man, but he was the man who cared for everyone no matter what their situation was. . . . What set him apart was the fact that he did not succumb to the false sense of masculinity. He treated everyone the same no matter how many houses they owned, the type of car they drove, or the size of their wallets. . . .

These young men, on the morning of the last game of their high school career, are reading their own obituaries in front of the brotherhood they will soon be leaving as they move on to the next stage of their journey. In writing their obituaries, our players are catapulted into the future with an opportunity to look back and assess their own lives. During this ceremony, as Biff and I sit among our players, we relish the rewards of coaching that reinforce our WHY: *to help boys become men of empathy and integrity who will lead, be responsible, and change the world for good.*

We see someone who was a boy when he came to us and who is leaving a young man. We are sending him forth, often with a new vocabulary, a new vision of the world, and a new sense of himself. We are honored to have played a critical role in this transformation from a boy to a man who can begin to think and act in new ways. We have led our players through a season-long rite that culminates in a quiet, simple ceremony. And the power of transformation rises up and is felt by every player and coach during that very powerful morning.

Our players, like all people, move toward and become that which they believe about themselves. They seek or avoid relationships and opportunities based on their perceptions of their self-worth. Like my coaching model Dorothy from *The Wizard of Oz*, we want them to envision themselves with all their gifts and potential. In taking the time to look back over their lives, they can look ahead and make choices about who they want to be. "What kind of citizen was I?" "What kind of friend, brother, father was I?" These are the kinds of questions we challenge our young athletes to ask themselves when they are summarizing their lives. It is a powerfully moving ceremony and one that inevitably sets parents, coaches, and other players on their own internal searches.

THE LAST ANTHEM

By the time the game begins, the players are always jacked up. In keeping with our ritual of recognizing and emphasizing our players' accomplishments in other endeavors, a senior musician or singer from the team will perform the national anthem at midfield whenever we host the game at home. One year it was a viola player; another year a piano player; often a singer. Then the team plays its heart out. And so do the McDonogh boys. We win some years, McDonogh wins other years. But the game is almost always beautiful, transcendent, and joyful.

THE LAST BANQUET

After the game, we perform the third ceremony of the day, and it is the last step of our hero's journey: reentrance to family and community. We hold our team banquet that evening and the celebration dulls the sting of defeat or enhances the thrill of victory. We realize that what we are celebrating is the new status of our players and our togetherness as a community. Ceremony encourages us to focus our thoughts on the basic sensation of being a man, a parent, a team, and a community. This banquet is a time for our families to come together, break bread, and celebrate our young heroes. After players read their obituaries to the entire community, we have an open mike and everyone is welcome to share their feelings. It is usually a time of laughter, tears, and reminiscing about the season's high points, low points, and most often, the powerful and transformative changes that occur in the lives of our young men.

THE LAST CEREMONY

For a few years we were able to save one final ceremony in the spring before graduation, a sort of postscript to the football season that resurrected the remembrance of the players' joy and transcendence one last time before we sent these young men into the world to be men for others. But with spring sports concluding, final exams, baccalaureate service, and graduation it became increasingly difficult to schedule.

This postscript ceremony entailed gathering the entire football community at Gilman, including rising eighth graders, freshmen, junior varsity, varsity, and all of their parents in an auditorium.

With Rod Stewart's "Have I Told You Lately That I Love You" playing loudly on the speakers as the seniors filed in, the tears and emotions immediately flooded the room. As the graduating young men took their places with their families, their coaches stood before them and congratulated them, honoring their passage into adulthood. Then, two by two, a senior and his presenter (mom, dad, or significant adult) walked up front and sat facing the entire community.

The senior was presented with a plaque by his parent or significant adult that was engraved with his name and the words "A Man Built for Others." The plaque was a tangible memento of the high school journey completed. But the more important and memorable ceremonial keepsake was the speech that the father, mother, or other loved one gave as he or she presented the graduate with his plaque.

Instructed to speak about the growth and maturation they had seen in their young man, the presenters were given one rule: They couldn't talk about sports.

All young people need to know three things before they graduate from high school. One, they are loved. Two, they are loved and accepted for who they are, not what they do. Three, they need to know that they have something of importance and significance to offer to the world.

The presenters were sometimes awkward and stumbled for words, especially without the language of sports, but this ceremony provides an opportunity for parents and loved ones to say the things they want to say but don't know how to say. We often hear fathers say things and show feelings that their sons have never experienced with them before that night. We hear mothers express love and pride with words that rival those of the great poets, and we see young men realize that they are loved and that they are being charged with a mission to go out into the world to love as they have been loved. And we witness it together as a community. It is a moving and profound experience for all.

This past year at Georgetown University, we gathered for dinner and ceremony with the senior lacrosse players and their parents after the Hoyas' last home game. With the moms once again leading the way with their hearts, they reserved a room at a restaurant, played a DVD they created filled with childhood pictures, music, and fond memories, and created the perfect environment for the perfect night. Together we enjoyed an evening in which fathers and mothers and sons publicly expressed their love, admiration, and support for one another.

The unexpected bonus came at the end of the evening.

The young men collectively gathered in the front of the room. Each son personally and publicly expressed his love and gratitude to his parents for the support, sacrifices, and encouragement he had received throughout his journey. Then, they thanked their teammates for their friendship, their support, and the memories they will never forget. Another phase of the hero's journey concluded, celebrated and cemented by ceremony.

We had a wonderful experience with Barney and his teammates' parents at Georgetown. A group of us went on vacation together before the season began and, even though many of our sons have moved on to answer the next call of life's adventure, we are planning a cruise for next year. This is what sports can do—build lasting community—long after the game is over for players and their parents!

I've wondered what Coach Simmons might think of this sort of ceremony. I would love for him to see how Biff and I, always aspiring to be transformational coaches, are merely implementing what he taught me forty years ago about beauty, transcendence, and joy. He gave me a transformative model and the permission to step outside the traditional Coach Box to coach from my life narrative and not from society's script. He combined his artistic temperament with the lessons he learned from a life alongside the Native Americans of Syracuse to structure a program that encouraged ceremony at practices, games, and museum visits. He was not a guru or priest; he was a master of ceremonies. Those rituals led to and fed our spirituality as players. He knew many of us craved them; he knew our culture rarely provided the opportunity for them; so he took sports and transformed them into communion.

Beauty, transcendence, joy. Those three words are usually associated with "art," not sports. You hear those words when people talk about paintings or music. But for an InSideOut coach on the last game day of the season, when his seniors are leading the team through a ceremony that usually blows their minds, beauty, transcendence, and joy are the best words to describe a sporting event. Sports can do that—just as great art can. So we insistently, even defiantly, use ceremonies to bring our players into the artful and spiritual realm of beauty, transcendence, and joy.

Sports have the power to unite us because they enable us to transcend together—to seek the highest values for the greatest common good, be it for a team, a school, or a country. Once an InSideOut coach realizes this, he can help his athletes cherish those transcendent moments. Coaches can be ceremonial figures—orchestrating, choreographing, and even ministering—but most of all ensuring that their athletes walk away with the understanding and experience of virtue.

An InSideOut coach knows that the process of becoming good and involved men never ends: The turn inward to adjust and improve our outward behavior is continual. Writing this book has been part of that very process for me. It has been arduous, painful, revelatory, joyous, and enriching. I am ever becoming an InSideOut coach, but the inside work of writing this book has been yet another critical step in mastering the outside effort to transform young people.

I want more than anything to see young athletes replicate glorious days like the ones Biff and I have experienced. But I want it for them every day. There is no reason why every practice cannot be a beautiful, transcendent, and joyful experience for young people. This possibility was one of the first things Biff and I discussed: We would strive to make every day a healthier day for our players. At the least, we wanted to find a way to minimize the confusing and negative days and multiply the moments of rightness.

I see clearly now what Chief Oren Lyons and Coach Simmons meant years ago when they taught us that sports were spiritual activities. To me spirituality is the quest for self-transcendence—moving beyond self-preoccupation and self-aggrandizement. Spirituality is enhanced when we can rise above ourselves and connect with others in the pursuit of a higher purpose. Spirituality in sports is often referred to as "chemistry" or "flow," but it is much richer and more holistic than these terms suggest. The quest for transcendence lays the foundation for authentic community, honorable competition, life-affirming communication, and other-centered classroom teaching.

It took me a long time to understand that the best way for me to bring this spirituality into the lives of my athletes is through the ceremony inherent in sports. Sports are, quite simply, a ceremony: a season of life containing all the rituals and spiritual exercises necessary to mark, internalize, and publicize the internal growth in each hero's journey.

I now see that what I needed all along from sports, more than the fame and ego boosting, was the ritualized transcendence inherent in the spirituality of team sports. It is those moments that have helped me survive difficult aspects of my childhood in Buffalo, moments when I realize that life can feel right and I can feel something called peace. They, like many pain-filled moments, were sports-related, too, but they were the spiritual moments. They are what athletes need more of. Transcendent moments are what we aspire to provide for them.

Inside/Lesson

I began this journey in a fog—literally and figuratively. I was driving home with my then four-year-old son Barney on a misty night in Baltimore City. It was the beginning of my search for truth: truth that uncovered painful parts of my past, revealing the gap between who I thought I was and who I was capable of becoming. The painful parts of my life were not an enemy to hide from. They were not something to deny, ignore, or repress. They were to be explored, understood from an adult perspective, and integrated into my life story. That night was the beginning of my establishing a coherent narrative, the start of my In-SideOut journey and my effort to become a transformational coach. But the more immediate payoff was the dawn of a new path to becoming a better husband and father.

My father died October 5, 1987. I conducted his funeral service and gave the eulogy. It was one of the hardest things I've ever done.

Upon receiving news of his death I found I had no tears, no emotions. I was numb. Despite all the confusion he created in my life and in the lives of my mother and my siblings, I loved him and sought his acceptance and approval. It is the power that dads, good or bad, have over their children and especially their sons. After the funeral I continued to deny my experiences and repress my emotions. Ever since I was a twelve-year-old boy abused in a country shack, I had dissociated from all that had hurt and haunted me. I spent a lifetime walking away from memories and pushing away from people for fear of exposure, hoping the next person or position would stop the hemorrhaging of my soul.

That night back in 1991 with little Barney, supported by the security of Paula's love and strength, I began another phase of the hero's quest for authentic manhood. As I write I am still engaged in this process, still journeying for healing and wholeness as a man, a husband, a father, and a coach.

It was Paula's love and the practice of contemplation that provided the skills I needed to put one foot in front of the other. Through her, I had learned to use the spiritual disciplines of silence and meditation to create balance and coherence in my life.

When I felt uncomfortable or peculiar, I worked to hold on to that feeling of contemplation until I could sit, ponder, and try to connect it to something that made sense. If I heard of someone else's success or achievement and a feeling of envy arose, I would contemplate where it was coming from and why I might feel threatened or insecure. Why would I be jealous of someone's good fortune? It was on one of these mornings when I started to reflect on Dah. And in my own mind, sitting on my sofa, I mentally walked back down the basement steps of my childhood.

As a grown man, holding the hand of five-year-old Joey Ehrmann, scared and frightened to reenter the scene that shamed me for a lifetime, I confronted the mighty Dah. I was there to advocate for that five-year-old boy who had no way of standing up to the power of my father. I needed that boy to understand that what had happened in that basement was never about him.

Five-year-olds are not supposed to know how to throw punches just right. Five-year-olds are supposed to cry. They are to be tenderly held, tucked in at night, and reassured about how much they are loved. Dah's behavior was never about me; it was always about him.

An amazing thing happened when I allowed myself to go back down those stairs. Once I could see Dah's full responsibility for hurting me, I was mystically enabled to feel empathy for him. He wasn't evil; he was ignorant and wounded. I started to wonder, who hurt him in a way that resulted in his treating us the way he did? What happened in his life journey? What was his relationship with his parents like? How many generations before me had repressed, denied, and then passed on their problems to their children? I know this—hurt people hurt people. Wounded boys become wounding men unless there is an intervention, an enlightened witness or mentor-coach to guide them. Wounded adults have to make an honest assessment of their life narratives. If men and women don't transform their pain, they will transfer it to their own children, no matter how much they love them. They will transact with people and players to get what they think they need to quiet the voices echoing in their minds.

The morning that I reentered the source of my shamed masculinity, I felt all of the emotions, the tears, the rejection, and the agony of failing to meet my father's expectations. As I started to release myself from his grasp, I was finally free to forgive him.

And I started the InSideOut process knowing that all meaningful and lasting change had to begin on the inside before it could be manifested outwardly.

InSideOut coaching is not just a program; it is a process. For me it culminated in this book. The relationships, the learning, the teaching, and the coaching have all been one long, arduous, and ultimately liberating ceremony. The beauty of transformational coaching is that the transformation works both ways—it transforms us as coaches, too. Our players teach and challenge us. And if we listen, they tell us how to love them.

ACKNOWLEDGMENTS

Writing this book required the support of the people Paula and I work with every day and who kept so many balls in the air as we organized a lifetime of experiences and emotions. Thank you to Cathy Chamberlain, Brenda Merrill, and Johnna Harvey for daily support and encouragement. To Greg Jordan, Greg Helvey, and our editor, Bob Bender—thank you for helping to connect the dots. To my readers Bo Dixon, Dr. Jan Boxhill, Jason Harper, and Jim Thompson, thank you for your insights and affirmations. Jeffrey Marx's friendship and support helped me through difficult parts of this book. I would also like to thank a lifetime of wise mentor-coaches who have spoken into my life at various stages of my journey: Dr. Ray Bakke, Reed Carpenter, Dr. Wendell Johnston, Bishop Douglas Miles, Ron Shapiro, Bill Devon, and my uncle Jim Yeates, who has always been my best man.

To all the players I have had the privilege to coach: You are Men Built for Others and signs of hope that a more just and hospitable world is possible. To my fellow coaches at Gilman and other members of the Gilman community: Tyrone Barnes, Buzz Battaglia, Lori Bristow, Sherm Bristow, Chris Dawson, Johnny Foreman, Jeff Gouline, Tim Holley, Keith Kormanik, Ray Mills, Carol Schuch, Rob White, and Stan White. While I tell the story of building our program through my relationship with Biff Poggi, it never would have happened without your contributions and commitment.

I also would like to thank transformational coaches everywhere who make the daily sacrifices of time, energy, and finances to utilize their platform to build boys and girls into healthy men and women of character and substance. I stand on your shoulders.

INDEX

256

Index

Spend a season with Joe Ehrmann in the bestselling

SEASON
of
LIFE

I I I I I I I I I I I I I I I I I I I I I I I I I I I I I I I

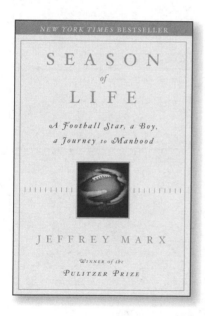

After renewing his friendship with a childhood hero, writer Jeffrey Marx chronicled a year in the most extraordinary sports program he'd ever seen. *Season of Life* is an inspiring story that will resonate with athletes, coaches, parents—anyone striving to make the right choices in life.

Available wherever books are sold or at
www.simonandschuster.com